LIBERATION AS AFFIRMATION

SUNY series in
CHINESE PHILOSOPHY AND CULTURE

Roger T. Ames, *editor*

LIBERATION AS AFFIRMATION

The Religiosity of Zhuangzi and Nietzsche

GE LING SHANG

STATE UNIVERSITY OF NEW YORK PRESS

Published by

STATE UNIVERSITY OF NEW YORK PRESS, ALBANY

© 2006 State University of New York

For information, address
State University of New York Press,
194 Washington Avenue, Suite 305 Albany, NY 12210

Production by Kelli Williams
Marketing by Susan M. Petrie

Library of Congress Cataloging-in-Publication Data
Shang, Geling.
Liberation as affirmation: the religiosity of Zhuangzi and Nietzsche / Ge
Ling Shang.
    p. cm. — (SUNY series in Chinese philosophy and culture)
Includes bibliographical references and index.
ISBN-13: 978-0-7914-6667-4 (hardcover : alk. Paper)
ISBN-10: 0-7914-6667-1 (hardcover : alk. paper)
ISBN-13: 978-0-7914-6668-1 (pbk. : alk. Paper)
ISBN-10: 0-7914-6668-X (pbk. : alk. Paper)
1. Philosophy, Taoist. 2. Philosophy. 3. Philosophy, Comparative.
4. Zhuangzi. 5. Nietzsche, Friedrich Wilhelm, 1844–1900. I. Title.
II. Series.
BL1920.S45 2006
181′.114—dc22

                                                            2005007995

10 9 8 7 6 5 4 3 2 1

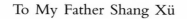
To My Father Shang Xü

CONTENTS

ACKNOWLEDGMENTS

This book would have been an impossible task for me to accomplish without the direct and indirect contributions by a great many people to its production.

I wish to thank late Charles Wei-Hsun Fu, who encouraged me to come to study in the United States and worked with me on this topic at the outset. His delicate taste and acute criticism of philosophy, his passionate and exuberant will to love and friendship, and his conscientious study and continuous search for knowledge kept reminding me how to live and work as a philosopher. Many of the ideas in the book originated from our conversations and discussions during the years we spent together at Temple University.

Special thanks to Joseph Magolis, Yü Ying-shih, Thomas J. Dean, Sandra Wawarytko, Lisa Portmess, and Louis J. Hammann whose critical comments and constructive advice through most parts of my graduate studies are invaluable for its further development. I am happy to acknowledge specifically the help and support I received from Donald Munro, Peimin Ni, and Stephen Rowe. They read my final manuscript and provided very concrete advice and serious corrections for its completion. I would like to thank my friends Weiming Tu, Yanming An, Yong Huang, Zao Zhang, Tania Oldenhage, Kui-de Chen, Wansheng Huang, Guorong Yang, Xuanmeng Yü, Jianchu Chen, and Elizabeth Rossmiller for their constant support and stimulating conversations, which have always been the most precious wells of my inspiration. My special appreciation goes to Douglas Berger, because almost every step I made and every pain I went through for this work has to do with his care, patience, and wisdom.

I am grateful to Harvard-Yenching Institute at Harvard University for a fellowship (in 1999–2000) which gave me tremendous support both academically and financially. I would also like to acknowledge the philosophy department and The Institute of Modern Chinese Thought and Culture at East China Normal University for giving me the opportunity to teach and do research in China (2003–2004). It enabled me to exchange ideas with many Chinese scholars, which benefited my study enormously.

Finally, I appreciate Roger Ames, Nancy Ellegate, and State University of New York Press for their interest in my work and all the supporting work they have done for its production. And of course, I am thankful from my bottom of heart to my family, my wife Yu Lin, my sister Lingguo Shang, my mother Xiaoyun Wei, and my niece Jiawei Wang, for their selfless care, love, and support.

CHAPTER 1

INTRODUCTION

As a Chinese intellectual living in China in the 1980s, I cheerfully anticipated China's political and economic reform after the closure of Mao's reign, but felt pessimistic about whether such reform, based as it was on communist ideology and a vast bureaucracy, would bring prosperity and well-being to my country. This predicament evoked my fascination in the great philosophers, Zhuangzi (庄子, 399–295 BCE) and Friedrich Nietzsche (1845–1900), who were frequently seen by Chinese intellectuals as having nothing in common except their marginalization. On the one hand, I found consolation in Zhuangzi's advocacy of detachment and disengagement from secular concerns, and I admired his independent and noble spirit of freedom (*xiaoyaoyou*, 逍遥游), which most Confucian, activist, and communist intellectuals had fervently opposed. On the other hand, Nietzsche's devastating attack on traditional and modern values had enormous appeal to, and in fact intoxicated, me and my generation of intellectuals, as his writings had intoxicated intellectuals in earlier turbulent periods of Chinese history.[1]

It was only later that I was able to articulate the two main purposes of this book. One is to interpret Zhuangzi and Nietzsche's texts from a new perspective of religiosity,[2] which crosses and transcends the boundary of philosophy defined conventionally. Here, religiosity is seen as a religious feeling or sentiment characterized by a "religiously" profound and passionate concern for things in life that are believed to be particularly meaningful, sacred, or sublime. I tend to set religiosity or religiousness free from the narrow but prevailing Western notion of religion premised solely on the God-human relation and directed exclusively toward a supernatural being or beings. Following some important thinkers of our time such as Emile Durkheim (the distinction of sacred and profane), Paul Tillich (ultimate concern, hidden theology), and John Dewey (religious experience), I define religiosity broadly to include religious feelings that are not necessarily directed toward a god or supreme truth. The feelings or "spiritual sensibility" (Roberts, 5) toward life, totality, infinity, perfection, responsibility, freedom, and liberation, etc., are for me religious in quality. Religiosity as such has existed throughout human

1

history and served as the original inspiration and immanent drive of the development of religion and philosophy. In this respect, religiosity is not something external to philosophy but an indispensable part of it. From the perspective of religiosity, I believe, we can get a better understanding of philosophy including those aspects that may appear nonreligious or even antireligious. I found that both Zhuangzi and Nietzsche exhibited profound religiosity, which is essential for understanding their works.

The other purpose of this book is to compare Zhuangzi and Nietzsche, by encountering their philosophical writings through the perspective of religiosity, in order to provide two great examples of philosophers in the history of world philosophy who made their philosophies capable of dealing with the fundamental problems regarding human liberation and spiritual freedom.

REINTERPRETING ZHUANGZI AND NIETZSCHE

As I pursued my post–Cultural Revolution fascination, I discovered that generalizations about the two philosophers abounded among Chinese intellectuals: Zhuangzi, the escapist, the relativist, a successor of egotist Yang Zhu (扬朱, ca. 440–360 BCE) or a mystic skeptic; Nietzsche, the rebel, the passionate worrier and relentless destroyer. The first attempt I encountered to make a serious comparative study of Zhuangzi and Nietzsche was by Chen Guying, a Chinese professor who in 1984 lectured in Beijing on the two philosophers.[3] I was invited to that lecture, which struck me as sensational rather than convincing, inspiring rather than referential. But it opened my mind to the gradual reconsideration of the two philosophers that has become the work of this book.

My decision to explore Zhuangzi and Nietzsche had in fact very little to do with Chen's lecture. The decision came instead from a great deal of reading and reflection on the writings of the two philosophers. The more I read, the more suspicious I became of previous stereotypes of them, and the more intertwined instead of opposed their fundamental orientations began to seem. Gradually I discovered in their writings more and more affinities, not only in their life experiences, writing styles, use of allegories, and common experience of being misunderstood in history, but also in their philosophical temperament and spirituality amid their respective worlds.

The most profound meeting point of the two is, as I now put it, their religiosity, their original drives and ultimate concerns for freedom and liberation from traditional values in order to affirm life. More surprisingly, I have found Zhuangzi and Nietzsche to be neither negative nor destructive, as reflected in common perspectives, but positive and constructive; not passive but active, because their concerns for human liberation and freedom ultimately rest upon the affirmation of life as it is, a very special kind of affirmation that is rid of any reservation or calculation. With this conviction the course of my interpretation was set—to bring these two philosophers together to explore in each how the route toward human liberation is built and what human freedom might be conceived to be.

Most commentators have interpreted Nietzsche's philosophy from various perspectives[4] and raised countless controversial issues from analysis of his writings. Questions are debated among Nietzschean commentators: whether Nietzsche is a metaphysician (Heidegger, Kaufmann) or not (Jaspers, Derrida); whether he is a nihilist (Danto, Nishitani) or not; whether he rejects the existence of truth entirely (Rorty, De Man) or not (Heidegger, Kaufmann, Clark). Nearly all of these interpretations I found to be inspiring and in some cases quite plausible. But most commentators try to interpret an unconventional, "abnormal," or artistic philosophy by means of a conventional method, so that something significant in Nietzsche's work seems missing to me in their arguments. Most critics miss what I believe is the deep religious orientation of his writings, a misunderstanding that derives from the apparently antireligious, especially anti-Christian writings of Nietzsche and his outrageous proclamation that "God is dead." This aspect of Nietzsche's work lures or distracts one's attention easily away from Nietzsche's own religiosity as the soul of his philosophy.[5]

Curiously enough, some Western scholars have tended to interpret Zhuangzi as no philosopher at all, but as a mere mystic and rhetorical thinker (Schwartz, Wright, Creel), or representative of religious mysticism in association with Laozi, Nagarjuna, and the late Zen Buddhists (Smart). Measured by the ethnocentric standard of European philosophy, Zhuangzi was read by them with little attention to the distinct religious dimensions of his stylistic philosophical work, such as his critiques of language, reason, meaning, and morality, his unique art of paradoxical discourse, his reconstructing humanity based on *ziran* (自然) or "spontaneity," and finally his ultimate concern for human liberation and freedom. On the other hand, some scholars have perceived Zhuangzi as a relativist (Chad Hansen, David Wong), or a skeptic (Paul Kjellberg, Lisa Raphals), in a debate which cannot give readers a full understanding of Zhuangzi's philosophy. The misunderstandings of Zhuangzi in Chinese history are much more serious than in the West,[6] and all these misunderstandings finally resulted in the severe and mistaken accusations against Zhuangzi by modern communists: that he is a pessimist, a reactionary, a relativist, a skeptic, a subjective idealist, a nihilist, and an escapist.[7] These perspectives derived from customary methods of philosophical analysis and interpretation, which have failed to grasp what I believe is essential in Zhuangzi's philosophy.

My own perspective on Zhuangzi and Nietzsche is quite different. In my analysis I give attention, as most commentators do, to the philosophical questions and themes in the writings of each philosopher. But what I have termed the religiosity of each philosopher is the Ariadne's thread which I use to pass through each labyrinth. From this perspective, both Zhuangzi's and Nietzsche's attack on traditional values was not so much an attempt to present another system of human values as an attempt to overcome and transcend all traditional values to reach a state of liberation and freedom. For, according to Zhuangzi and Nietzsche, liberation itself is not a value in a customary sense, but the transcending of all previous values. So, unlike other commentators, when I examine the philosophical themes in the works of each, themes such as metaphysics, truth, knowledge, language, and morality, I think about how their arguments intimately relate to their ultimate concern with human transformation and liberation. I then return from this height to shed light on how they cope with these traditional philosophical questions. I hope my effort will provide a new horizon from which to look at both Zhuangzi and Nietzsche and will deepen as well as broaden our understanding of their great philosophies.

PERSPECTIVE ON COMPARATIVE PHILOSOPHY

I am not ignorant of the debates that exist over the possibility of comparative philosophy. Some scholars such as Richard Rorty argue that the difficulties of communication across boundaries of language, customs, and cultures make us virtually unable to understand each other. In Rorty's view it is impossible to do comparative philosophy at all. Postcolonialists, in a similar skeptical vein, argue that the work done thus far in comparative philosophy is flawed because its foundations rest solely on a Eurocentric colonialist mentality. They claim that such an approach tends to draw *other* cultures and philosophies into European categories and thus necessarily fails to arrive at fair comparisons. I am sympathetic to these concerns and recognize the difficulty in comparative study, yet I do not agree with them.

In my view, except for the very first philosopher, whose existence is shrouded by time, every philosophy must be comparative because every interpretation originates under the condition of the existence of *others*. The problems of communication are always present not only interculturally but also intraculturally. Even within the same tradition people still have difficulty in understanding each other. However, the existence of obstacles does not stop the ongoing communication and mutual understanding among different people. By the same token, Western philosophy is itself comparative. For example, contemporary American philosophers writing in English must confront Greek or German philosophical writings that emerge from cultures now removed in many ways from their own. Though the gap between contemporary Western philosophy and classical Greek philosophy may not be so large as the one between Chinese and Western philosophical traditions, nonetheless the contemporary Western philosopher is a stranger to much of Greek culture and philosophy in subtle as well as conspicuous ways. And yet the search for understanding continues in careful textual and linguistic study, in cultural and historical analysis and in comparative studies that attempt to bridge different cultures and different time periods.

Furthermore, the fact that colonialism and ethnocentrism have had a deep impact on the contemporary study of the East, as Said has maintained, and on comparative philosophy, is undeniably true, but it should not lead us to renounce the possibility of comparative studies. Modern philosophy in the West began with the rediscovery of the Greeks, some of whose works were brought to Europe through Arabic texts. Who can prove that the Golden Age of Athens about twenty-five hundred years ago had nothing to do with influence that came from the East? In this postcolonial age, the important thing we must do, both former colonizers and the formerly colonized, is to overcome the colonialist mentality in active and positive ways, not through angry confrontation but by comparative studies. As a matter of fact, comparative study or dialogical strategy is one of the best antidotes for the colonialist illness, so that we might bring to the fore a real pluralist, open, and free intellectual environment.

Through a healthy dialogue with each *other* and with different traditions, we will become more and more aware that every philosophy is indeed a perspective, and not a final and exclusive truth. That being so, what we should disdain is absolutism and dogmatism, which are the hidden foundations of colonialism, just as fiercely held particular beliefs are its apparent foundation. We should not disdain the search itself for understanding across cultures. Refusing to grant meaning to such comparative studies precludes the possibility of finding any common ground for mutual understanding. Just as two individuals can only hope to understand one another through conversation, two cultures can only hope for mutual understanding through an attempt to communicate, and if the process of communication is pronounced impossible before it begins, the two individuals or cultures will seem irrevocably alienated from one another. This attempt at a conversation between cultures is the work of comparative studies. Whatever difficulties in understanding may appear, they appear in the course of conversation and comparison, not before the process begins, and only an engagement in comparative thought can confront these difficulties, not a refusal to engage. No matter what difficulties indeed confront us in comparative studies, we still must search for such common ground to respect the plurality of our world.

Such common ground I believe I have found in the two seemingly disparate thinkers, Zhuangzi and Nietzsche. Divided by culture, by language, and by centuries, Zhuangzi and Nietzsche reflect a common concern with spiritual emancipation. This is why I have chosen to bypass interesting debates over comparative studies in spite of the important epistemological questions they raise. Interesting as these debates are, I have worked on this project from the conviction that comparative studies are both inherent in the work of philosophy as well as meaningful.

METHOD AND PLAN

Since the two philosophers I have chosen to examine are among the most intensively studied, it is impossible for me to consider exhaustively the commentaries their work has inspired. As a result the methodology of this study has been primarily textual and thematic. I will focus basically on the original texts rather than their commentators, though they too have been the focus of my reading and research. In dealing with the full corpus of each author, some works of which remain controversial in significance and authenticity,[8] I have developed my thesis based on my research and my understanding of their writings. In the *Book of Zhuangzi*, I follow the consensus that the seven inner chapters were written by Zhuangzi himself. I base my analysis of his thought on these chapters; the rest I use as secondary sources. In Nietzsche, I will pay more respect to his own selection of his published writings than I will to the *Nachlass* published after his final breakdown (1888–1889). The *Nachlass* I will use occasionally as supplementary references.

During the process of this research, I found many problems in existing translations of Zhuangzi[9] that do not harmonize with my understanding of the text. I made some changes by translating most of the cited text myself with the help of my predecessors.

Again, this is a thematic study based on original texts and philosophical analysis rather than a study of Zhuangzi's and Nietzsche's thinking in its socio-cultural and historical context. I have concentrated particularly on those elements in the works of Zhuangzi and Nietzsche in which I could best point to the ultimate religiosity of their writings. The significance of sociocultural and historical factors is undeniable, and I have explored such factors throughout my research for this project. But to attend fully to these historical and sociocultural factors requires the concentrated attention of another work.

In what follows I shall present an overall interpretation of both philosophies respectively within their own contexts. My considerations in choosing such an approach are these: First, in my own reading of Zhuangzi and Nietzsche, I have found a unique brand of "religiosity" in their works that emphasizes the need for human liberation from all traditional values in order to affirm life. This will best be shown by first bringing to light how this religiosity manifests itself in the respective contexts of the two philosophers, whereas an attempt to glean this religiosity through a point by point comparisons of themes would not be convincing to those who are well versed in the texts of these thinkers. This particular reading of each philosopher in his turn is the first contribution of this book, a reading which I do not believe has previously been given to either.[10]

Secondly, having discovered the religiosity of human liberation in both, I try to present the thematic similarities in both that make this religiosity possible. That is to say, what is of central importance for this study is the articulation of a philosophy of human liberation that can be found in both Nietzsche and Zhuangzi, and in order for this particular articulation to be relevant to cross-cultural philosophical reflection, I first take it upon myself to show how this theme of liberation and life-affirmation is expressed by each philosopher, and only then show how the "philosophical religiosity" which I have discovered from my own readings can be formulated in a thematic comparative dialogue between Zhuangzi and Nietzsche.

Thirdly, I will reflect on what sort of relevance and impact this philosophical religiosity can have for both Western and Chinese philosophical contexts in an age of thinking challenged by postmodernism on the one hand and cultural confrontation and dialogue on the other. The philosophical religiosity of human liberation is relevant not only to the Western or Chinese philosophical scene in isolation, but is of importance to both in their confrontation and dialogue with one another.

The main body of this book is divided into five chapters. In chapter 2, I examine closely Zhuangzi's main ideas, interpreting his writings in light of how he arrives at his sense of human liberation and life affirmation. I examine the concept of Dao and its background in ancient Chinese history from which Zhuangzi's unique philosophy derives. I then describe how Zhuangzi deconstructs the "metaphysical" meaning of Dao and *wu* and examine his critical yet creative approach to knowledge, truth, language, and morality, liberation from which is the precondition of ultimate emancipation. In the final section I illustrate a religiosity manifested in Zhuangzi's perspective of Dao as *xiaoyaoyou*, as realized freedom in this world.

In chapter 3, I examine carefully Nietzsche's writings, from his "revaluation of all values" to his method of genealogy, from his negation of metaphysics, true knowledge, religion, and morality to the creation of his own perspective of the world. I analyze the doctrine of the will to power, the notion of the *Übermensch*, the Dionysian spirit, and the doctrine of eternal recurrence as expressions of his ultimate affirmation of life and the core of Nietzsche's religiosity.

In chapter 4, by looking at each philosopher in light of the other, I propose a way of seeing the two as complementary in philosophical outlook. Bringing attention to several aspects of their philosophies, such as their linguistic strategies, their conceptions of truth, knowledge, and interpretation, their critiques of morality and their ideas of nature as a unity of differences and as the world of life, I argue for seeing each as ultimately concerned with human liberation.

In the concluding chapter 5, I reflect on some of the implications this philosophy of human liberation has for the philosophical as well as religious discourse of the contemporary world, both in China and the West. First, I take a look at the recent philosophers such as Derrida, Foucault, and some other poststructuralist thinkers, to examine critically their relation to Nietzsche and Zhuangzi and to show that the philosophical religiosity of the latter may offer something positive to the epoch after the death of "God" and "Man." Then I illustrate historically the studies of Zhuangzi and Nietzsche in China to see how my project can enrich or "multiply" the scholarship of the subject. Finally, I return to my main thesis to elaborate how the concept of religiosity, shown in Zhuangzi and Nietzsche's philosophies, would possibly affect the studies of philosophy and religion in the future.

After all, in the creative and vital spirit of Nietzsche's work, as in the tranquil and inward spirit of Zhuangzi's work, a surprisingly similar vision of human freedom exists—one in which spiritual transcendence is possible by affirming life "religiously" as sacred and divine. To argue in this way for the religiosity of Zhuangzi's work may be less idiosyncratic, but the strange and paradoxical position of arguing for the religiosity of Nietzsche's work has proved surprisingly fruitful for philosophical analysis. Only those who would narrow all religious sensibility to forms of otherworldly theism would find Nietzsche's philosophy atheistic and antireligious. I do not, and thus find in Nietzsche's writings, as in Zhuangzi's, religious striving, liberation, and the promise of spiritual transformation.

CHAPTER 2

ZHUANGZI'S DAO: A WAY OF FREEDOM

Zhuangzi, originally Zhuang Zhou (庄周, 399–295 BCE), was said to be a contemporary of King Hui of Liang or Wei (梁惠王, 370–319 BCE), King Xuan of Qi (齐宣王, 319–301 BCE), and Mencius (371–289 BCE) though they never met each other. Zhuangzi was a resident of Meng, which belonged to Chu State, now probably somewhere in Anhui Province near Long River in mainland China.[1] According to *Shi Ji* (史记) or *The Historical Record* by Sima Qian, Zhou had worked as a low-ranked clerk in a small town. He wrote more than one hundred thousand words, most of them allegories. King Wei of Chu State heard Zhou's reputation and wanted him to be the prime minister of Chu. Zhuangzi laughed at this and told the messenger, "Go away, don't insult me! I shall never be a politician. I just want to enjoy my free spirit"(*Shi Ji, Zhuangzi Liezhuan*, 庄子列传). The story of Zhuangzi's life became the legend and symbol of an independent intellectual who has been respected generation after generation. But the most important contribution of Zhuangzi is his philosophical teachings recorded in *The Book of Zhuangzi*, "one of the most entertaining as well as one of the profoundest books in the world"(Arthur Waley). *The Book of Zhuangzi* in current edition has thirty-three chapters.[2] The first seven chapters, called *Inner Chapters*, are most commonly thought to be Zhuangzi's own writings; the *Outer Chapters* contain fifteen chapters, and seem to have been written by his disciples as a record of Zhuangzi's teaching and interpretations of the *Inner Chapters*. The rest of the chapters belong to the *Miscellaneous Chapters* and are mixtures of stories and theories, including the last chapter, "The World" (*Tianxia*, 天下), which examines the different schools of thought at that time and is considered the first historical review of Chinese philosophy.

A few words should be added at this point about how *The Book of Zhuangzi* is used in the following chapters as evidencing the philosophy that I take to be the philosophy of the historical Zhuang Zhou. The more or less common view among scholars, as mentioned, is that Zhuangzi himself authored the *Inner Chapters*, while the remaining chapters were the products of either Zhuangzi's students or disciples belonging to different schools of thought. As

9

a result, the question arises as to how to locate the thought of Zhuangzi within the fragments of the classic book that, compiled over several centuries, bears his name. For the most part, I have remained faithful in my citations to the *Inner Chapters*. I have, however, also cited from specifically selected passages in other chapters of the book. I have carefully selected materials from chapter 27, *Yuyan* (寓言), "Allegory," and chapter 33, *Tianxia*, "The World," especially in connection with issues on language that are pertinent to the following discussions. I have also employed chapter 33 to elucidate the differences between Zhuangzi's and Laozi's thought, as well as the distinctions between Daoist, Confucian, and other schools.[3] Selections have been made from chapter 22, *Zhibeiyou* (知北游), "Knowledge Wandered North," in connection with the antimetaphysical import of Zhuangzi's philosophy that coincides with passages from chapter 2, *Qi Wu-lun* (齐物论). Chapter 23, *Gengsangchu* (庚桑楚), has been referred to for the purpose of highlighting this theme further, also in connection with the logical implications of chapter 2 and chapter 5, *De Chong Fu* (德充符). Quotes have been taken from chapter 13, *Tiandao* (天道), "The Way of Heaven," in order to thematize metaphysical questions that were current in classical Chinese thought in the time of Zhuangzi, with which he would have been familiar. Chapter 17, *Qiushui* (秋水),"Autumn Floods," figures into an explanation of self-transformation and the concept of *ziran* or "spontaneity." I have also made use of a story in chapter 18, *Zhiyue*, or *Zhile* (至乐), "The Ultimate Music/Joy," in connection with biographical details about the death of Zhuangzi's wife. These selections have hardly been made indiscriminately. With the exception of the citation from chapter 18, all of the material selected for use in what follows has come from chapters attributed to the "School of Zhuangzi," Shu Zhuang Pai (述庄派). Liu Xiao-gan and Zhang Cheng-qui have classified the chapters of the Zhuangzi as having been penned by various subsequent schools of Zhuangzi commentary, among which are the Shu Zhuang Pai, a Yangist School, Confucian School, Legalist School, and what A. C. Graham calls a Syncretist School.[4] These separations are based not on any concrete historical evidence of actual schools of interpretation, but rather on thematic differences among the various chapters, and so the basis of such a division of the text, while it has gained a general consensus among scholars, is still conjectural. I have limited myself to those chapters attributed to the "School of Zhuangzi" because of the thematic continuity between these chapters and the *Inner Chapters*. The justification for my use of these chapters can only be found in what they contribute consistently to the understanding of the *Inner Chapters*, and so there can be no question that my selections are interpretative ones. In what follows, therefore, it needs to be understood that the philosophy of Zhuangzi that I shall appeal to below is an exegetical construction, and my invocation of Zhuangzi's name in the argument is a result of this construction, to a certain degree. It is certainly easier to refer to the historical Nietzsche, for instance, in reference to his texts, though I would suggest at the same time that it is difficult at best to gainsay that speaking of something like "the philosophy of Nietzsche," or any other historical philosopher whose thought is spread out over many years of writing and development is also not an exegetical construction. One only needs to remember that the only work we have that came from Aristotle's own hand was the *Nicomachean Ethics* to understand how tenuous our constructions of philosophical identity in fact are. With these necessary qualifications, however, I shall proceed to refer to Zhuangzi as the textual, exegetical construction that I believe best represents the philosophical thought of the historical Zhuang Zhou.

THE CONCEPT OF DAO IN EARLY CHINESE HISTORY

Oswald Spengler, in his *The Decline of the West*, depicts Chinese culture as "the culture of Dao." He said that Dao is the primary symbol of Chinese culture. The Chinese word *Dao* embodies that significant understanding of the world in which *mensch* and nature, individual and society, person and person celebrate their great harmony (II, 287). Although this kind of assertion is too general to be relevant to characterize Chinese culture as a whole, it would be safe to say that Dao—what it is and how it works—had been the basic conception and central theme of early (pre-Qin) Chinese thought during the Spring and Autumn period and the Warring States period (600–221 BCE), the dark age of political turbulence and the golden age of intellectual creativity, to which Laozi, Confucius, Mencius, Zhuangzi, and many other great names all belong.

It was a productive age of great Chinese thinkers, historically called "the age of a hundred schools of thought" (ca. 600–221 BCE). The splintering and decline of the Zhou Dynasty perhaps catalyzed this great production of Chinese thought because the chaotic and disintegrated nation demanded guidance (*daoshu*, 道术) so that the dukes could expand and strengthen their states to compete with each other for predominant political power, and the royal family of the House of Zhou could restore the order of the aged Empire and preserve the unity of China. The political vicissitudes adversely impacted the lives of ordinary people who were confused about everything they experienced. They too needed to find a *way* (Dao) to move on. Thus, all kinds of theories, political, moral, philosophical as well as religious, "a hundred schools" (*baijia*, 百家), were brought into being to present different understandings of the Dao, the Way, or the Art of the Way (*daoshu*, 道术) that could, as was believed, either restore order or bring justice to the entire world.

The origin of the concept of Dao in Chinese history may be traced to an early time. On the early Zhou bronze inscriptions, the graph for Dao (道) is composed of two semantic parts: a word *shou* (首, head) on the top and another word *zou* (走, walk) underneath, representing an image of a person who is walking. The message conveyed by the image is obvious: Dao stands for the path, road, or way by which people can walk. According to the earliest lexicon "Explanation of Words and Elucidation of Characters" (*Shuo Wen Jie Zi*, 说文解字), Dao is what one walks on. As Dai Zhen (戴震, 1724–1777)

later observed, "Dao" used to be a synonymy of "*xing*"(行, going or action) and "*lu*"(路, road) for the very early Chinese. "The three-hundred-piece Book of Poetry (*Shi Jing*, 诗经) often uses '*xing*' in place of the word 'Dao'"(Dai Zhen, Introduction 绪言, Vol. I). Derived from this original meaning, words such as *da* (达) or arrival, *tong* (通) through, *shun* (顺) or smooth, and *zhi* (直) or straightforward, are often associated with and even interchangeable to the word *Dao*. The implication of this message is primal and decisive for the Chinese way of thinking. To be able to walk there must be a way or road available; to have or to build a way is to have someone walk on it. Since walk (*xing*), the same word for action, conduct, behavior and practicality, is not idle wandering but always to go somewhere (or to reach a goal), the way could certainly be necessary and essential. Without a way or knowledge of it one could go nowhere and accomplish nothing. Zhu Xi (朱熹, 1130–1200) said explicitly in this regard, "Men and things go with their own intrinsic natures, therefore they must follow respectively their own paths in routine occurrences. This is what is called Dao"(Zhu Xi, 29). Indeed, it is from this seemingly plain matter of fact associated with our everyday life that derived quite a number of connotations of the word *Dao*, some of which are in relation, explicitly or implicitly, to many significant themes in Chinese philosophy.

For instance, to walk is to go somewhere along a path that can lead to one's destination. In the same respect, natural phenomena move or change in a *way* that leads the ten-thousand-things to exist in an ordered and harmonious universe; societies unite and develop in a *way* that leads to the promise of peace, prosperity and happiness; people act and think in a *way* that leads them to accomplish different meanings and purposes of their lives. This *way* or Dao could be conceived of as principle (*li*, 理). "Dao is *li*," says the *Book of Zhuangzi* (16/1). In other words, "When Dao is spoken, it always refers to the principle of necessity in things, the principle all men should follow"(Zhu Xi, 75). Ancient Chinese liked to speak of Dao as a principle of things both in nature and society, such as *tiandao* (天道, the way of heaven or nature), *rendao* (人道, the way of human beings), *wangdao* (王道, the way of princes), *daoshu* (道术, the art of Dao, or the strategy or technique of the Dao), etc. Many believed that an overall or ultimate *Way* or Principle must exist, for without such a Principle the world would be in a state of chaos. On the other hand, this *way* or Dao contains a meaning of guidance as the graph of *shou* (首) indicates the head of a person. Dao often stands for "to guide" or "to lead" one to get somewhere or to do something right. For example, in the *Analects*, Confucius said, "Lead [*dao*] by governmental order, regulate by law, and people will know nothing about shame . . ." (2:3). As well as in the *Zhong Yong* (中庸, The Doctrine of the Mean), it stated, "To guide our nature is called Dao"(1/1).[5] Furthermore, with *shou* or head as the home of spirit (*jingshen* 精神) and primary senses, Dao somehow symbolizes spirituality, rationality, and morality, all of which are of great significance in terms of personal cultivation and transformation.

Another meaning of the word *shou* is initiation or beginning (*qishou*, 起首, beginning, *shouxian*, 首先, first). It is quite likely that the word *Dao* could have a kind of sense of origin or originator of things, for nothing could be completed or achieved without a Dao or way of becoming. Perhaps this is why early philosophers such as Laozi, for example, had used the word *Dao* to signify the origin or root of the universe.

Dao sometimes refers to language, especially oral language or speech, whereas "name" (*ming*, 名) often refers to the written language. When Dao is used as a verb it usually means "to speak" or "to say." The very first sentence of Laozi's *Dao De Jing* says that the Dao that can be daoed (as a verb) is not the constant Dao. Here the verb *daoed* could mean, at least in part, "spoken of," "said" or "told." For most ancient Chinese, the Dao was supposed to be the universal principle or guidance so that it should be "heard" or "told" in order to be known. Dao speaks (*daos*). By speaking, Dao gives things names and puts them in a proper order; therefore, "having name or named is the mother of all things"(*Dao De Jing*, 1/2). Furthermore, in ordinary usage and modern Chinese, Dao could also mean "thinking," "expectation," "skill," etc. Dao is one of the most common and polysemous words and has a vast multiplicity and plurality of usage in Chinese language.[6]

In brief, as Charles Fu once noted in his investigation of Laozi's philosophy, there are six philosophical dimensions or meanings of the concept of Dao: (1) Dao as Reality (*daoti*, 道体) designating the essence, or being/nonbeing in the Western terms, of the world; (2) Dao as Origin (*daoyuan*, 道原) of all things; (3) Dao as Principle (*daoli*, 道理); (4) Dao as Function (*daoyong*, 道用) representing the dynamic and functional nature of things; (5) Dao as Virtue (*daode*, 道德); (6) Dao as Technique (*daoshu*, 道术). The first five dimensions, according to Fu, combine in the Dao as Manifestation or Form (*dao xiang*, 道相).[7]

Again, all these possible meanings and usages are derived from the original meaning of Dao as way and walk. It is from this very point that Dao eventually came to be the central concern of Chinese philosophy. During the mid and late Zhou Dynasty these connotations of the term *Dao* had been commonly understood and used in various contexts. It is very easy to become confused if one does not read the word *Dao* carefully within the right context of the text. Therefore, the above clarification of the term *Dao* will help us to sort out the proper meaning of Dao in the Zhuangzi.

It is hard to trace when, in the history of Chinese thought, the word *Dao* first became a cosmological or "metaphysical"[8] term, designating the cosmological origin or "metaphysical reality" that determines the form, meaning, and being of everything. Although many other earlier terms such as *tian* (天, heaven), *tianming* (天命, mandate of heaven), and *di* (帝, Lord) were still used with similar metaphysical connotation as the term *Dao*, the trend to develop a philosophical theory of Dao had already been initiated. In the *Book of Guanzi*, it is recorded that Guanzi (?–645 BCE) had used Dao and *tian-dao* to represent the universal truth or principle.[9] By the time of mid Zhou Dynasty (ca. 600 BCE), the word *Dao* began to refer to the ultimate reality, cosmological origin, or universal principle by various schools. Laozi believed that it was the Dao that produced (*sheng*) the vicissitudes of the universe, vitalized the whole world of lives, and legislated and justified patterns of human life and social relationships. For Confucius, too, the term *Dao* takes on its extended abstract and general meaning. As Benjamin I. Schwartz remarks, the Dao is the Dao of "an achieved universal" and "the word *tao* (Dao) would thus be Confucius' inclusive name for the all embracing normative human order" (Schwartz, 60, 63). Once the Dao was ignored, denied, or devastated by any cause, nature or society would lose their harmony and peace, and people would suffer from all kinds of disasters. Most early Chinese thinkers agreed that the meaning of human life, the content and purpose of true knowledge, the advance of morality, and the success of governance were simply manifestations of the ultimate Reality or Order that they called Dao. All great thoughts created during the early age of Chinese culture were based on Dao as philosophical presupposition and religious belief.[10]

In his *Disputers of the Dao*, A. C. Graham depicts the inquiry of Dao in early China in terms of a sociopolitical perspective. He thinks that since the decline and disintegration were perceived by most early Chinese thinkers as the inevitable consequence of the loss of Dao,

> their whole thinking is a response to the breakdown of the moral and political order which had claimed the authority of Heaven; and the crucial question for all of them is not the Western philosopher's "what is the truth?" but "where is the Way?", the way to order the state and conduct personal life. From the viewpoint of the rulers who listen at least to the more practical of them, they are men with new answers to the problem of how to run a state in these changing times; and this problem is indeed central to all of them, whether they have practical answers (Legalist), or ponder the moral basis of social order and its relation to the ruling power of Heaven (Confucians, Moists), or as defenders of private life think the proper business of the state is to leave everyone alone (Zhuangzi). (3)

Hence, the major schools of early Chinese thought can be viewed as diverse studies or teachings of Dao (*zhidaoshu*, 治道术). This does not mean that there was a unitary concept of or belief in Dao among those schools. As a matter of fact, different schools and thinkers presented their own understandings and interpretations of Dao, which not only were heterogeneous but contradictory or conflicting. What they shared was one goal, which was to explore, to learn, and to practice the Dao, the Truth or the Way. In his essay "On the Essentials of the Six Schools," historian Sima Tan (died 110 BCE) says:

> In the "Great Appendix" of *The Book of Change (Yi)*, there is the statement: "In the world there is one purpose, but there are a hundred ideas about it; there is a single goal, but the paths toward it differ." This

is just the case with the different schools of thought ... (*Shi Ji*, ch.130)

Based upon this primary purpose of searching for the Dao, different schools and individual thinkers created "a hundred ideas" about it, and some of them subsequently became the mainstream of Chinese philosophy and religious thought, such as Confucianism, Daoism, Legalism, and some of the Buddhist schools.

WUWU: A DECONSTRUCTION OF METAPHYSICAL PERSPECTIVES OF DAO

Most thinkers at the time were to present their own concepts of the Dao, such as Confucius's Dao of *ren* (仁) or human morality and Mozi's Dao of *jianai* (兼爱) or universal love. For Zhuangzi it was fine to create one's Dao in one's own fashion. The problem was that "[t]here are many who have studied the art of the Dao,[11] and each believes he has possessed a truth that cannot be improved" (33/1, cf. Watson, 363). They simply took what they thought of as the Dao itself and insisted on it as absolute and exclusive. Anything other than *my* Dao must be wrong. From then on, the endless debate had taken place, "the world was in great disorder, the valuable and sacred became equivocal, the Dao and its virtue were no longer One, most in the world were obsessed by their one partial point" (33/1). Instead of the Dao itself, there were only opinions of Dao in this world, the opinions that segmented and distorted the harmonious unity of the world, the opinions that alienated human nature and thereby made life inauthentic and coercive. How could one live on freely and happily without distracting oneself with, or simply forgetting, these fundamentalist beliefs or what Zhuangzi described as fixed mind/hearts (*chengxin*, 成心)? Hence, one of the crucial undertakings for Zhuangzi was to subvert or deconstruct the conventional or predominant ideas, especially Laozi's metaphysical utterance, of the Dao.

Historically, many have construed Zhuangzi as merely a follower or successor of Laozi who made the first metaphysical utterances, and hence have failed to detect or understand what original and subversive moves Zhuangzi made in his philosophy.[12] The two great founders of the Daoist tradition may look similar in various ways. But if we looked at them carefully, we would hardly miss that Zhuangzi presented his very unique philosophy and methodology as significantly different in many aspects from those of Laozi. This is perhaps why in Chinese history, especially in the tradition of Daoism, there used to be a particular school of Zhuangzi, which produced the *Book of Zhuangzi* and a special "learning of Zhuangzi" (*Zhuangxue*, 庄学) distinctive from the teaching of Laozi.

In the last chapter, *Tianxia* (天下) or "The World," of the *Book of Zhuangzi*, Zhuangzi is carefully separated from Laozi as symbols of two different schools. In comparison with Laozi's Dao as nonbeing, Zhuangzi's Dao is described as "Obscure, boundless, and without pattern; changing and trans-forming, without constancy. Is it birth or is it death? Is it the merger of heaven and earth? Is it where the spirit goes? Never clear where to go, never decisive what to be? Even if all the ten-thousand-things are counted, there is still no clue to locate it" (33/6). These few words successfully bring out the unique-ness of Zhuangzi's position on Dao. I will elaborate this point in the next section.

Guo Xiang (郭象, 252–312), the most influential commentator on and the editor of today's version of the *Book of Zhuangzi*, proclaimed in his "Intro-duction to the *Book of Zhuangzi*" that Zhuangzi was on the top of all "hun-dreds schools" because he attained the ultimate Dao. Wang Fu-zhi (王夫之, 1619–1692), another prominent philosopher in the Qing Dynasty, was one of the few who did not treat Zhuangzi as a mere follower of Laozi. He said in his "*Interpreting Zhuangzi*" (*Zhuangzi Jie*, 庄子解):

> Zhuangzi's teaching followed Laozi at the beginning; after his "morning enlightenment" [*zaoche*, 朝彻] and "seeing the self" [*jiandu*, 见独], he has realized that solitude and vicissitude are actually one, from which one is able to walk both ways [*liangxing*, 两行] smoothly without hindrance ... and he has created his own teaching which differs from Laozi's. (284)

It is from the notion of *liangxing*, or walking both ways, instead of Laozi's *wu* or nonbeing as the arbitrary origin of all beings, that Wang keenly sensed the major difference between the two masters.

Until very recently some scholars explored the difference between the two in terms of metaphysical and ontological perspectives, perhaps under the influence of Western philosophy. Charles Wei-hsun Fu is one of the few who have further detected the fundamental discrepancy between Laozi and Zhuangzi, especially from their perspectives of Dao. He said,

> Zhuangzi was in fact such a genius philosopher who, for the first time in the world history of thought, attained an ultimate recognition that the metaphysical and transmetaphysical [meanings of Dao] are actually two sides, which could be both separated and synthesized, of the same body. If, say, regular metaphysicians were guilty of cling-ing to "Being" and Laozi was guilty of attaching to "Non-being" [*wu*], Zhuangzi could be seen as the first transmetaphysician who surpassed the duality of Being and Non-being by his notion of *wu-wu* or no-nonbeing, five hundred years before Nagarjuna was born in India.[13]

The contribution Fu made here is that he revealed between the two masters' very different understandings of Dao, which were normally taken for granted as something homogeneous that Laozi and Zhuangzi had obviously agreed upon. I would like to investigate Zhuangzi's unique notion of Dao from the same starting point where Fu has begun, but with a different approach of my own.

Zhuangzi's unique articulation of Dao consists of two parts in general, by which he departed from Laozi: (1) a critique of Dao as metaphysical reality and cosmological originator, a deconstruction of truth, knowledge, and language as something final, absolute, and unchangeable (this was the central objectives of the second chapter, *Qi Wu-lun*, 齐物论or "equalizing opinions on things"); (2) an establishment and reconstruction of a positive Dao of the world and an affirmative attitude toward life itself, and thus a way to attain the ultimate liberation of the human spirit. Let's begin with Zhuangzi's deconstructing metaphysical Dao as an indispensable preparation and necessary *dao* for the ultimate realization of freedom (*xiaoyaoyou*).

In *Dao De Jing*, Laozi seems to come up with the conviction that, notwithstanding how hesitant or ambiguous his words sound, there is an ultimate reality which is the "root" (*gen*, 根), the base or origin (*ben*, 本) of the apparent world:

> We look but see it not; it is named "the Invisible." We listen but hear it not; it is named "the Inaudible." We try to seize it but find it not; it is named "the Intangible." These three cannot be scrutinized, and thus are undifferentiated into One. (*Dao De Jing*, 14)

This "One" is not supposed to be told by any name because it is the Name of all names or constant Name (*changming*, 常名). In another words, the Name that names all names cannot be named. Laozi was "forced to give a provisional name Dao" (25) as the Dao of all *daos*, or the constant Dao (*changdao*, 常道). Perceived by Laozi as the root or reality (*ben*) of ten-thousand-things, Dao unfolds or manifests itself into things and thus creates the whole apparent world. For Laozi, Dao is logically and cosmologically the origin of all things or beings of the world. Dao produced (or produces) one, one produced two, two produced three, and three produced all things (42). This is often seen as a cosmological claim that Dao is the origin of a temporal process of cosmological creation, such as from one to two and to three and so on. It is also important to note that Laozi might be understood as articulating how the ultimate or primary reality manifests and constructs the phenomenal world. From one to many here means from the ideal root or innermost nature (essence) to many apparent things or beings. As the origin and reality of *things* or *beings*, Dao cannot be one of them but is No-thing or Non-being (*wu*, 无). Everything comes into existence from nothingness and ceases into nothingness. For Laozi, things cannot be produced from things themselves. So *wu* is the quality and nature of Dao that enables Dao to be the reality and origin of the world: nonbeing or nothingness produced being (*you*, 有), being has two energies (*yin* and *yang* or *tian* [天], heaven and *di* [地], earth), and finally ten-thousand-things were created. In this respect, *wu* is understood also as the final source or real dynamic which makes everything in the world happen.

Furthermore, "The movement of Dao is reversal (*fan*, 反)" (2). From *wu* to *you*, from *you* to *wu*, Dao moves from one pole to the other, turns around like a circle from the beginning, over and over. Finally, Dao is *ziran* (自然),[14] spontaneous or natural, which has nothing to do with any personified God or magic power or moral virtue but nature itself—"man follows earth; earth follows heaven, heaven follows Dao, Dao follows its spontaneous nature [*ziran*]" (25).[15]

Yet on the other hand, Laozi says in the very beginning of his *Dao De Jing*: "Dao that can be *daoed* is not the eternal and constant Dao" (1/1). In other words, Laozi might have well been aware that any metaphysical explanation of the Dao is not Dao itself but only part of it. Whichever sense one chooses, whether material, Idea, Form, Goodness, *ren*, or *tianming*, to define the Dao is incomplete, and therefore not final. The more we think or talk about it the farther the real Dao slips away. Zhuangzi agrees with Laozi that Dao is not something we can speak of or learn as knowledge from textbooks but the "Dao that is not *daoed*" (不道之道, 2/5). Metaphysical claims about what Dao is are only opinions constructed by very limited human language and knowledge which cannot grasp Dao but only give rise to constant argumentation. For Zhuangzi, Laozi might have discovered at the outset that metaphysics and cosmology were impossible means to know or attain Dao even if Dao was the reality or origin of the universe. However, Laozi couldn't help talking about Dao metaphysically. The whole work he wrote rested on the foundation of Dao as the metaphysical reality, universal principle, and cosmological origin of all things.

When we learn from Laozi that the Dao is "Nothingness" or "Nonbeing" (*wu, wuyou*), we might expect him to dismiss the metaphysical or ontological concept of Dao. If the Dao is nothing, or *is-not* as nonbeing, how can it be thought of as something that exists? Some scholars have tried to interpret this *wu* as his "trans-ontological" or "trans-metaphysical" breakthrough (Wu Kuang-ming, Charles Fu), since the conception *wu* actually could have undermined any possibility of metaphysical device. Yet unfortunately, Laozi took the other way. He turned the Non-being/Dao into "something (not nothing) undefined and complete, coming into existence before Heaven and Earth" and "the Mother of all things" (*Dao De Jing*, 25/1). As Charles Fu has argued, Laozi did render the Dao as the metaphysical and cosmological meaning of Reality and Origin or Originator.[16] This is why Laozi has often been called "the first Chinese metaphysician." It was Zhuangzi who took Laozi's thought of *wu* into an antimetaphysical position: Dao, as metaphysical Reality or cosmological origin is simply nothing (*wu*), not nothing-ness as something primary or substantial, not Non-being as Being, but just *is-not*.

Laozi was great, Zhuangzi would say, because he had revealed that what is *prior* to things or beings is *wu*, while everybody else fixed their sight on the realm of things or beings. No matter what kind of thing one chooses as *a prior*, it would still be in the realm of things but not of Reality. The Dao as primal Reality of things, or Being of beings, such as Plato's Forms and Hegel's

Idea, cannot be a thing, because it is the Reality that produced (*sheng*) the existence of things, not vice versa. Therefore, "Dao that can be *daoed* is not the eternal and constant Dao"(*Dao De Jing*, 1/1). That No-thing-ness that cannot be seen and named is the real Dao, in other words, the Dao is No-thing, or Non-being is the Being of beings, or simply, Being or Dao *is not* (*wu*). The Dao as metaphysical Reality and cosmological origin is actually No-thing, which means no Dao as such exists. It is at this point that Zhuangzi departed from Laozi's metaphysical interpretation of Dao. He did not force himself to deploy *wu* to pursue a metaphysical and ontological presupposition, or to trace the origin of the cosmos as Laozi did. Rather, he first questioned and then denounced such presuppositions.

Therefore, Zhuangzi would accuse Laozi of hypostatizing No-thing into something, as root, beginning, or reality. Laozi maintains that *wu* is the "Beginning or Origin of the Heaven and Earth" (1/2), because "the ten-thousand-things in the world were originated from Being (*you*), Being originates in No-thing/Non-being (*wu*)" (40/2). By this metaphysical effort, Laozi inevitably slipped into a trap: the un-daoable Dao was daoed, the No-thing became a *thing*, an ontological *Being*. He says: "Dao is '*something*' elusive and evasive. Evasive and elusive! Yet within it there is 'image'. Elusive and evasive! Yet within it there is '*something*' . . ." (21). Again: "There is '*something*' nebulously complete in and by itself, which comes before Heaven and Earth" (25/1). What is this *something*? Why? Zhuangzi has frankly shown his skepticism about this. In chapter 2 he says,

> There would be no self without the other; the other would not stand without the self. This comes close to the matter of fact. But no one knows what is behind all this. It would seem as though there is the True Master, yet no one finds a trace of it. We believe that it functions, yet see no forms of it in so far as it has no form but affection. The hundred joints, the nine openings, the six organs, all come together and exist here [as my body]. But which part should I feel closest to? I should delight in all parts, you say? But there must be one I ought to favor more. If not, are they all of them mere servants? But if they are all servants, then how can they keep order among themselves? It would seem as though there must be some True Lord among them. But whether I succeed in discovering the fact of it or not, it neither adds to nor detracts from the authenticity of them. (2/2, cf. Watson, 38.)

The True Master (*zhenzai*, 真宰) and True Lord (*zhenjun*, 真君) here might refer to that metaphysical or cosmological *something*. Or, perhaps they are what account for the regular movements of things (as in "from life to death"), that is, a nontheistic pattern things of certain categories must follow. What Zhuangzi has to say is that we are not able to know what or who or when originated the world and ten-thousand-things, except a constant flow of becoming (*sheng*,

生), change (*bian*, 变), or transformation (*hua*, 化) of things. Neither can we know what or who makes things what they are, things become what they are by virtue of their correlation, interaction, and interdependence with each other, as all joins, openings, and organs of one's body. We are not entitled to name or appoint one of the things the True Master or True Lord. If we do, the only result is to make our mind fixated (*chengxin*) with certain idea or discourse of Dao instead of living with the true Dao (2/2). Moreover, our opinions of Dao would not make any difference to the natural world and its course of becoming. This could be another proof that we know *nothing* about whether there is such a True Master of the universe. A further illustration of this point in chapter 14 is worth quoting here.

> Does Heaven turn? Does the earth sit still? Do sun and moon compete for a place to shine? Who masterminds all this? Who pulls the strings? Who, resting inactive himself, gives the push that makes it go this way? I wonder, is there some mechanism that works it and won't let it stop? I wonder if it just rolls and turns and can't bring itself to a halt? Do the clouds make the rain, or does the rain make the clouds? Who puffs them up, who showers them down like this? Who, resting inactive himself, stirs up all this lascivious joy? The winds rise in the north, blowing now west, now east, whirring up to wonder on high. Whose breaths and exhausts are they? Who, resting inactive himself, huffs and puffs them about like this? May I ask the reason, why? (14/1, Watson, 154)

Is there a reason or final cause (master) for everything that is going on in the world? Winds blow and rain falls on their own, sun and moon shine without purpose, No-one or No-thing is the Master or Lord who creates and controls the course of the nature itself. We never know whether there is such a Dao as Creator, Originator, and Reality. The world worlds, things thing, being beings as such, all by themselves. Everything becomes, changes, transforms by its own rhythm, its own cause and its own will with *no-thing* else behind. This is what Zhuangzi meant by *ziran*, spontaneous nature, or simply self-so, thus-so.[17]

From this point, Zhuangzi advanced the notion of *wu* into a radical claim of *wuwu*, a double *wu* that deconstructs the entire metaphysical account. First, if *wu* was designated as the beginning of the universe it would be no more No-thing or Non-being but something. Secondly, if *wu* was conceived as the real Being of beings, the whole world of becoming would be denied as a real world. For Zhuangzi, therefore, it is not enough to realize the No-thing-ness of things, or Non-being of beings, the *wu* itself must be "*wued*" (deconstruction itself should be deconstructed).

In chapter 2, Zhuangzi thus reasons:

There is a beginning. There is a not yet beginning to be a beginning. There is a not yet beginning to be not yet beginning to be a beginning. There is being (*you*). There is Non-being (*wu*). There is not yet beginning to be Non-being. There is a not yet beginning to be a not yet beginning to be Non-being. Suddenly *There-is* Non-being, I am no longer sure whether Being and Non-being are actually Being and Non-being. (2/5, Watson, 42)

From this reasoning, we have seen that (1) one can not reach the beginning and end or finality of *wu*; (2) the dividing line between beginning and not yet beginning, *you* and *wu* is no longer clear, because in the course of nature there is no such dividing point but ever flowing flux of mutation and transformation.[18] Hence, Zhuangzi tries to go beyond the boundary of *wu*, creating his unique theory of *wuwu*, No-No-thing, which used to be called Non-being of Non-being. A passage in chapter 23 says:

There is life, there is death, there is a coming out, there is going back in—yet in the coming out and going back there is no sign to trace. This is called the Gate of Heaven. The Gate of Heaven is No-thing or Non-being. The ten-thousand-things come forth from Non-being. Being cannot create being out of being; inevitably it must come forth from Non-being. And Non-being is itself Non-being or No-thing. This is the home in which a sage stores [his mind]. (23/6, Watson, 256–57)

The Gate of Heaven (*tianmen*, 天门) refers metaphorically to the mysterious origin (Dao as Origin and Reality) from which everything comes forth and goes back in. This is Laozi's idea of *wu* For Zhuangzi it is not enough to designate Non-being as the Gate of Heaven. When Laozi says that Non-being beings or produces ten-thousand-things, it is no longer No-thing but something else, which could be mysterious forces and divine beings (developed later by religious Daoism). In order to avoid such a dilemma, Zhuangzi goes further to point out that nonbeing itself is Non-being, No-thing itself is no-thing, *wu* itself is *wu* (*wuwu*). From the new concept of *wuwu*, Zhuangzi intended to tell us, nonbeing is not the Being of beings, there is simply no Being in this world. Therefore, Non-being *is-not* or does *not be*; do not try anything to make up a Being, such as an Originator, Lord, Creator, etc., out of nonbeing.

No-thing, according to Laozi and the majority of his disciples, is the opposite pole of things, or the negation of things. This means No-thing cannot be independent apart from the existence of things. To be attached to or obsessed by *wu*, Zhuangzi has pointed out, would obstruct one's view to see the world as a whole and block the Way for one to attain ultimate enlightenment. *Wuwu* has reached a new state that transcends the opposition between no-thing and things, nonbeing and beings. The Gate of Heaven has opened up with no Gate; it is nowhere and everywhere. The world worlds, "it comes out from no base, it goes back in through no aperture; it is real yet has no spot to reside; it has duration yet neither beginning nor end" (23/6).

And this is the home in which the sage of Dao wants to abide, the real root Zhuangzi wants to return to. Listen to this allegory:

> Guangyao (Brilliant) asked Wuyou (Non-being), "Sir, would you tell me if you *are* (*you*) or you *are-not* (*wu*)?" Wuyou didn't answer. Guang-yao stared intently at the other's appearance—all was vacuity and blankness, all day long he looked without seeing, listened without hearing, touched without contacting. "This is perfect!" Guangyao mumbled, "How could he reach such perfection? I can only conceive of the No-thing, but not of the No-no-thing. If one stay at the position of No-thing, he will never reach this kind of perfection." (22/9, Watson, 244)

The perfect state of Dao is *wuwu*, the real *wu* that embraces the self-negation and self-destruction. With the perspective of *wuwu* Zhuangzi has departed from the traditional and prevailing ways of thinking toward a very different perspective of philosophizing Dao: (1) *wuwu* as a thoroughgoing negation leaves no room for any metaphysical, foundational, and substantial meditation on Dao, and dismisses attempts to think of Dao as a transcendental Being supposed to be external or above this world. In conjunction with the ideas such as *wufen* (无分, undifferentiation), *huanzhong* (环中, the middle of the ring), *wuji* (无极, no-beginning), *wuzhi* (无知, ignorance, no-knowledge), *buyong* (不用, not-to-use), and the practice of *liangxing* (两行, walk in both ways), *tong* (通, throughness, clearing, openness), *zuowang* (坐忘, sitting and forgetting), *xinzhai* (心斋, mind fasting), etc., Zhuangzi provided an alterna-tive way of overcoming and transcending all metaphysical positions. (2) *Wuwu* is an ever open process of nature as *ziran*, a process with no beginning or end, no limit or boundary, no concept of right and wrong, No-no-thing whatsoever, except its original force or dynamic of changing and becoming. (3) *Wuwu* has completely overcome the duality between thing and No-thing, or Being and Non-being, it is both *you* and *wu*, or neither *you* nor *wu*, it is a real affirmation of this existing world through negation of negation. (4) As such a nonduality (*wudai*, 无待, or *du*, 独), *wuwu* has dismissed the human or artificial distinction of the world into Dao (as reality, being, Lord) and things (as appearances, differences), truth and error, being and nonbeing, big and small, birth and death, etc. Everything gains equality and identity as One with Dao; everything becomes Dao. Dao, at the same time, becomes One with everything or "ten-thousand-things" (manyness or differences). Finally, the destructive or deconstructive process of *wuwu* now ends up with a constructive or reconstructive state of itself, through which Zhuangzi enables himself to complete his unique and paramount perspective (*jingjie*, 境界): Dao/道

throughs/通 as/为 One/一 (*daotongweiyi*, 2/4), in other words, Dao is–not being or nonbeing or *wuwu* but throughs or *tongs* as One.

DAO THROUGHS AS ONE

The last quote above is from the *Book of Zhuangzi*, chapter 2/4: "Things however peculiar, ridiculous, wondrous and mysterious, they are all One as Dao throughs (道通为一)."[19] If read by sentence itself: "Dao throughs as One." Many English translations available today have so far misinterpreted this important assertion of Dao made by Zhuangzi. They, including most Chinese commentators, have not realized that this sentence contains in Zhuangzi the fundamental understanding of Dao. Two key words "*tong*" and "*yi*" have been either lost or underrated as if this sentence makes sense only with the previous sentences. Not that the Dao "makes" or "connects" things into one "unity" (Burton Watson, Victor H. Mair, A. C. Graham, Yu-lan Fung). That would put Zhuangzi back to Laozi's position as a metaphysician, but that the Dao is One whence through (*tong*). For Zhuangzi, One is what Dao is while throughness is the positive state of One. The word *tong* often missed in translations and interpretations plays an extremely significant role in Zhuangzi's philosophy. Without the connotation of *tong*, one could not fully understand and characterize Zhuangzi's distinctive notion of Dao and One. Only if a path is through, I mean *tonged*, free of blockage, is one able to walk by. This is why Zhuangzi speaks of *tong* in conjunction with *dao* as *daotong* (道通). Whence the throughness is reached, in another words, whence Dao is clear, open, or *tong*, One is realized, or, ten-thousand-things become One, this is what Zhuangzi meant by *weiyi* (为一). Without throughness, Dao is no longer Dao, for no one can actually walk through it to get anywhere. By the same token, being blocked from each other, things would lose their correlations and connections with each other and hence the totality of themselves. According to Zhuangzi, the way or Dao has to be clear, connected, or through as an ideal condition for the change, transformation, and becoming of all things as a harmonious whole. This is what Zhuangzi meant by "Dao throughs as One." In order to understand Zhuangzi's teaching, I would suggest strongly, one should always keep in mind that *dao*, *tong*, and *yi* are themselves One; they go together and identify each other as a whole to accomplish Zhuangzi's reconstruction of Dao perspective (*daoguan*, 道观) and Dao discourse (*daoyan*, 道言). Dao throughs as One; Dao is One that throughs; throughness as One is Dao—that is Zhuangzi's understanding of Dao, the way of throughness. For Zhuangzi, it is not some ultimate substance, being, idea, nor nothingness hypostatized by metaphysical reasoning but throughness (*tong*) that makes possible the ways all things become what they are and get together with each other as a harmonious whole. Again, without throughness one could hardly understand Zhuangzi's Dao and his notion of One.

On many occasions Zhuangzi talked about *yi* in reference to Dao. In the *Inner Chapters* alone, *yi* is mentioned or discussed more than twenty times

(1/2, 1/3, 2/1, 2/2, 2/3, 2/4, 2/5,2/6, 2/7, 4/1,4/3, 5/1, 6/1, 6/2, 6/6, 6/7, 6/9, 7/1). The frequency of the appearances of the word *yi* even exceeded the word *Dao*, especially in chapter 2. If we read Zhuangzi close enough we will easily find that the *yi* Zhuangzi incessantly emphasizes is synonymous and interchangeable with the word *Dao*. The significance of *yi* as Dao in Zhuangzi, however, is far more complex and intriguing than one may first think from its literal and traditional meaning. As far as I know, Zhuangzi's notion of *yi* as Dao has not yet been well thought out by his commentators, partly because they did not pay enough attention to his different or creative use of *yi* in contrast to its use by Laozi. The reason for this oversight has been due to the conventional meaning of *yi* in a Confucian context as the "harmony" of heaven and earth (*tianrenheyi*, 天人合一). When Daoist commentators found *yi* in Zhuangzi, they often accepted and understood it in this cosmological sense. The one major exception to this trend was the third-century eclectic commentator Guo Xiang. [20] This successor of the magnificent Daoist exegete Wang Bi rethought the meaning of Zhuangzi's notion of *yi* in a very novel way, and the interpretation that follows is in part indebted to him.

Laozi was perhaps the first who used *yi* to designate the ineffable Dao as the cosmological origin and thus a metaphysical reality. He said in the *Dao De Jing*, "Dao produces one [*yi*]; One produces two; two produces three; three produces ten-thousand-things"(42). In his interpretation of this verse, Wang Bi explained that, as one is the beginning of all numbers, it is thus the origin of all things (Wang, 105). Since every number can be reduced to a collection of ones, One is also construed by Laozi as a universal metaphysical reality or Dao itself. "It is by acquiring the One, sky becomes clear, the earth becomes peaceful, spirit becomes alive, the valley becomes fulfilling, ten-thousand-things come into being and the king brings justice to the world ..."(39). Following Laozi, commentators have conceived of *yi* as the ultimate origin, reality, and principle, synonymous with Dao.

When Zhuangzi wrote that Dao throughs as One or Oneness (*yi*), one could easily be convinced that he was talking about the same thing Laozi had before him. But as a matter of fact, Zhuangzi's notion of *yi*, based on a non-metaphysical stance, is very different from Laozi's. According to Zhuangzi, *yi* is not the cosmological origin, or original One that is supposed to be the creator or producer of things. Nor is *yi* a metaphysical reality (*wu*) that determines the Being of all beings and represents the only truth of the phenomenal world. For Zhuangzi, as we discussed before, does not admit any metaphysical connotation of the concept of Dao. He has no intention to conceive of *yi* as some sort of absolute entity or to construct any kind of monism when he says, "Dao is One," or, "Ten-thousand-things are One."

For Zhuangzi, "one" is not a number that initiates numbering, nor a single entity that excludes or opposes many; instead, One (*yi*) is, first of all, a general designation which is parallel to words such as "*tianxia*" (the world), "*tiandi*" (heaven and earth), "*yüzhou*" (宇宙, universe), and "*wanwu*" (万物, ten-thousand-things), designating the togetherness, the inclusiveness, the integration or whole of all things. "Thus," as Fung Yulan has pointed out, "ten-thousand-things and I mixed up as One. The words 'mix up'(*huntong*, 混同) used here fit fabulously, for the One is indeed reached in virtual of such a mix up without any differentiation"(Fung, 372). One as such characterizes nature or *ziran* as an undifferentiated, all-inclusive, all together totality, which does not produce or unify things but is simply a sum total of things, that is to say, one is the ten-thousand-things put together. Everything that exists relates or is relative to other things. One is not something that determines any particular relationship but the fact of relationship itself. As far as the relationship is concerned, the distinction of self and other is relativized and dissolved into the Oneness of self and/or with others. The One of individual being becomes a One of togetherness or totality or all the ten-thousand-things as a whole. Furthermore, inasmuch as one (*yi*) is just the totality of everything all together, it does not dismiss or repress but affirms the existence of every single being. The differences between individuals are not dissolved into some grand and abstracted universal, but are distinguished or characterized by the Oneness of their togetherness. This is what Zhuangzi meant by "undifferentiated" Oneness. In this respect, *yi* is associated with the meaning of *zhou* (周, all-around), *quan* (全, comprehensive, all included), and *he* (和, harmony, combination) that all have something to do with the meaning of togetherness, wholeness, and the totality of the ten-thousand-things.

Another meaning of *yi* however is *tong* (同) or "sameness." Zhuangzi does not advocate any notion of ontological Being that represents the truth of all beings. What he called "same" refers to the spontaneous activity that makes all things what they are. What produces, transforms, and "things" is not the Being of beings but rather the "things themselves" (*zisheng*, 自生, *zihua*, 自化, *zide*, 自得). Things become, exist, change, and transform all by themselves with no recourse to any super-beings; this is what is called *ziran*. Within the course of all these particular movements of *ziran* there underlies the "sameness"(2/4). Guo Xiang has a great comment on this:

> It is a matter of fact that the stalk is horizontal and pillar vertical; that a leper is ugly and Xishi beautiful. But so called equalizing (qi, 齐) cannot be construed as equalizing forms or uniformising norms. Therefore [Zhuangzi] uses the instances such as vertical, horizontal, ugly and beautiful, ribald, shady, grotesque and strange to show that they are all *so* and all *okay* by themselves respectively. Though principles (*li*, 理) are ten thousand times different, they contain the very same nature (*xing*, 性). This is what is called "Dao throughs as One."(Comment on 2/4)

Yi as sameness in Zhuangzi means the sameness or commonness of difference rather than uniformity. All things are different, everything has its own identity, which belongs uniquely to itself; this exhibiting of difference is the same for all things. On the other hand, difference itself is not fixed; it changes provisionally according to one's changing relation to the other. If everything is different, then the differencing of things is a common or same activity of things. So, "Analogy (*lei*, 类) and difference (*bulei*, 不类) are the same in the way they come across"(2/5). In other words, *yi* is sameness (analogy) and difference come across into each other and become one, the one (*yi*) that does not deny, exclude, and condemn either sameness or difference but affirms and embraces both—different things are equally or identically different. This is also what Zhuangzi meant by *hezhiyitianni* (和之以天倪) or harmonizing or undifferentiating the differences of the natural world (2/6). In this sense, *yi* as employed by Zhuangzi is often equivalent to *tong* (same, analogy), *qi* (齐, equal, identical), *jun* (均, equal), *lei* (kind, specie, analogy).

The third meaning of *yi* or One stands for the appropriate way (Dao) of how human beings look at things and the world, or the ideal state of an enlightened human mind. A true person (*zhenren*, 真人) or person of Dao always sees and treats ten-thousand-things as one and in virtue of that she can wander around the capricious world, let go within the flux of life and become one with nature by casting off the obsession of the self (*sangwo*, 丧我, 2/1 and 6/1). A mind of *yi* or Oneness is also a mind that has overcome all kinds of attachment, obsession, dualism, dogmatism, prejudice, and discrimination. It is important for people to see that things are different and that our perceptions or opinions of things are different, but it is more important to see the affinity or oneness of all different things as well as our perceptions or opinions on things (5/1). Furthermore, a mind of *yi* is a mind of no mind or no-self-mind which finally transcends one's own ego into the harmonious and spontaneous oneness with all things around. Such a mind of *yi* does not distinguish differences but simply lets difference be, just like cook Ding who has forgotten the differences between himself and an ox, so that his knife can go over different parts and bones with tremendous ease (3/1). The story says,

> What I care about is Dao, which goes beyond skillfulness. When I
> first began cutting up oxen, all I could see was the oxen itself. After
> three years I no longer saw the whole oxen. And now—now I meet
> it by the spirit of instinct (*shen*, 神) without my eyes looking at it.
> My body knows where to stop and the instinct goes wherever it
> wishes. I go along with the natural makeup, strike in the big hollows,
> guide the knife through the big openings, and follow things as they
> are (*guran*, 固然). (3/1)

Here, "not seeing the whole oxen" and "looking without eyes" imply not having differentiated mind; "meeting it by the spirit of instinct" (shenyu, 神遇) implies the state of casting self or no-self; "following things as they are" refers to the oneness with nature; and "my body knows where to stop and the instinct goes wherever it wishes" gives an image of the state of *tong* or throughness, which is the key to understand Zhuangzi's notion of One.

After all, *yi* as a state of mind is the way of the kind of human liberation or spiritual freedom from the bonds of attachment, obsession, prejudice, dualism, dogmatism, or any form of fixation of one's mind. In this respect, *yi* can be read as a verb "to *yi*" that is equivalent to *qi* (to equalize, identify, or not distinguish), *tong* (通, to get through, to access, to connect with, to join), *he* (to harmonize, conciliate, combine, and blend).

Finally, *yi* represents a thorough throughness and openness (*tong*, 通) between heaven and earth, nature and human beings, self and others, which prevents a mind from being fixed or attached to any metaphysical presupposition, self-centered prejudice, and dualistic mentality. *Dao-tong-wei-yi*, "Dao throughs as One" (2/4), so that nothing can block the way of anything's or anybody's self-transformation, and no prejudice, knowledge, and moral principle will confine one's own spontaneity. As soon as one's mind opens through oneness, one liberates oneself from human alienation and returns to the natural, instinctive, and healthy life. One can in "imagination" move from one limited perspective to another, while never attached to any.

Dao became the undifferentiated One (*yi*) of myriad things, which keeps nature away from any subjective or artificial division and thus preserves the true diversity and differences of the world unharmed. Everything that *is* right here right now *is* Dao. A story was told by the unknown author of chapter 22, "Knowledge Wandered North" (*Zhi Bei You*, 知北游):

> Master Dung Guo asked Zhuangzi, "Where does the so called *Dao* exist?"
> Zhuangzi said, "There is no place it doesn't exist."
> "You must be more specific, please."
> "It is in the ant."
> "Why is it so low?"
> "It is in the panic grass."
> "Even lower?"
> "In the tiles and shards."
> "Isn't this the lowest?"
> "It is in the piss and shit!" (22/6, Watson, 240–41)

At the end of this conversation the Dao seeker Sir Dong Guo was stunned, either enlightened or confused. This was a stunning statement that threatened and challenged the traditional concept of the Dao: it exists everywhere even in the lowest things in *this* world. In other words, Dao is every thing; everything is Dao. Everything composes and transforms everything by itself (*zihua*), No-thing determines everything's own destiny. There is no-thing which sits behind the scene of the world of the ten-thousand-things controlling the coming and going of the appearances; it is the "thing-as-itself" (*ziji*, 自己) that moves, changes, lives, dies, presents, and absents all by itself. Therefore, Zhuangzi's Dao as One does not designate any universal principle or unitary system of the world but refers to the togetherness (Oneness) of all things in the world. This togetherness embraces all existences as they are without distinction (*wufen*, 无分).[21]

Dao is nothing but the One of everything, of the world as it is. Unlike most of his contemporaries, Zhuangzi's One as throughness identifies and equalizes all things into the togetherness of Dao. Since Dao is no-thing that controls and determines the ways of existence, every way of existence or self-transformation is supposed to be the way of Dao or *ziran*, every way of *ziran* must be affirmed as a part of the togetherness. Zhuangzi's notion of "Dao as One" does not connote any monistic meaning or dualistic mentality that holds uniformity or singularity against multiplicity of things, identity against differences, or reality against appearances, but a real Oneness that has overcome all duality by affirming multiplicity and differences. For Zhuangzi, the affirmation of differences is to realize the ONE or identity (*jun*, *qi*, or equality) of different things; when we see different things as different we tend to fight for a distinctive difference among them, but if we see different things as same, as non-different, as equally different, then we will comfortably let difference be naturally. This One and harmony of differences composes the ultimate music that is called "the sound of heaven" (*tianlai*). Anyone who reaches the realization of Dao as the One of the ten-thousand-things is able to hear it: a blowing (of *ziran*) on ten-thousand differences that lets every sound come out spontaneously (1/1).

There is a parable told in the second chapter that can be a very good example of how Zhuangzi's Oneness affirms differences:

> So it is that long ago King Yao consulted King Shun, "I will attack the Zong, Kuai, and Xu-ao,[22] but as I sit on my throne I don't feel at ease with this decision. Why is this?"
>
> King Shun replied, "These three rulers are only little dwellers in the weeds and brush. How can you not be disturbed like this? In old times, ten suns came out together at once, and ten-thousand-things were all lit up without exception, let alone that the luminary of virtue (*de*) must be greater than sunshine today." (2/6, Watson, 45)

The world of Dao in Zhuangzi's mind is a world that has "ten suns" shining differently together, a world that is a harmonious unity of ten-thousand-things. One should have no reason to attack "other" suns because of their differences.

As One, Dao represents the infinite flux of the ever-becoming nature in which everything comes to be and ceases to be and cannot help but be what it is. "Heaven cannot help but be high; earth cannot help but be broad; sun and moon cannot help but revolve; the ten thousand things cannot help but flourish" (22/5, Watson, 239). In Zhuangzi, the terms Dao, *tian* or heaven, *ziran* or nature, are often interchangeable; they all refer to the thus-so or self-so nature in a very original sense. Since Dao could be identical with the totality of nature, Dao has lost completely its metaphysical meaning and no longer needs to be perceived as something fundamental. Dao as nature itself is actually No-Dao (*wudao*, 无道) or Dao of No-Dao (2/5), because Dao does *not* do anything (*wuwei*, 无为) to control, to guide, to force, to change, to decide what is or what is to become; everything becomes, transforms itself all by itself (*zihua*).

The deconstruction of metaphysical Dao is for Zhuangzi the primary step to open and liberate one's mind from all kinds of repression or manipulation by conceptions envisioned as Reality, Lord, and Originator. Human mind is used to attaching itself to these conceptions (*chengxin* or fixed mind) and wasting all its life pursuing such a metaphysical Dao, which Zhuangzi thinks is no-thing or no-nothing (*wuwu*). This sort of mind or *cheng-xin*, he tells us, is the main source of our suffering and agony, because it grounds itself upon nothingness. To deconstruct metaphysical Dao is to get ready to demolish all that is fixed, artificial, and dogmatic and let oneself go with the spontaneous rhythm of self-so (*ziran*) and self-transformation (*zihua*). *Wuwu* or no-nothing therefore is not a nihilistic notion of the world; on the contrary, it is for Zhuangzi indeed a very affirmative state of mind by *wuing* or *no-ing* those hypostatized conceptions for the sake of returning to the actual flow of life or becoming one with nature. Therefore, it can be argued that Zhuangzi's deconstruction of metaphysics is actually motivated by his religiosity, his ultimate concern of freeing one's mind, rather than his philosophical interest. It is for the same reason that Zhuangzi goes on to critique human knowledge, language, and morality, which are all responsible for constructing the metaphysical reality of the world.

WUZHI: EQUALIZING OPINIONS IS THE WAY OF TRUE KNOWLEDGE

In the following sections I will illustrate Zhuangzi's position on knowledge, language, and morality. Zhuangzi is concerned with the enslavement of humankind caused by the construction and deification of knowledge, language, and morality. In order to free oneself or become *xiaoyao*, Zhuangzi asks us to overcome and go beyond conventional concepts and applications of knowledge, language, and morality. Again, we will see that in his critique there always lies a deep religiosity, a passion for ultimate liberation and freedom.

People following traditional ways of thinking believe that as soon as we find knowledge corresponding to the metaphysical Dao, we possess the absolute Truth. It is the same belief that most philosophers and theologians all over the world have developed, around which they have formulated their theories and generated numerous controversies. As an outsider to this mainstream of human thought, "Zhuangzi neither presupposes nor does his doctrine entail that a single ineffable Dao exists, nor that there is such knowledge of a single, ultimate Dao, nor that we ought to follow such a Dao, and so on."[23] The reason for Zhuangzi to hold this is very simple. Since there is no metaphysics or metaphysical basis in the real world, as we have just seen, how can we possibly have a knowledge that corresponds to it? What people used to call truth is not the real truth but mere human imagination and artificial opinion, because it cannot be called truth if it corresponds to nothing.

Zhuangzi was not interested in criticizing any particular metaphysical theory; instead, he was concerned with the nature of common knowledge in general, and its negative impact on human life. What is knowledge? What is its actual function? Does knowledge provide the perfect Way (Dao) to guide our life? Is there a knowledge that can be the final Truth? Is there a standard that can judge what is right and wrong? What is the relationship between knowledge and life? Can knowledge benefit life in the ultimate sense, as most of us have believed?

Before I discuss these issues, the word *knowledge* (*zhi*, 知) needs to be clarified. Zhuangzi used this word as it was commonly used and understood, designating human knowledge (as a noun) and the activity of knowing (as a verb). But in his writing, he made a clear distinction between common knowledge and true knowledge (Dao) attained by sages. His critique of knowledge examines common knowledge and the conventional understanding of knowledge. When he says that true knowledge is *no*-knowledge (*buzhi*, 不知, *wuzhi*, 无知), but rather awareness or realization of Dao, he means that in order to know Dao (*zhidao*, 知道) one must overcome the enslavement to common knowledge and surpass the conventional understanding of knowledge. To deconstruct the common understanding of knowledge, therefore, seems a more crucial task for Zhuangzi than to do metaphysics, because metaphysics itself is a kind of knowledge or what Zhuangzi called *wulun* (物论, opinion of things).

More important, to deconstruct and go beyond common knowledge for Zhuangzi is the indispensable path to free oneself from the melancholy of an alienated life, which is controlled and disturbed by common knowledge. What is the problem of our life? What has restrained our freedom and spontaneity? Why can we humans not live in a carefree condition? What causes our anxiety, misery, and confusion, which tear our lives apart? Zhuangzi did not approach these questions from the aspect of economics and politics as others did, but directly from considerations of our way of thinking and the construction of knowledge. Zhuangzi appeared to believe that people used to live happy lives, for the ancestors knew (without knowing) how to live with Dao spontaneously. But once human beings created different forms of knowledge, they lost their natural integrity and the harmonious relationship they once had with each other and the world. Laozi had pointed out before that things only first became evil when we started knowing goodness, and first became ugly when we started knowing beauty (*Dao De Jing*, 2/1). In other words, the trouble came from the interference of human opinion, or, came from using dualistic categories wherein one (good) implies the existence of the other (evil). Human beings no longer dealt with nature or their genuine lives but with opinions they constructed by themselves. People construct themselves, their identities, and are thus controlled by their own knowledge or opinions on things (*wulun*). With such a diagnosis based on his religiosity or ultimate concern of life, the first thing Zhuangzi wants to do is deconstruct opinions of all kinds, especially the metaphysical claims concerning Dao, for this is the most crucial step toward human freedom and liberation.

The very foundation of Zhuangzi's philosophy is in his second chapter, called *Qi Wu-lun*, or "Equalizing or Identifying Opinions on Things" in my literal translation. The title of this chapter is still controversial for many scholars. Most translations have separated the last two words as *wu* and *lun*, which literally means *things* and *opinions*. Watson, for example, translates the two words as "the Discussions on Making All Things Equal"; Fung as "Equality of Things and Opinions"; Legge was right to translate the two together as "controversies," I believe. He said: "Mr. Balfour has translated this title by 'Essay on the Uniformity of All Things;' the subject of the Book being thus misconceived . . ." (Vo.I, 128.). Chen Gu-ying held that this title has two meanings: (1) to equalize all things; and (2) to equalize different opinions (Chen, 33). I don't think Zhuangzi would advise that anyone take such an action as "equalizing all things,"[24] inasmuch as things don't need be equalized, they are what they are. In light of the entire content of the chapter, I agree with Legge's comment, yet his translation of the title, "Adjustment of Controversies," seems inaccurate to me. *Wulun* literally means the "opinions of things" or opinions determined by "things," referring to theories and perspectives held by different individuals or groups. This chapter sometimes specifically refers to the views, not necessarily controversies, of the various schools. Zhuangzi's thesis is not to "adjust" or synthesize those controversial opinions, as if he were an eclectic (Fung), but to assess all the opinions as such, to examine how and why human beings formulate metaphysical opinions in the first place and thus help them to see the equal (*qi*) nature of different opinions so that entrapment within the web of these opinions can be avoided. I would rather translate the title *Qi Wu-lun* as "Equalizing or Identifying Opinions on Things," with the awareness that the author means by "opinions on things" views on metaphysics and ontology, on language and opinion itself.

What does Zhuangzi mean by *qi*, equalize or identify? The dual meaning of the word *qi* was implied in the chapter: (1) to equalize all *wulun* even in virtue of their relative nature, or to identify them as equally limited perspectives; (2) to sort out or tidy up, to put all different opinions into their right locations by means of examining their nature critically. Many understood or interpreted *qi* only from the first meaning and attributed to Zhuangzi some kind of relativism or skepticism. The mistake they made is that they overlooked the second meaning of Zhuangzi's action of *qi*. In the chapter, Zhuangzi did not criticize any particular opinion or form of knowledge to show whether it is right, but rather he dealt with the common problems of different opinions or knowledge as a whole. His purpose in *Qi Wu-lun* is not to reach a conclusion that every perspective is equally right or equally wrong, but to get rid of the bondage they made.

The first reason why we should not put any ultimate faith in knowledge or make it an absolute value is its limitations. Many have believed that human knowledge has an infinite power to know and to master nature, or, that even though we have not yet reached absolute knowledge, one day we will. For Zhuangzi, those who have such beliefs do not know what knowledge is and how limited and uncertain it is. Had they realized the limitations of knowledge, they would not have had such faith in it. Therefore, according to Zhuangzi, to recognize the limitation of knowledge is to realize the nature of knowledge.

Knowledge, as Zhuangzi sees it, is the outcome of the human activity of reasoning. We perceive information by means of immediate contact with things. Without sense information our reason would have nothing to schematize and categorize. On the other hand, the way we perceive information is determined by the structure of our reason, the structure that corresponds to our biological and cultural nature. How could objective or factual knowledge ever be possible? If knowledge lacks an objective foundation, how could we legitimize its authority, and why should we take it seriously?

As Zhuangzi has argued, to reason is to differentiate the object of reasoning. Along with the process of reasoning—clarification, analysis, deduction, induction, and argumentation—the oneness of life and the genuineness of a thing have been concealed or lost. Nature (*ziran*) does not reason and differentiate itself into various categories and conceptions. It is an undifferentiated one of many and different in which everything becomes and appears in its own way yet without distinction (*wufen*, 无分). There is no "flower" but rather blooming in the mountain; there is no "moon" but that which is hanging in the sky. There are no "life" and "death" but a constant flux of becoming; there are no "thises" (*ci*, 此, *shi*, 是) and "thats" (*bi*) but an undifferentiated world of *ziran* as an integration or unity of heterogeneity. It is the process of reasoning or forming of knowledge that differentiates things from the oneness of nature, abstracting them into different concepts and categories. In the first place, there is the differentiation between the object (the known) and subject (the knower), and between the world (*tian*) and human beings (*ren*). In the second place, there is differentiation among things, such as trees, mountains, and persons. In the third place, all kinds of *wulun* have generated one after another. And the differentiation between you and me, this and that, right and wrong come into being thereafter. In other words, as a consequence of the development of knowledge or *wulun*, Dao or nature as it is withdraws itself (2/2).

The process of reasoning is preshaped by the structure of language and logic, which violently projects its structure on the phenomenal world, calculating and regulating it according to the demands of linguistic principles. What Zhuangzi tries to point out is not whether language and logic are useless, but their inevitable limitation. Knowledge relies on language and logic, therefore its limitation also relates to the limitation of language and logic. Things are changing, the whole world is moving constantly, yet the process of reasoning just picks up one moment from the whole course of the changing world, making it a static concept or motionless theory. Could we say that this concept or theory is the correct representative of the ever-changing world? We never know, Zhuangzi would say, for the speaker (knower) needs words, yet the signified that words signify is never certain or clear (2/3). If words or language are uncertain, how can knowledge be certain?[25]

The existence of a human being is limited. The space and time we have lived in are only a small portion of the whole universe. We cannot even imagine what the word *big* could mean actually. In an infinite or boundless universe we can never reach the knowledge of what is biggest or smallest. The human ability to learn and to know is limited. For "life has its end but knowing (knowledge) has not. It is dangerous for one to pursue the endless with his limited life" (3/1). According to Zhuangzi, the limitation of knowledge also entails its endlessness, an endless interpretation or reinterpretation that could never be proved as "right" representation or final truth of things, and thus evokes an endless argumentation of "right" and "wrong." For Zhuangzi, there is no end for knowledge to complete itself because of its limitation, and there is no way for such a limited and endless knowledge or theory to reach the final conclusion through equally limited and endless reasoning. It is wasting time or devastating to our finite life to pursue in vain a completely true knowledge that does not exist.

The second reason why we should not take knowledge seriously is, according to Zhuangzi, that there is no standard to judge whether the knowledge we believe we have is true or false. Everything we perceive, every idea we form by means of knowledge, language, and logic is relatively true or false, relatively good or bad. There is simply no absolute knowledge that gives the final truth of the world. Zhuangzi says,

> Suppose you and I have had an argument. If you have beaten me instead of my beating you, then are you necessarily right and I necessarily wrong? If I have beaten you instead of your beating me, then am I necessarily right and are you necessarily wrong? Is one of us right and the other wrong? If you and I don't know the answer, then other people are bound to be even more in the dark. Whom shall we get to decide what is right? Shall we get someone who agrees with you to decide? But if he already agrees with you, how can he decide fairly? Shall we get someone who agrees with me? But if he already agrees with me, how can he decide? Shall we get someone who disagrees with both of us? But he already disagrees with both of us, how can he decide? Shall we get someone who agrees with both of us? But if he already agrees with both of us, how can he decide? Obviously, then, neither you nor I nor anyone else can decide for each other. Shall we wait for still another person? (2/6, Watson, 48)

Or, shall we wait for a master, a Lord or God? If there were such an ultimate Being who could decide for us, we would not argue so urgently in the first place. The endless arguing about right and wrong itself disproves the existence of a final judgment about right and wrong. In this way, there is no difference whatsoever among different opinions: they are identical in their limitation and are equally relative, including the opinion that all opinions are relative. It is the human mind (*chengxin*) constructed by specific traditions and discourses that has decided or judged the rights and wrongs of various opinions, not truth itself. Nature (Dao) has no rights and wrongs of its existence and movement. There is no "True Lord" that determines or plans or drives the vicissitude of the process of worlding; everything becomes and goes the way it becomes and goes without any absolute trace (*wuji* 无迹) of its cause, reason, and origin. Out of what can we possibly assert an opinion, final truth, or absolute knowledge? Zhuangzi would say that no one is able to find it.

Therefore, truths are in fact opinions, opinions are mere interpretations which are not in accordance with truth "in-itself" but with different perspectives. From different perspectives we *see* differently how things are and the world is. The important thing we should do, instead of arguing for right and wrong, is to realize it is some particular perspective that causes us to look at things in a particular way. More importantly, from such realization we may open up and free our mind to different perspectives which could be decisive for our ultimate transformation and liberation. Therefore, Zhuangzi proposed his "perspectivism":

> Viewed from the perspective of Dao, things are neither precious nor cheap; viewed from the perspective of things, one regards himself precious and the other cheap; viewed from the perspective of the marketplace, one cannot even figure out precious and cheap by himself. (17/1, Watson, 179)

We need to transcend our usual perspective of the marketplace and *wulun* to achieve the perspective of Dao, the perspective that has equalized or identified (*qi*) all opinions and viewed ten-thousand-things without prejudice. Here Zhuangzi's Dao becomes a stage of perspective (*jingjie*, 境界),[26] a paramount condition of mind, and an immanent achievement of life. But it is not one of all opinions, it is a perspective with all opinions equalized and overcome and transcended. Based on this Dao perspective with a height of religiosity beyond reason and common knowledge, we are able to see things in a totally different way:

> Viewed from the point of differences, if we regard a thing big because it is bigger than the other, then ten-thousand-things are all big; if we regard a thing small because it is smaller than the other, then everything is small. If we notice that heaven and earth are as small as a tiny grain and the tip of hair is as big as mountains, then we have seen the account of difference. Viewed from the perspective of utility,

if we regard a thing as useful because there is certain usefulness to it, then ten-thousand-things are all useful. If we regard a thing as useless because there is certain uselessness to it, then everything is useless. If we notice that east and west are mutually opposed but cannot exist one without another, then we can clarify the measure of utility. Viewed from the point of preference, if we regard a thing as right because there is a certain right to it, then ten-thousand-things are all right; if we regard a thing as wrong because there is a certain wrong to it, then everything is wrong. If we notice that King Yao and Rob Jie each thought himself right and condemned the other as wrong, then we may understand what is the real virtue of preference. (17/1, Watson, 180)

From the Dao perspective of the Oneness and identity of things and the world, we are now able to see and treat things as equal in the sense that all things are different by being what they are. *Wulun* enslave themselves in concrete or tangible things, like the frog in the bottom of a well that sees the sky as being as little as the mouth of the well. Isolating it from the integration, *wulun* customarily fix themselves in one thing or one idea as the privileged perspective. The Dao perspective, on the other hand, *wuwuerbuwuyuwu* (物物而不物于物), sees things as they are yet never fixes itself in judging which is right and which is wrong. Thus, one can never be enslaved by any particular opinion as *wulun*. It sets the mind free in order eventually to wander about the infinite world. This perhaps is why Zhuangzi does not condemn any particular opinion as wrong. All he does is to point out their limitation, partiality, and exclusiveness. He does not intend to engage in debate but to disengage and deconstruct (*qi*) opinions from a Dao perspective. What Zhuangzi suggests here is that we must overcome or surmount the common knowledge in order to liberate and free ourselves by attaining a Dao perspective, a *jingjie* of religiosity, or what he called "true knowledge with no-knowledge."

Here and there, Zhuangzi has told us what "true knowledge" is. True knowledge is the knowledge of no-self (*wuwo, sangwo*). All prejudices and arguments originate from our obsession with self as if it were the ultimate being. But in fact, the self exists only because the other exists; without the relation to the other there is no self. If the self is forgotten, there will be no fixed mind; without fixed mind, there will be no opinion, no argument and prejudice. Thus, one returns to nature (*ziran*) and attains true knowledge of Dao.

True knowledge is "no-knowledge." According to Zhuangzi, the significance of the notion of no-knowledge is twofold. First, in terms of his religiosity, common knowledge needs be abandoned or transcended for it is only an obstacle separating us from nature (Dao) or differentiating things from the oneness of nature. Second, the knowledge of no-knowledge also means our realizing the limits of knowledge and that only partial truth but never the totality of the world can be grasped. For Zhuangzi, the former leads us to reach the height of a religious state of spiritual freedom while the latter confirms that no-knowledge is not a rejection of knowledge, but a detachment or nonattachment to the common belief in knowledge, which is in fact a condition of the former. An important point worth noting here is that Zhuangzi's position on knowledge does not parallel that of skeptics and "anti-intellectual" people, in that his deconstruction and transcendence of knowledge should go through knowledge itself. One cannot liberate oneself from knowledge without having gripped knowledge at the outset; this is why Zhuangzi calls the no-knowledge "true knowledge."

True knowledge is also knowing when to stop seeking what cannot be known (2/5). Searching for what is beyond knowledge, such as metaphysical reality, God, the mandate of heaven ends in fruitless argument. So a Daoist sage never talks about what is beyond the Six Realms,[27] never argues over what is within the Six Realms (2/5).

Furthermore, true knowledge transcends the rationality of ordinary knowledge, which relies fundamentally on human logic, language, reasoning, text, and principle. Zhuangzi reminds us that our natural instinct, spontaneity, irrational spirit, sensual perception, and even physical body are more primal than rationality. Only if one surpasses reason and self-consciousness is one able to reach the higher state of freedom. With a mind of no-knowledge, no-self, no-thinking, and no-mind, one is able to do things with least effort yet greatest success. The stories such as that of cook Ding cutting a cow (3/1), a wheel maker making fun of the king who was reading (13/7), a swimmer playing with the waterfall that even fish could not stand (19/9), an artisan drawing a perfect circle without compass (19/12), are all examples demonstrating that the ultimate skill of acting is to forget thinking of it, simply act spontaneously in accord with nature, after years of practice.

Of course, Zhuangzi did not mean to negate the ordinary utility of knowledge. His notion of no-knowledge means no attachment to and no dependence upon opinions and knowledge. One seeks liberation from partial knowledge and arbitrary opinion.

After opinions are equalized and deconstructed, we finally arrive at the ground of "non-dependence" (wudai, 无待). Our minds are no longer fixed upon ideas but are clear and spontaneous, like a mirror reflecting the real course of nature. Nothing stops or stays still; everything goes and comes in accord with nature. This movement leads to the state of xu (虚, vacancy or emptiness), a mind "hears" or perceives, not through conceptual knowledge but qi (气, air or clearing in the sense of emptiness), things as they are without discrimination (4/1). The mind of xu as such becomes independent (wudai), which relies not on anything intelligible, conceptual, or artificial, knowledge that is external to itself; it reflects on and identifies itself to things as they are and as the flux of ziran thereby becomes itself ziran. Through the mind of xu, everything is conceived of as an "absolute," for it is what it is, with nothing more than what it is, with no differentiation and dichotomization of life/death, right/wrong, here/there, good/evil, big/small, and self/other. This is Zhuangzi's Dao of nature (Heaven and Earth) that is beyond the relativity of differentiated knowledge or opinions.

> Therefore, knowledge that stops at what cannot be known is perfect knowledge. Don't you understand the apologia that is beyond language, or, the Dao that is no-Dao? If you understood this you could call it the Reservoir of heaven. Pour into it and it is never full, dip from it and it never runs dry, and yet it is not known where the supply comes from. This is called Preserved Light (*baoguang*, 葆光). (2/5)

After all, we see that Zhuangzi's critique of knowledge is rather a step of human liberation from the illusion and manipulation of any humanly constructed knowledge than a pure philosophical or scientific observation of knowledge. We will continue to see from his critique of language and morality the same affection for religiosity that makes his critique amount to a sort of practice and cultivation of self-transformation and self-liberation.

LANGUAGE WITHOUT WORDS: BEYOND LANGUAGE AND SILENCE

The problem of knowledge relates to the problem of language. We often think that language represents meaning and truth. Our thinking is composed of or constructed by the form of language, but the problem is whether words can present the truth of things. Many have believed so. They take words seriously as representing things themselves. In this section, in relation to his critique of knowledge, I will elaborate Zhuangzi's opposition to such belief and his active deconstruction of the nature of human language. Language, according to Zhuangzi, is what constructs and fixes our thinking so that it opens a gap between man and nature and suppresses our spontaneity and freedom. With his religiosity in mind, Zhuangzi tried to overcome limitation by language, as he did with knowledge, and obtain emancipation from being manipulated by language. We will also see how Zhuangzi experimented to transcend language through language itself and thus enabled a religious or ecstatic play, or *xiaoyaoyou*, with the flux of life.

Words are signs we use for communication and for the sake of knowing. The principal characteristic of language is to verify, catalogue, name, and conceive things. These linguistic devices are created by the specific structure of human consciousness and the peculiar way of living that is distinctively human. For Zhuangzi what we talk about is still what humans talk about, and is never a kind of universal talk or truth-reflecting discourse that can capture nature as a whole.

Differentiation is the basic function of language. In order to name, signify, and conceptualize things, language cannot help dividing undifferentiated nature into different signifiers, names, and categories; they may represent some features of things but never correspond to the oneness of them. Zhuangzi says:

> Dao has no distinction; word has no constancy. It is because of our drive for what is right that there came to be distinctions. These distinctions are: there is left, there is right, there is hierarchy [of human relations], there is righteousness, there is discrimination, there is debate, there is competition, and there is struggle. These are eight consequences (*de*, 德)[28] of distinctions. (2/5, Watson, 44)

Nature is constantly changing, becoming, transforming; there is no beginning and end, and no fixed reality or certain, static, and unmoving entity can possibly be found. Yet language can make sense only by fixing a meaning in words and names. It freezes the course of changing nature and constructs another fictitious or linguistic world "grammatically." So "words are not blowing breath. Words have worded, but what a word worded is never determined" (2/3). In other words, language does not represent nature accordingly and properly, so why should we trust it or take it seriously?

Even in itself, there is no one thing we can speak of as language, because language "that can be spoken of" is not universal. When Zhuangzi says that a word worded or a signifier signified is undetermined or indefinite, we can take this to imply that words signify in their own way, in their own context of being spoken. By extension, in a more contemporary vein, we recognize that language manifests itself in different discourses, and different people in different times and circumstances have used different discourses to represent their own needs, will, understandings, and interpretations. Beyond the edge of discourse we cannot understand each other precisely even with the same words. So language is always limited within particular human contexts. By claiming for itself the name of truth, language became the source of the quarrelsome history of human beings. The original meanings (worded) of words have been lost in the process of using them, and finally, rhetorical functions replaced the descriptive ones. "Dao is concealed when being fixed. Worded (meaning) is lost when words become extravagant" (2/3). According to Zhuangzi, to talk is to convince others that "I am the truth." The aim is to be victorious over others and to appropriate different discourses under "mine." Thus, the fight for right (I) over wrong (other) has been brought up into human life.

In our own manner, we can see how all through history, not merely within the context of one culture, language or discourse becomes ideological, political, and moral. Through the power of language one seeks the authority to interpret the world and life in a privileged way—an exclusive truth to which all others should be subjugated. Language is no more a game within itself but a power struggle. This is why Confucians, Moists, and other schools have contested without end. Were they contesting for truth? Were their words representative of real things and truths? Not really, for as Zhuangzi relentlessly pointed out they were just abusing the use of language for the purposes of winning the battle of right and wrong.

In contrast to Laozi, Zhuangzi did not reject language as the means of expressing Dao. Laozi points out that Dao cannot be talked about, but he talked at length about it. This paradoxical situation does not bother Zhuangzi; instead, he takes this paradox as the feature of Dao language, a new way of expressing Dao as it is. This is what he called "speaking of what cannot be spoken of" or "speaking without language" (yanwuyan, 言无言). For Zhuangzi, language could become a twofold means to approach the ultimate Dao of liberation: (1) by deconstructing language through and within language itself, (2) through the recognition that language as an instrument to express things is indispensable, so long as we are aware of its limitations and do not mislead ourselves into taking it as having ultimate reference to Dao. It is even possible that we can use language to reveal some kind of meaning that may help us in achieving enlightenment.

Based on the above theory, Zhuangzi created his idiosyncratic way of using language, perhaps the first in Chinese history. As summarized in the *Book of Zhuangzi* (chapters 27 and 33), there are three types of discourse that characterize Zhuangzi's writing: allegory (*yuyan*, 寓言), double words (*chong-yan*, 重言), and goblet words (*zhiyan*, 卮言).

Yuyan has been translated as "metaphorical language" by Creel, "imputed language" by Watson, and "metaphor" by Mair. They all sensed the multiple meaning of *yuyan* in the *Book of Zhuangzi*, so they used different English words to translate it. These translations are not wrong, but neither are they wholly accurate. First of all, *yuyan* is commonly used in Chinese as allegory, as found in fables and parables. The application of allegory has been popular since the Zhou Dynasty in Chinese literature. Most great thinkers and writers used allegory to express opinion, teach wisdom, give advice, and make arguments in an indirect and nonprescriptive way.[29] For Zhuangzi, direct statements often result in a true or false conclusion that could block the access to truth. Allegory works better because it gives readers freedom to interpret the story in their own fashion. Zhuangzi was the best storyteller and creator of his time, frequently using allegories, fictional and historical, in his writings. Through allegory he sought to inspire readers to grasp something ineffable. The above mentioned translations do not show clearly what is meant by *yuyan* in this sense.

Second of all, *yuyan* refers to indirect language as well. In chapter 27 *yuyan* is "to say something by borrowing others (*jiwailunzhi*, 籍外论之)." Guo Xiang interprets this to mean that the author did not think the readers would trust his words so he let other persons speak for him; and he thinks that this is why Zhuangzi has borrowed many names, such as Confucius, Jian Wu (肩吾), Lian Shu (连叔), and so on (Guo, 948). Guo Xiang's interpretation does not sound correct to me, though most commentators have followed him, because: (1) Zhuangzi would not worry about whether people would accept his thought or not, so he needed not rely upon anyone's power or authority to get hold of readers; (2) to borrow another person's words is not an unusual feature of Zhuangzi, since such borrowing was customary in early Chinese literature; (3) the author did not say that the word *wai* refers to other person's words, it could mean something else. Perhaps this mistake in understanding is caused by misunderstanding the following sentences:

> A father does not act as go-between for his son because the praise of the father would not be as effective as the praise of an outsider. It is the fault of other men, not mine [that I must resort to such a device, for if I were to speak in my own words], then men would respond only to what agrees with their own views and reject what does not, would pronounce "right" what agrees with their own views and "wrong" what does not. (27/1, Watson, 303)

Guo Xiang takes the father reference literally, not metaphorically. Father here is a metaphor that refers to a word or name that people use to signify things (to praise his son). These words people usually use are not relevant or effective according to Zhuangzi's critique of language. And it is words or names that make people put stock in their own opinions of "right" and "wrong." Therefore, Zhuangzi decided to use something "other" (indirect words) than "father" (direct words) to express things, especially the ineffable Dao. This interpretation agrees with Zhuangzi's coherent theory of language and with his way of "speaking without words." To this extent I think Legge and Mair are right to think of *yuyan* as metaphorical language or metaphor, for that is what Zhuangzi meant by *jiwailunzhi*. Metaphorical and symbolic language are what Zhuangzi "borrows" to overcome the limitation of ordinary language.

Thirdly, *yuyan* is the inclusive language that speaks but never imposes any personal judgment upon what it talks about, nor excludes anything that is commonly thought of as wrong. The word *yu* (寓) has three basic meanings: (1) to lodge, abide, to be at home, or "to rent a house"; (2) to borrow, to utilize something or somebody to do or say (what you want to do or say); (3) to include, to embrace, to cover things or meanings. Because Dao is all-inclusive and the undifferentiated One that cannot be differentiated by analytic and conceptual language, the language used to access Dao must be inclusive as well. Many stories told in the Zhuangzi are not prescriptive but suggestive; no actual assertion is made in a traditional way. In the *Book of Zhuangzi*, no matter who is speaking, Confucian or Daoist, he must speak in a very inclusive way. By means of *yuyan*, language and stories speak not for the sake of argumentation but for themselves. There is no determined presence of the presence of *yuyan*; it is only a demonstration of non-language or Dao language, which shows that language cannot represent the Dao of things. Language is only language, not things themselves. Through *yuyan*, language deconstructs

itself and thus opens up our minds to the vivid or vital nature of things. This
is why in the *Book of Zhuangzi* the most important thing is not what he says
but how he says it, because what he intends is to reveal the nature of language
itself. Only after one has realized the nature of language is one able to overcome the limit of language.

Chongyan means double words or dual discourse. The interpretation of
chongyan is still controversial. Guo Xiang explains *chongyan* as *zhongyan* (*zhong*
means heavy or weighty alluding here to respectful words said by elders or
sages): "They are the words from the elders that everybody has respected.
Seven tenths of them are truthful" (Guo, 947). Wang Fu-zhi opposes such a
reading. He argues that *chongyan* means the repeated, or duplicated words of
elders (Mair translates it as "quotation," and Watson "repeated words"). Most
interpreters follow one or the other of these interpretations, since in the text
it says, "*chongyan* which makes up seven tenths of it are intended to put an
end to [common] language, for they are the words of the elders" (Watson,
303).

I agree with some contemporaries[30] who reject both of the above readings. *Chongyan* is neither respectful words nor quotations. First, Zhuangzi never
intended to rely on any authority to legitimize what he was talking about. In
the *Inner Chapters*, he rarely used quotations or repeated the words of others.
According to Zhuangzi, words are just dead corpses of spirit or meaning, the
words of old sages are "the chaff and dregs" of them (23/8). So why should
Zhuangzi repeat "the words of the elders"? *Chongyan* should be something
else. Second, in the same paragraph Zhuangzi is talking about elders who are
not necessarily respectable: if they "have not grasped the Way of man, they
deserved to be looked on as mere stale remnants of the past" (27/1). Why
should he quote them? Third, Zhuangzi seeks to deconstruct the common
view of language and to indicate that language is incapable of conveying the
truth. Why would he be so serious about the words of elders? Fourth, to
repeat (or borrow) words from others has been included in the form of *yuyan*.
If *chongyan* is just to repeat or quote, then how does it differ from *yuyan*?

Chongyan, dual words or double discourse, could be understood as paradoxical language as well. *Chong* refers to dual, overlapping and double, so
chongyan contains dual or opposite meanings and might also be spoken in a
paradoxical manner. For Zhuangzi, paradox or duality is a trait of language.
When people try to get rid of it, the quarrel begins and the truth becomes
clouded. So he created his eccentric discourse to follow the nature of language,
which is also the manifestation of Dao. The meaning of a word can vary easily
into its opposite when the context is changed. Take the word *qiai* as an
example. *Qiai* refers to respected or trustworthy elder. If,

> however, one is ahead of others in age but does not have a grasp of
> the warp and woof, the root and branch of things, that is commen-
> surate with his years, then he is not really ahead of others. An old
> man who is not in some way ahead of others has not grasped the

Way of man, and if he has not grasped the way of man, he deserves
to be looked on as a mere stale remnant of the past. (27/1, Watson,
304)

Here the same word *qiai* could mean both the "respected" and "disrespected";
there is no either/or situation for us to decide which is right and which is
wrong. This is what he meant by *chongyan*—to display the paradoxical nature
of language in order to ridicule the traditional either/or discourse. In this way,
language has freed itself by means of *chongyan*.

Chongyan could also be used to demonstrate the self-negatability and
contradictory nature of any statement or judgment. Neglecting all logic, *chongyan* makes a paradoxical statement: A is both A and Non-A, for example, *qiai*
(elder) is *qiai* and is not *qiai*. In the entire *Book of Zhuangzi*, especially in the
Inner Chapters, *chongyan* appears most frequently in association with *yuyan*.
Zhuangzi often defines a conception by its negation: "When it is born it is
dead, when it is dead it is born; when it is positive it is negative, when it
is negative it is positive; it is right because it is wrong, it is wrong because it
is right ..." (2/3). He asks questions such as this: "Do I say something? Do I
not say anything?" "Is there 'this' or 'that'? Is there no 'this' or 'that'?" He
constantly makes this kind of dual and contradictory statement which is called
chongyan.

What is Zhuangzi trying to say? What sense does he make by this understanding of *chongyan*? Isn't he just playing a language game, trying to confuse
the reader? Although he is playful with language, the purpose of *chongyan* is
not to play. (1) What matters for Zhuangzi is not what he says but how he
says it. He does not want the readers to judge whether he said something
correctly but to realize that language itself is paradoxical and has no boundary
between right and wrong, this and that, self and other. Language in general
did not create the argument over right and wrong, but rather a certain use
of language. *Chongyan* is a special discourse in which language speaks by and
for itself. It does not signify anything but the process of signifying in which
there is no identification of the object as signified. The use of *chongyan* requires
that no determinate signified be singled out as the topic of the discourse, and
by this kind of use, one comes to see the indeterminacy of language in general
with regard to the signified. (2) By speaking *chongyan* we actually speak not
about anything beyond language, we do not refer to something that is nature
or Dao. Dao is neither right nor wrong, or it is both right and wrong. It has
no preference concerning an object of reference as we humans do between
"this" and "that," since it embraces all. (3) *Chongyan* has deconstructed the
language that has been commonly trusted as the only vehicle that conveys
Dao, though speaking it paradoxically. We get frustrated by reading those
chongyan and may suddenly be awakened from the nightmare of language. Only
then are we able to detach or liberate ourselves from language, with a language
that has freed itself from the argument of right/wrong, from the mentality of
differentiation.

Zhiyan or goblet words is the name for Zhuangzi's special discourse as a whole. Goblet (*zhi*) in the past was a sort of container or cup for liquor, which would remain upright when it was empty and would turn upside down when filled. Guo Xiang says that it has no uprightness of itself but depends on the one who drinks. In reference to language, it describes the words that change in accordance with the change of things, renewing themselves every day (Guo, 947). Chen Xuan-ying says there is another interpretation: *zhi* means branch or dismemberment (*zhi*), *zhiyan* is dismembered and irrelevant words (ibid.). I think both are right about Zhuangzi's discourse or Dao language. *Yuyan* are goblet words because they can never be filled with fixed meaning. Their space of meaning will never be permanently occupied and exhausted. *Chongyan*, on the other hand, dismembers, deconstructs, and dissipates the language of rights and wrongs. It says nothing and everything without any trace left behind. The whole discourse Zhuangzi applied in his teaching, including *yuyan* and *chongyan*, can be characterized by the name of *zhiyan*. So in the Zhuangzi, "Nine tenths are *yuyan*, seven tenths are *chongyan*. It is *zhiyan* that comes forth like new days, completely in harmony with the natural diversity (*tianni*, 天倪)" (27/1). *Zhiyan* is the real secret of Zhuangzian discourse, which does not differ from but includes *chongyan* and *yuyan*.[31] This discourse is different from any other discourse:

> Day after day *zhiyan* comes forth in harmony with natural diversity, flows over spontaneously with no-mind, this is how one completes his life. There is equality [of nature] when there is no word, word and equality are not equal, equality and word are not equal, this is so called no-language (*wuyan*, 无言). We should speak without words. One may speak all his life, and may have spoken nothing; one may speak nothing all his life, and yet have spoken something. It is the self that makes one say "okay" (*ke*, 可); it is the self that makes one say "not okay" (*buke*, 不可); it is the same reason for saying "so" (*ran*, 然) and "not so" (*buran*, 不然). Why it is "so"? It is so if it is so. Why "not so"? It is not so if it is not so. Why it is "okay"? It is okay if it is okay. Why "not okay"? It is not okay if it is not okay. Things have their own "so"; things have their own "okay." Nothing is not okay, nothing is not so. Without *zhiyan* coming forth and harmonizing with natural diversity, therefore, how could it [language] last long? Myriad things are [equally] One, only passing on in different forms, coming and going like circles, yet nothing could be traced as their principles, this is called natural equality (*tianjun*). Natural equality is no other than the natural diversity. (27/1, Watson, 304)[32]

The major attributes of *zhiyan* could be summarized as follows:

1. *Zhiyan* comes forth from spontaneity, as every day begins (*richu* 日出). Contrary to common language, there is neither self (*zi*) nor fixed mind

(*chengxin*) to divide things in accordance with human categories of right and wrong. It speaks as nature speaks (*tianlai*, 天籟) by and for itself, solely according to the diversity and equality, or simply the dao, of nature. Such discourse reflects perfectly upon the Dao, which creates and transforms all by itself.

2. *Zhiyan* does not rely on words (*wuyan*, 无言). For words have failed to represent nature from the perspective of the undifferentiated oneness and the ever-renewed flux of things. We should forget the fixed meaning of words (as the signified of a signifier) and let words flow with the ever-changing world. This is what is called speaking "with no words," which means words have no fixed definition and thus grip no poles of duality. *Zhiyan* does not speak, in a conventional sense, and yet has spoken everything.

3. It takes no stand regarding right/wrong, permissible/impermissible, and so on. Common language is the reflection of human intentions or consciousness rather than an object. So long as we are naming things we are imposing or projecting our intentions on them, consciously or unconsciously, and thus the named objects either explicitly or implicitly have contained in them a human sensibility, evaluation, or judgment that has nothing to do with the things themselves. *Zhiyan* makes no assertion of right/wrong, but stays in the middle with no demarcation of the world, harmonizing itself with the natural equality and diversity of things.

4. *Zhiyan* as the Dao discourse is also the discourse of the sages, the liberated persons who have no attachment to language and do not argue. They simply follow the way of nature, "transforming the dependent (*xiangdai*, 相待) sounds (disputable words) into independent (*buxiangdai*, 不相待) discourse . . . forgetting time and righteousness, hovering around the realm of infinity, and abiding in the unlimited universe" (2/6).

To sum up, *zhiyan*, including *yuyan* and *chongyan*, is how Zhuangzi was speaking and writing, which transcended the boundary of common sense or conventional language. Like Laozi he realizes the limitation of language, yet he *speaks* without and simultaneously within language. It is quite ironic that when the edge of the limitation has been reached the possibility of overcoming it will appear. *Zhiyan* is such a language that leads to this edge and consequently makes words the sound of Heaven.

Zhuangzi and his school, without doubt, were the pioneers of philosophy of language and linguistic study. They have shown cunning insight in breaking through what is essentially problematic in language, an opacity with which we have just begun to cope after more than two millennia. The most distinguished contribution of the Zhuangzian theory of language is the exploration of the relationship between words and things or names and substances (*ming*, 名, *shi*, 实), language and meaning (*yan*, 言, *yi*, 意), which in modern linguistic theory we describe as signifier and signified (*zhi*, 指, *suozhi*, 所指). In the early history of China, these issues were discussed widely within the circles of various thinkers. Confucians, Moists, Sophists, Legalists all talked about them. Yet most of them considered name or language as the perfect represen-tation of reality; only the misuse of language could devastate the congruence between name and things themselves. Zhuangzi, contrary to them, pointed out that language in its common fashion could not represent the reality of things; words and things could not be equal (see 27/1). Things change but words are static. Things are naturally in a harmonious relationship but words are selective and judgmental. Things exist as they are within an undifferentiated oneness yet words demarcate and categorize them. Hence, "words are not wind. Words worded, yet what a word worded is not determined" (2/3). If we rely only on language to pursue the truths of nature, not only will we fail but we will become entangled in the endless debate over what is real, what is right, and so forth. Through the deconstruction of language, Zhuangzi has destroyed the foundation of all kinds of dogmatism and authoritarianism which are dependent, foolishly, upon words.

Language is only a means that may help us to realize the Dao of true life. Its performative, not prescriptive function provides suggestions or "traces" of access to what is meant by the word *Dao* but not the Dao itself:

> The fish trap exists because of the fish; once you've gotten the fish, you can forget the trap. The rabbit snare exists because of the rabbit; once you've gotten the rabbit, you can forget the snare. Words exist because of meaning; once you've gotten the meaning. you can forget the words. Where can I find a man who has forgotten words so I can have a word with him? (Watson, 302)

Language is something that should eventually be forgotten. To forget language here means to forget the word as truth or reality itself. This is what Zhuangzi meant by "language without words."

Zhuangzi did not hesitate to reveal that the nature of language is differ-ence and paradox: (1) Signifiers or words do not match the signifieds or things, words are not things. (2) Words signify and clarify things by dividing them into different categories. Language as naming things is actually the process of differentiation, through which "things become the things thus named" (2/4). (3) Any temptation to unify the differences of language will necessarily lead to unsolvable paradox.[33]

How Zhuangzi believes we can overcome the limitation of language is unique as well. "Neither language or silence are capable of expressing the difference between the Dao and things. Only non-language and non-silence (*feiyan* and *feimo*, 非言非默) may speak of the ultimate" (25/11). Language and Dao are no longer two; they are one resounding of the "music of heaven" (*tianlai*), the melody performed by myriad things with their own different voices (2/1). It may sound eccentric, incoherent or even crazy, but Zhuangzi plays it as perfect music (*zhiyue* or *zhile*, 至乐):

Then I played it with unwearying notes and tuned it to the nature of spontaneity. Therefore it seemed to be a chaotic symphony that emerged from everywhere, mingled with different tones which were chasing and embracing each other but left no forms behind them. They developed and unfolded independently with no trace [of their cause], mysteriously and dimly with no voice. Such music came from enigmatic darkness and moved toward nowhere. It could be called death, or called life; it could be called reality, or called flashiness, because it was flowing and scattering constantly, would never be captured by any unchanging notes. The world might be confused by it but a sage would keep it as it was.... So I ended the music all with confusion, confusion therefore ignorance, ignorance therefore *dao*, the *dao* that could be carried out and undifferentiated from you. (14/4)

In the performance of such music of heaven, all human prejudices and anxieties that have stemmed from language and senseless debates on metaphysics, truth, and knowledge have ceased; we return to our home of nature. Now we clearly see how Zhuangzi's religiosity manifested in his deconstructing and reconstructing language and what kind of liberation his dealing with language was leading to. For him, freeing language from its traditional function of fixation, differentiation, and prescription amounts to freeing human spirit. In this respect, Zhuangzi's philosophy of language is very different from his sophist contemporaries, such as Gonsun Long (公孙龙) and Hui Shi (惠施), and some of the modern thinkers in the West, such as Derrida, who like to play or deconstruct language only within the territory of language.

WUWEI OR NON-DOING: AGAINST THE TRADITION OF MORALITY

Now we turn to Zhuangzi's notion of morality. Again, I will follow Zhuangzi's religiosity as I did in preceding sections, to show the importance of his critique of morality as an indispensable means to reach his ultimate state of human liberation (*xiaoyao*) as life affirmation (*ziran*). Morality, in association with knowledge and language, is another major cause of human suffering and alienation because it works against our spontaneity and instinct of living with nature in constructing a human-made moral world. Many attribute to Zhuangzi relativism or even nihilism inasmuch as he does not advocate any final judgment or categorical imperative of morality. I would like to argue that Zhuangzi's thought does not fit into the shoes of either relativism or nihilism, because his critique is deeply motivated by his religiosity, or his longing for a genuine state of human existence, which is unfortunately alienated and lost in the course of human civilization.

According to Zhuangzi, the world that worlds does not rely on knowledge, the thing that things does not depend upon its name; by the same token, human existence is not determined by moral codes and obligation. From the perspective of Dao as the undifferentiated unity of the world, there is no distinction between right and wrong, good and evil, moral and immoral. The sun rises and sets, the four seasons turn around, people live and die. Does it matter if we insert any moral evaluation or alternative upon them? My body is composed of different parts and organs; is there one that works as master and others as servants? Or is there a True Lord that controls the movement of the body? Which one of them should be my favorite? If I could not find the "Lord" or "Truth" of the body, would the body fall apart or would the organs work anyway (2/2)? If I could not find the "Lord" of the world, how am I supposed to imagine a universal goodness that determines my existence? These are the questions that would be asked by Zhuangzi if he were compelled to discuss morality.

Morality was believed by most Chinese to be an absolute imperative that was transcendentally given. The ancestral emperors enacted the moral code in accordance with the "mandate of Heaven" (*tianming*, 天命). Rooted in nature, morality made humankind differ from other species. It is also the fundamental ground on which the whole political and social system is based. When a society no longer practices morality, it loses its integrity and order. Therefore, the disorder and decadence of a society, according to Confucianism and Moism, is caused by the degeneration of moral conscience and activity.

Against the mainstream, Zhuangzi indicates that all the virtues we are obliged to follow are merely human inventions. Nature does not need morality to make its move, neither do human beings. In the very beginning of human society, according to Zhuangzi's account, there was no morality (*renyi* 仁义) ever employed, for people lived peacefully by their inborn spontaneity. Nothing needs be done to restrain oneself in order to be harmonious with the other and the environment (*wuwei*, 无为), because the Way of nature is to let everything be itself in its own development and transformation (*zihua*, 自化). To live by spontaneity is to live in the world of "constant naturalness" where "things arced not by the use of the curve, straight not by the use of the plumb of line, rounded not by compasses, squared not by T squares, joined not by glue and lacquer, bound not by rope and lines" (Watson, 100–101). It was the emperor Shun, the successor of Yao, who started forming morality for his governance. Since then, people lived under the guidance of those moral ideas at the cost of their spontaneity. For Confucius, that is, the triumph of human society consists in the invention of morality, which serves as its basis, whereas for Zhuangzi, society is a form of mass manipulation in which morality attempts to fix human life into prescribed social roles and thereby suppresses human freedom, which flows from the spontaneity of all things.

Since moral imperatives are created by human beings, Zhuangzi would argue that it is impossible to legitimize any imperative to be the absolute measure of all values. Moral values are relative because they depend on human

intention and volition. When Wang Ni was asked if he knew whether there
is a universal agreement in truth, he said he did not. When he was asked:
"Why?" He thus replied:

> Now let me ask you some questions. If a man sleeps in a damp place,
> his back aches and he ends up half paralyzed, but is this true of a
> loach? If he lives in a tree, he is terrified and shakes with fright, but
> is this true of a monkey? Of these three creatures, then, which one
> knows the proper place to live? Men eat the flesh of grass-fed and
> grain-fed animals, deer eat grass, centipedes find snakes tasty, and
> hawks and falcons relish mice. Of these four, which knows how food
> ought to taste? Monkeys pair with monkeys, deer go out with deer,
> and fish play around fish. Men claim that Mao Qiang and Lady Li
> were beautiful, but if fish saw them they would dive to the bottom
> of the stream, if birds saw them they would fly away, and if deer saw
> them they would break into a run. Of these four, which knows how
> to fix the standard of beauty for the world? The way I see it, the
> rules of benevolence and righteousness and the paths of right and
> wrong are all hopelessly snared and jumbled. How could I know
> anything about such discriminations? (2/6, Watson, 45–46)

Therefore, there is no fixed truth or moral norm that can be applied universally to different species, different times, and different persons. People with
different intentions would create, change, or choose different values. Zhuangzi
had no objection to those values. The problem he saw is that people like to
universalize and absolutize the value or morals they created, ignoring completely the fact of the relativity and the diversity of the natural world and
human beings. Dao has no fixed boundaries. Speech has no static constancy.
Virtually every being-in-the-world has a *right* to exist the way it chooses, for
there is no violation whatsoever of the Dao of nature as long as one acts or
transforms by one's own nature (*zihua, zixing*, 自性). Only when people
started contending over what was right and wrong or good and evil were
they caught up within the boundaries of the dichotomies they had created,
such as left and right, hierarchical relationship (*lun*, 伦) and righteousness (*yi*),
humanity (*ren*), or benevolence and propriety (*li*, 礼); with this entrapment
they began a life of differentiation (*fen*, 分) and (*bian*, 辨) dispute, emulation
(*jing*, 竞) and contention (*zheng*, 争) (2/5).

The creation of moral principles, according to Zhuangzi, ruined the
harmony and naturalness of human life, generated among people a ceaseless
campaign for dominant moral ideas. Ethical norms and moral fame, often
accompanied by names (*ming*) designating one's social status and moral regard,
became the aim and meaning of human life and self-cultivation. Different
schools of moral teaching came into being and the peace of people's minds
was disturbed by various arguments. The unity of Dao was broken into pieces

of superficial opinions and moral judgments, such as good/evil, right/wrong, this/that, and beautiful/ugly. Everybody attempted to generalize their opinion as the universal truth, trying to dispense with or exclude other opinions that were different. In such a noisy world of artificial morality, Dao is compelled to conceal itself (2/3). Because of the arguments of right and wrong Dao gets lost; it is because of the loss of Dao that the love (of profit and goodness) is prompted (2/4).[34]

Life became a means to acquire moral values that were believed to be the very nature of human beings (Menzi, 孟子, Xunzi, 荀子). One should sacrifice oneself for the sake of moral ideals (shashengchengren, 杀身成仁). The purpose of morality is supposed to be the preservation of human life and happiness. Unfortunately, Confucians and Moists have turned morality from a means of life into the ultimate goal of life. Confucius once said: "If one has heard the Dao in the morning, he would die without regret in the afternoon" (Analects, 4/15). Under such a teaching, people have been driven for moral fame (ming, 名) and knowledge, disregarding what their inherent nature (de, 德) is and what life is. Striving for moral perfection, the superior man (junzi, 君子) dedicates his whole life to morality, just as a vicious robber strives for money and goods. The sage kings attacked adjacent states to disseminate their moral ideals, while brutal dictators invaded other states for their material resources. We cannot neglect the discrepancies between sage kings and dictators, but we cannot deny their commonality. In the first place, they all strive for goals that are estranged from the nature of life itself. In the second place, they often end with the same result—killing or being killed. Sages are killed for their fame and robbers for goods. All kinds of wars, no matter whether they are just or unjust, moral or immoral, always bring chaos and disaster to the world of life. In this respect, Zhuangzi calls such moral fame and knowledge "murder weapons" because they destroy the innate nature of man and generate endless contention among people (4/1). According to him, morality, especially the Confucian teachings, could be the cause of confusing people's minds and devastating the harmony of the society.[35]

Morality is a sign of degeneration and alienation of human existence. Pursuing moral perfection, our nature is dissipated, minds clouded, vitality exhausted, we are no longer ourselves but "horses with haltered heads and oxen with strings in pierced noses" (17/1). Being haltered and stringed, horses and oxen are not what they were originally but tools and slave laborers dragged around by others. Is this the life we human beings deserve to live? Is this the way we were born to be? No, this is a life of punishment or imprisonment (tianxing, 天刑). In order to free oneself from such punishment, one should break the bondage of morality and return to the natural spontaneity of human existence: "Being together with heaven and earth; being one with ten-thousand-things" (2/5). When one lives in the world of nature one should not worry about right and wrong, moral and immoral, distractions unnecessary for a spontaneous life as it is. Fish spew each other trying to save each other with a little spit, when they are left stranded on the ground. Is it not better for them to forget each other in the river and lake? By the same token, people would like to complain about Je (桀, an evil ruler) and praise Yao (the good king), but is it not much better for them to forget about both and live spontaneously (6/2)?

What did Zhuangzi mean by returning to the genuine life? It is the life of spontaneity and non-action (*ziranwuwei*, 自然无为). The idea of *wuwei*, created by Laozi, suggests that Dao *daos* or world *worlds* by its natural course and rhythm, as water flows without compulsion. There is no Lord who determines or commands the existence and movement of ten-thousand-things. The effort made or action taken by forces other than spontaneity may not do any good but may disrupt the natural process and the process of self-transformation. So try not to help, try not to do anything extra, everything will be accomplished by its natural course of transformation (*ziran*). Without the help of morality, Laozi and Zhuangzi believe, a society would be much better maintained and governed than the one in which we now live. Sun and moon shine, the mother loves her daughter, Zhuangzi dreams of being a butterfly, everything comes, happens, goes spontaneously and harmoniously, without notions of benevolence and righteousness.

From the idea of *wuwei* Zhuangzi brought up his concept of do-not-use (*buyong*, 不用). After he has pointed out that there is no way to find out the resolution of the argument regarding who is right and who is wrong, he suggests that we had better keep our mind clear (*moruoyiming*, 莫若以明, 2/3). The way to keep the mind clear, Zhuangzi tells us, is to "embrace all functions and utilities of the world by not using or utilizing them" (2/4). To use is to engage one's evaluation or judgment upon things and thus attach oneself to the function that he or she would expect from things. As a result, one could be trapped in the meaningless debate of right and wrong, good and evil, losing sight of things as they are. On the other hand, the real function and nature of things would be distorted by those rational speculations and moral evaluations. Making no use of things is the way to leave things to themselves and free from any unnatural destruction, like trees being cut for the use of plumbs. Making no use of our mind is the way to see the world as a whole or One and to attain Dao as throughness and spiritual freedom from all partial opinions. This is called "useless usefulness" or "useful uselessness" (*wuyongzhiyong*, 无用之用). Unfortunately, "The ordinary people know only the use of usefulness but know not the useful uselessness" (4/7). With such a mind of useful uselessness, one would never be concerned about the trouble that is generated from human knowledge, language, and morality. This is the mind of a sage of Dao, clean as a mirror, "going after nothing, reflecting but not storing. Therefore he can win over things and not hurt himself" (7/6, Watson, 97). Furthermore, it is the mind of no-mind (*wuxin*, 无心); nothing can be used in it. It becomes a part of nature and is itself nature or Dao. In this state genuineness and innocence are restored and one becomes a true person, a person of Dao and *de* (virtue).[36]

In contrast to the Confucian gentleman who presumably possessed all moral virtues, Zhuangzi promotes the person of *daode*. In modern Chinese, the word *daode* refers to morality. But during the pre-Qing period, perhaps not many people would equate "*daode*" (道德) with "morality"; they would rather use "*ren*" (benevolence) or "*yi*" (righteousness) for what we now call morality. For Daoism, Dao and *de* have very little to do with morality; they are words that represent the Daoist understandings of nature and the nature of things. In the book of Laozi, Dao is the metaphysical reality and the cosmological origin of the world. And it is through *de*, which refers to individuality and the actual or tangible existence of things, that the Dao manifests itself. Wang Bi in his commentary on Laozi often interpreted *de* as "to gain or acquire," which means things that have gained their existence from nothingness. He said: "Dao is where and why things are [created]; *de* is what things have gained [their nature]" (Wang, 95).

In the *Book of Zhuangzi*, *daode* is considered one of the ways to cure the illness caused by morality. Zhuangzi refers to *de* as virtue or genuine, spontaneous, and excellent nature of actual human beings and things, while Confucians refer to it in terms of moral virtue. He maintains that we "gained" (*de*, 得) virtue directly from nature, that it is the manifestation or actuality of Dao within our existence. To live in such virtue means to live with or as Dao. Morality, knowledge, and language are refuges only for those who have lost their *de* or virtue.

Zhuangzi wrote an entire chapter articulating his idea of *de*. Chapter 5, entitled "*De Chong Fu*" (德充符), "Virtue Adequate and Conformable,"[37] suggests that when *de* is adequate inside a person and simultaneously conformable to the outside world, one becomes a great sage. Instead of exhibiting various famous moral exemplars, as Confucius used to do, Zhuangzi tells us stories about the ugly and deformed as his ideal models of *de*.

These people are imperfect or deformed in their appearance, but they often have shown great integrity and personality, being revered, loved, and even followed by others. Why? Because they are persons of *de-chong-fu*. Their minds are filled with *de* with no room left for any "all-too-human" things. This is because (1) they don't stand up teaching (morality and knowledge), they don't sit down arguing (right and wrong), yet people like to follow them and learn from them (5/1); (2) they have no attachment to anything, treating everything as equal and identical, therefore nothing that has happened could move or change their *de* and peace of mind. No difference exists for them between good and bad, right and wrong, big and small, high and low, life and death, simply following or being the course of nature; (3) they never try to do anything they cannot accomplish, nor complain about their incapability, yet always enjoy their fate as it is. Therefore, no conflict arises but only harmony between the person of *de* and nature, the person of *de* and other people. This is what *dechongfu* means by virtue that is adequate inside and conformable outside.[38]

From the above discussion, we see that Zhuangzi did not dismiss morality for nothing, but for the alternative, a height of *de-chong-fu*, another aspect of his ideal of freedom and life affirmation, or what I call "religiosity."

XIAO YAO YOU: A SPIRITUAL FREEDOM REALIZED IN THIS WORLD

All the work of deconstruction and reconstruction that Zhuangzi has done so far on such phenomena as Dao, knowledge, language, and morality has been aimed at attaining the ultimate perspective (*jingjie*) of Dao, a spiritual state of freedom and joyful life—*xiaoyaoyou* (逍遥游). Perhaps the best term we can think of in the *Book of Zhuangzi* to characterize Zhuangzi and his philosophy must be *xiaoyaoyou*, the thesis of the very first chapter and the spiritual destination of his whole teaching.

The *book of Zhuangzi* begins with a stunning allegory, which illustrates the meaning of *xiaoyaoyou*:

> In the never known[39] Northern sea there is a fish named Kun.[40] The Kun is so huge you have no idea how many thousands of miles she measures. She transformed into a bird named Peng. The back of Peng measures I don't know how many thousand miles across and, when she rises up and flies off, her wings are like clouds all over the sky. When the hurricane comes to the fore, this bird sets off for the never known Southern sea.
>
> The cicada and the little dove laugh at this, saying, "When we make an effort and fly up, we can get as far as the elm or the sapanwood tree, but sometimes we don't make it and just fall down on the ground. Now how is anyone going to go ninety thousand miles to the south!" The one who goes around the green woods nearby needs only three meals to fulfill her stomach. The one who goes hundred miles away must grind her grain a night before. The one who goes thousand miles away starts collecting food three months in advance. What do these two little ones understand? (1/1, Watson, 30)

The two kinds of animals symbolize the twofold meaning of *xiao yao you*. *Xiao* refers to a kind of carefree mind or detachment, like the cicada and little dove jumping around without worrying at all about their life. *Yao* means faraway or distance, like great Peng who by flying can even reach the "lake of heaven." *You* stands for free movement, wandering, playing, or dancing amidst the world.[41] Of course, *xiaoyaoyou* in Zhuangzi is more of a spiritual state of freedom, liberation, and affirmation rather than physical or actual movement, even though he talks occasionally about some legendary godlike figures (1/2).[42] As a state of spirit, *xiao* specifically refers to nondiscrimination and nonattachment to the ten-thousand-things; *yao* means an open and vacant mind whose vision can go through the vastest and remotest space and time without hindrance and difficulty; *you* signifies the way one exists and moves with the spirit of *xiaoyao*, like a liquidized body and vaporized spirit flowing in the One, easy and happy. By using the metaphors of huge Peng and little creatures, Zhuangzi shows us how graceful and free the spirit of *xiao yao you* can be. However, when capable of *you*, one should have both *xiao* and *yao* together in one mind, otherwise the ultimate state will not be acquired.

The problem of human life began when people generated their consciousness of a self and a fixed mind (*chengxin*), like Peng and the little bird. When they started laughing at each other's disadvantage they lost their natural freedom and became defensive about their own limited and dependent positions. From this consciousness of self came into being all the productions of human beings, such as the knowledge for subduing nature and the other; language for argument; the use of morality for one's better name; and consequently the huge machine of the state government and military forces. According to Zhuangzi, the profit we gain from the "progress" of civilization was much less than the impairment it brought about. Therefore, he decided to return to the original and spontaneous Dao of life and attain spiritual freedom in *xiaoyaoyou*.

Zhuangzi's Dao of attaining the state of *xiao yao you* is twofold, both theoretical and practical. On the one hand, he uses conventional theories of knowledge, language, and logic to deconstruct their finality and universality, which serve as the rational foundation of our self-consciousness and fixed mind. On the other hand, he teaches a series of practical methods such as *wuwei*, *xinzhai* (心斋, fasting the mind), *zuowang* (坐忘, sitting and forgetting), *wuyong* (being useless), *yangshen* (养身, maintaining health), *xujing* (虚静, vacancy and tranquility).[43] Both the theoretical and practice exercises will rid us of the consciousness of self and fixed mind, the obstacles that have kept us apart from the world of *ziran* and the state of *xiaoyaoyou*.

Consciousness of self makes one's mind fixed or dependent (*youdai*, 有待) on specific forms of existence and styles of life. For example, the great Peng depends on a vast amount of air to hold her wings and a huge space to fly; little birds can only live in the bushes seeing a very limited universe. Since nothing can exist without relating to others, it is natural for things and people to be mutually related and dependent. The problem is that our minds are fixed, dependent on, and attached to the conditions and circumstances that limit and restrict our competence. We enslave ourselves in a closed, exclusive, and narcissist realm of the self, fighting, struggling, and protecting it as the only interest, only truth, only good, only Dao in the entire universe. This is why we are living not in a world of *ziran* anymore but in a human-all-too-human world which has become more and more a battlefield of miserable selves.

For Zhuangzi, therefore, the first and last thing we must do to release ourselves from this condition of enslavement is to dismiss the consciousness of self in order to transcend the limitations and dependence of the self (*wudai*, 无待). From the perspective of Dao, everything we earlier thought best is not true:

> Little knowledge cannot reach the broad knowledge; the short-lived cannot come up to the long-lived. How do I know this is so? The ephemeral worm knows nothing of twilight and dawn, the summer cicada knows nothing of spring and autumn. These are short lived (*xiaonian*, 小年). South of Chu there is a caterpillar which counts five hundred years as one spring and five hundred years as one autumn. Long, long ago there was a great rose of Sharon that counted eight thousand years as one spring and eight thousand years as one autumn. They are the long-lived (*danian*, 大年). Yet Peng-zhu alone is famous today for having lived a long life, and everybody tries to ape him. Isn't it pitiful! (1/1, Watson, 31)

Speaking of time, there is always a duration of time that is either longer or shorter yet never the longest or shortest. Speaking of space, there are always different sizes that are either bigger or smaller yet never the biggest or smallest. Big and small are relative concepts. Should we not stop discriminating between big and small, long and short and try to realize things as they are? Speaking of the perfection of a person, and the ceasing of such discrimination, Zhuangzi continues,

> Therefore a man who has wisdom enough to fill one office effectively, good conduct enough to impress one community, virtue enough to please one ruler, or talent enough to be called into service in one state, has the same kind of self-pride as these little creatures. Sung Rongzi would certainly burst out laughing at such a man. For the whole world could praise Rongzi and it would not make him exert himself; the whole world could condemn him and it wouldn't make him mope. He drew a clear line between the internal and the external, and recognized the boundaries of true glory and disgrace. But that was all. As far as the society went, he didn't fret and worry, but was still ground that he left unturned. Liezi could ride the wind and go soaring around with cool and breezy skill, but after fifteen days he came back to earth. As far as the search for good fortune went, he didn't fret and worry. He escaped the trouble of walking, but he still had to depend on something to get around. (1/1, Watson, 31–32)

Human talent, virtue, and perfection also compete endlessly since there are numerous different persons with different qualities. Why not stop the competition for the superiority of the self (*sangwo*, 丧我, 2/1), *which* Confucianism and Moism urge and is the cause of our dependent mind and life. Therefore,

> If one can mount on the middle-way of heaven and earth, follow the changes of the six phenomena[44] [of nature], and thus wander through the boundless, then what would she have to depend on?
> Therefore I say, the Perfect Person has no self; the Holy Person has no merit; the Sage has no name. (1/1, Watson, 32)

The key for *xiao yao you* is the state of *wudai*, nondependence or nonduality (sometime also called *du*, 独) of one's mind. *Wudai* is the ultimate state of *xiaoyaoyou*, because in this state one has overcome the consciousness of the self, forgotten all conventional conceptions of knowledge, morality, and argument, renounced dualistic ways of thinking and the fixed mind of dogmatism, disengaged from political, economic, and various social competitions and struggles. "But then what would she have had to depend on?"

With a mind of *wudai*, one becomes completely natural and spontaneous, having no attachment at all to any humanly desired things (*xiao*). With a mind of *wudai*, one also opens oneself to the entire universe, near and far, having no discrimination, boundary, and limit of any thing at all (*yao*). A new, spiritual, and free life of wandering, playing, and dancing thus starts (*you*). It *transcends* the artificial surface of the world and human life, *returns* to the genuine nature that is believed and experienced by Zhuangzi to be the carefree, harmonious, manifold, as well as one.

Xiaoyaoyou thus does not encourage any intention to leave or escape from actual life and this world. On the contrary, it affirms life, this life in this world, without denial or rejection. This ultimate affirmation, which has characterized Zhuangzi's special religiosity, is precisely the secret of *xiaoyaoyou*, from which derives all Zhuangzi's work of deconstructing commonsense knowledge and conventional beliefs.

What is the life that Zhuangzi has affirmed originally and ultimately? The answer could be very simple if given briefly: the life of *ziran* as such. The true person (*zhenren*, 真人) of *xiaoyaoyou* must be the person who is able to say, "I was born with heaven and earth; I am one with myriad things!" (2/5). In Zhuangzi's dictionary, "freedom," "liberation," "*xiaoyaoyou*," "*wudai*," "transcendence," and "return" all have the same connotation of unconditional and nondependant affirmation of life as *ziran*. Everything *ziran* ought to be affirmed.

Affirming life as *ziran* is to affirm Dao-throughs-as-One or the wholeness and togetherness of all things. But unlike other thinkers who believe the Oneness as something absolutely certain, steady, constant, unchangeable, eternal, and unitary, Zhuangzi attributes his concept of One to the nature of impermanence, change, chaos, uncertainty, openness, and diversity. The only thing constant is impermanence; the only real world is the world of becoming or transforming, There is virtually no beginning nor end in this ever-changing flux of life. Again, one's ultimate affirmation of life is to be one with the flux in a way that she or he is totally *through* or *tonged* (通) in this world. And this throughness or *tong*, according Zhuangzi, is freedom, is liberation, is *xiaoyaoyou*.

Zhuangzi does not believe in or rely on any Lord or God that creates and determines our world, nor does he believe that human beings can control and determine the course of *ziran*. *Ziran* goes its own way and we human beings can never know "why" and determine "how." To this extent, *ziran* is also called "*ming*" (命) or fate. In chapter 4, *Ren Jian Shi* (人间世) or "In the Human World," "Confucius says, 'There are two great decrees in the world: one is fate and the other righteousness (*yi*). That a son should love his parents is fate that cannot be explained. That a subject should serve his ruler is righteousness, since there are rulers everywhere and one cannot escape such service under heaven' " (4/2). A true person of *xiao yao you* does not fight against her fate but "understands that fate is inevitable and therefore follows it as it is at ease" (4/2). Whatever fate brings forth to one's life, that is, either fortune or poverty, either luck or pity, either success or failure, either life or death, this fate should not be protested or praised but all affirmed, accepted, and celebrated. Everything that is *ziran* must be affirmed equally and identically. Such unconditional and undifferentiated affirmation, Zhuangzi believes, will bring about the ultimate state of unconditional and undifferentiated freedom and liberation. In other words, with such an affirmative spirit in mind, one can live and enjoy life—*xiaoyaoyou*.

Based on this perspective of Dao or Dao of no-Dao (*xiaoyaoyou*), in which a profound and ecstatic religiosity or spirituality abides, Zhuangzi created his own philosophy and teaching of Dao, full of the spirit of uniqueness, openness, and creativity. The last chapter of the *Book of Zhuangzi* sums up Zhuangzi's work beautifully:

> Obscure, boundless, and without pattern; changing and transforming, without constancy. Is it living or is it dying? Is it the merger of heaven and earth? Is it where the spirit comes and goes? Never clear where to go, never decisive where to be. Even if all the ten-thousand-things are counted at once, there is still no clue to locate it. There was in ancient times the "art of Dao" as such that Zhuangzi heard[45] and was delighted. He'd like to play in odd and empty terms, in absurd and bombastic words or in boundless and abysmal discourse, being self-indulgent instead of being fixed by partial opinions and single-dimensional views. Since the world was considered muddy and turbid, and could not be represented by formal language, he relied on goblet words to embrace the boundless, on paradoxical words to make language adequate, on allegorical words to meet the plurality of meanings. He communicated only with the spirit and essence of heaven and earth yet never discriminated any one of the myriad

things. He did not scold over "right" and "wrong" so that he could get along with common people. Though his writing is a string of queer beads and baubles, they roll and rattle and do no one any harm. Though his words seem to be ambiguous, the paradoxical nature comes to the sight. His mind is abundant yet never full of being enriched. Above he wandered with the creating and transforming nature of things (造化者); below he made friends with those who have forgotten life and death, who are carefree about beginning and end. As for the foundation, his grasp of it is broad, expansive, and penetrating; profound, liberal and unimpeded. As for the principle, his articulation is flexible and accordant to the greatest height. Nevertheless, in adapting himself to change and unleashing himself beyond the fetter of things, his idea cannot be exhausted and his dynamic is never decayed. Obscure and concealing, his art of Dao is ever open for completion. (33/6, Watson, 373)

CHAPTER 3

NIETZSCHE'S PHILOSOPHY OF LIFE AFFIRMATION

The question, after a brief scheme of Zhuangzi's philosophy has been presented, now comes to the fore: Who is Nietzsche? Is there such a man, a writer, a philosopher, whom I can present? Who is that man asking, "Why am I so clever?" and, "Why I do write such good books?"? Some would think these are silly questions not worth asking because we have at hand all his texts, published before and after his final breakdown in 1890. But when we refer a name of a thinker to his or her special mode of thinking, the name becomes questionable. Since Nietzsche has attracted great attention in the twentieth-century world, the name "Nietzsche" has been diversified by numerous writers, commentators, and critics.

The question of Nietzsche's name was brought up by Heidegger and raised again by Derrida as the question of whether the thinking we know under the name "Nietzsche" was one single kind of thinking. In his essay *Interpreting Signatures*, Jacques Derrida accuses Heidegger of claiming that Nietzsche bears only "one single name" or that "his thinking is one." Derrida refers to Heidegger's claim that it is Nietzsche who *names* his thinking and "his naming takes place only once ... at the summit of Western metaphysics, which is gathered together under this name."[1] On the contrary, Derrida contends that Nietzsche, next to Kierkegaard, "was one of the few great thinkers who multiplies his names and played with signatures, identities, and masks."[2] The dispute over Nietzsche's name has been a watershed in the arguments by different groups of Nietzschean commentators on whether Nietzsche produced a unified philosophy (one name) or fragmentary thinking (multiplied names).

As a result of my reading of Nietzsche, which is neither Heideggerian nor Derridian, I would interpret Nietzsche, his life, his writing, and his philosophy as a whole, bearing one name but with many signatures. We can discuss many different theories and attributes of Nietzsche, his ambiguity, inconsistency, and contradictoriness. Yet these all belong to the same person whose name, the only name, is "Nietzsche." In other words, no matter how many times Nietzsche played with signatures the name he signed for himself is still one, Nietzsche. On the other hand, Nietzsche's thinking as a whole is not only *one* thinking, not even close to *one* systematic metaphysics as Heidegger has claimed. It is a whole with thorough openness and multiplicity, a name with many signatures and masks, a fragmented discourse with frequent self-contradiction and variation. In this respect I will view the entire corpus of Nietzsche's philosophy. To view Nietzsche's corpus will not involve the imposition of a systematic interpretation upon it, but will be an attempt to correlate his major works with one another, early and late, published and unpublished, in order to examine and detect what in these works are Nietzsche's major themes and whether there is any coherence and consistency to them.

This chapter will deal with Nietzsche's thinking as a whole, and will investigate the ideas that developed over the course of his life. Many postmodernist critics would argue that it is wrong to read Nietzsche as a whole because his thinking is fragmentary, ambiguous, and contradictory. But, are not his ambiguity and contradiction something unique in his thinking that has therefore characterized his name, "Nietzsche"? Is there something that consistently determines his style of inconsistency and ambiguity? Can we find it, under all kinds of masks and disguises?

Are there ideas that are clearly and explicitly presented in Nietzsche's thinking? Are there ideas that Nietzsche never ceased promoting through his life? I believe there are. The idea of "revaluation of all values," of "will to power," of "eternal recurrence," of "affirmation of life," of "genealogy of morals," are ideas that Nietzsche consistently and continually pursued in his life, even if at times contradictorily. It is these ideas or "signatures" that created the great name "Nietzsche." I also believe there is at least one thing that correlates Nietzsche's ideas, not as an onto-theological center but as a passionate longing for elevating or liberating human life from its course of degeneration, or affirming life as an endless flux of transformation or excess over (*über*) human-all-too-human limit. As Tyler T. Roberts acutely observed, "The place of religion in Nietzsche's writings begs to be reexamined. Nietzsche announces the death of God, but with Dionysus, the eternal return, and affirmation, he invokes a new spiritual sensibility—a new reverence, a new joy—that has yet to be fully explored by his interpreters" (Roberts, 5). This is exactly why I am so determined here to elaborate or "reexamine," though not necessarily "the place of religion" that Roberts has looked into, how this longing, this "new spiritual sensibility" or specific"religiosity" has characteristically and consistently affected Nietzsche's writings.

NIETZSCHE'S MISSION: REVALUATION OF ALL VALUES

In this section I try to examine Nietzsche's thought on "revaluation of all values," through which we will see that the underlying "religiosity," an "abysmal" concern or passionate longing for liberating human life, is a thread that runs through his thinking of "revaluation of all values."

No one who has truly read Nietzsche could possibly deny that the "revaluation of all values" was a mission that Nietzsche carried out enthusiastically and persistently in his writing. Although contradictions, inconsistencies, and ironies often cloud his writings, Nietzsche has made himself clear enough about such a mission: "*Revaluation of all values: that is my formula for an act of supreme self-examination on the part of humanity, become flesh and genius in me. It is my fate that I have to be the first decent human being; that I know myself to stand in opposition to the mendaciousness of millennia*" (*EH*, "Why I am a Destiny"). Not only is this the formula for his thinking and philosophizing as "supreme self-examination," but also for his flesh, his genius and his fate that formulated his whole life. And, in fact, the task made his life "wonderful," he said: "For the task of *revaluation of all values* more capacities may have been needed than have ever dwelt together in a single individual—this was the precondition, the long, secret work and artistry of my instinct" (*EH*, "Why I am So Clever," 9). Through this mission of revaluation, Nietzsche becomes who he really is, with all his uniqueness, idiosyncrasy, boldness, creativity, ambiguity. It is also by his formula of revaluation that Nietzsche created a philosophy of his own. We could hardly comprehend his work if we took away the thread of revaluation.

Nietzsche's general concern had been consistently, from his early writings to the end of his productive years, the problem of human life and the decadence of Western culture. All he wanted to do with his devoted life was to "improve" mankind (*EH*, 217, *TI*). In order to regain the health and strength of mankind, we should find out what has been wrong with the human-all-too-human life so far, of course, by *revaluation of all values*. For the purpose of diagnosis, Nietzsche designates his task or mission of revaluation "the supreme self-examination on the part of humanity," which means an action to seek out "everything strange and questionable in existence" (ibid.).

To begin the project of self-examination, Nietzsche argues, we should switch our focus from the question of "truth" to something deeper and more fundamental, which can put us on the right track of "supreme self-examination." In the beginning of Part One of *Beyond Good and Evil*, he asks the "strange, wicked, questionable questions" which "this will to truth has not laid before us!" "That is a long story even now—and yet it seems as if it had scarcely begun" . . . so, "*Who* is it really that puts questions to us here? *What* in us really wants 'truth'" (9)?

Look at these questions carefully. What all philosophers so far have taught does not even touch the nature of truth yet. For the questions asked were mostly about the truthfulness or falsehood of objects or ideas, under the presupposition that there is/are objective truth(s) and that we philosophers could one day reveal such truth(s) through constant inquiry. It is the "long story" of the history of Western philosophy, to the extent that such inquiry has been carried out well for such a long time, and yet "it had scarcely begun," to the extent that there is scarcely anyone in this "long story" who has revealed such truth(s). Because no one had ever been aware that there are questions, real

Sphinx questions, that are strange, wicked, questionable, which should be asked before those we are used to inquiring: "*Who* is it really that puts questions to us here? *What* in us really wants 'truth'?" Or simply: *Who* is the person who is questioning? Before we ask what truth is we should know who we are, really, and *what* in us wants "truth." It is an obvious secret of human beings and their will that we should reveal before we begin to talk about the truth *they* want. Thus, Nietzsche was, unlike other philosophers hitherto, looking for something other than truth per se, something that is at the origin of those traditional questions we used to ask, to wit, the *nature* of human beings, and the *nature* in us that *wills* and *wants* "truth." Nietzsche calls such questions the "questions of values":

> Indeed we came to a long halt at the question about the cause of this will—until we finally came to a complete stop before a still more basic question. We asked about the *value* of this will, suppose we want truth: *why not untruth? and uncertainty? even ignorance?*
>
> The problem of the value of truth came before us—or was it we who came before the problem? ... It is a rendezvous, it seems, of questions and question marks. (*BGE*, 9)

Arriving at this "basic question" of value, Nietzsche began his whole thinking, his "supreme self-examination." Instead of asking about what truth is, he brought up the question of what the *value* of truth is. It is not the *truth* that decides our will to truth but the *will* that wills truth. Philosophers have so far concentrated themselves on the will to *truth* yet have forgotten their *will* to truth. When the fact of will comes into light, we realize that truth is not something objectively "true" but something *valuable*, something we want or will. The concepts of truth or lie, good or bad, etc., are all dependent on human will or evaluation, which stands for the demand, or, more fundamentally, physiological demand for "the preservation of a certain type of life"(*BGE*, 11). Truths are values, the value of truth is in fact the value of life. "When we speak of values," Nietzsche says, "we speak with the inspiration, with the way of looking at things, which is part of life: life itself forces us to posit values; life itself values through us when we posit values" (*TI*, 490). Life and our judgment of life are the *what* in us that wants "truth," and what Nietzsche considered as the "gravity" of his thinking.

In contrast to other philosophies of life and value theories, which usually presuppose a universal nature or truth as the measure of values, Nietzsche conceived life and our evaluation of life (will) as heterogeneous and multitudinous. Different "types of life," different kinds (ranks) of people always will, value, and interpret their lives differently. Therefore, to answer that the will to truth is the will to life, or that the value of truth is the value of life, is not enough for Nietzsche's "philosophizing with a hammer." We should keep interrogating *who* this particular type of person *is*, and *what type* of life this person lives and wills. This *who* is crucial, for the specific qualities of this person, such as strength, health, psychological condition, social status, etc., could significantly decide what type of life he or she wills and values. With the awareness of this *who*, who is questioning and valuing, Nietzsche proposed his question of value prior to other philosophical questions of truth, knowledge, and morality. And from this awareness, he also developed his unique notion of "truth" and the remarkable theory of "perspectivism," which can be seen as the first action of revaluation. According to his perspectivism, all that we used to believe as unchangeable, absolute, objective "truth" is merely provisional interpretation, perspectives based on the condition of our existence and the way we will and value life. "Truth" can be false; lies can be "truths." In this way Nietzsche opened the door of his revaluation of all values.

Why is it "revaluation of all values"? As soon as we have deepened our view from the traditional belief of "truth" to the questions of values, to "modes of existence of those who judge and evaluate,"[3] "the problem of the value of truth comes to us," or, we "come before the problem" simultaneously and necessarily. Is the truth we have believed for so long real truth? Are the values we have valued so far real values? If the values of truth hitherto correspond with a *certain type of life*, then, what type of life is it? Whose life is it from which the existing values were invented? To answer these questions, for Nietzsche, means to re-value the values, hence the question of value became the question of "revaluation," a "supreme self-examination" of all values we have had so far: *"the value of these values themselves must first be called in question"* (*GM*, "Preface," 6).

The problem of prevailing or "highest" values,[4] in general, is the negative attitude (*resentment*) toward life and the world of our existence. In the history of Western civilization, the highest values dominant for so long were those of the Platonic and Judaic-Christian traditions. The values on which this tradition has rested are *opposite values*: Truth versus error; God versus man; Being versus becoming; Reality versus appearance; Good versus evil; Reason versus instinct; Morality versus free spirit; the "true" world versus the *real* world; etc. Everything this tradition devalues and resents belongs to the *real* world of life, and those it values the highest "must have another, *peculiar* origin—they cannot be derived from this transitory, seductive, deceptive, paltry world, from this turmoil of delusion and lust. Rather from the lap of Being, the intransitory, the hidden god, the 'thing-in-itself' " (*BGE*, 10). This fundamental faith in opposite values, demonstrated in Western metaphysics and Christian morality, rejects and denies the actual world for another, fictional one. "*In summa:* . . . in this world, in which we live, is an error—this world of ours ought not to exist" (*WP*, 585/A). To what type of life does this kind of evaluation reflect? According to Nietzsche, the type of life that has generated such values is the type of declining, weakened, weary, condemned life, the life of degeneration and decadence. Furthermore, "what kind of man reflects in this way? An unproductive, suffering kind, a kind weary of life" (ibid.).

The necessary consequence of this decadent culture was "the advent of Nihilism," for its belief or value has been grounded on *a true world* that does not exist. The shadow of nihilism accompanied popular values even from the outset when they were sought as highest values. Underneath the *true world* decorated with all the solemn ideals of Truth, God, Being, Morality, and so forth, there was the hatred or denial of *this* world, the world of contradiction, deception, change, and sensuality, which were condemned as causes of suffering. Platonic philosophy and Christianity are, by their nature, nihilistic because they negate the world as it is (becoming) by establishing an erroneous "true" world as their measure of all values. Everything that exists in *this* world is untrue, worthless, evil, and therefore *this* world is simply nothing; instead, the opposite values have been posited as highest values. The positing of such highest values simultaneously posits the possibility of their devaluation, which already begins when these values show themselves to be untenable. Life thus appears to be unsuitable and utterly incompetent for the realization of these values. Nihilism comes to the fore when the belief in Truth, God, and Morality seems by no means tenable (*WP*, 55). For Nietzsche, nihilism represents the ultimate logical conclusion of Western values and ideals—"*That the highest values devaluate themselves*" (*WP*, 2). As the final consequence of nihilistic devaluation it now seems as if there were no meaning, no value in existence at all. This was diagnosed by Nietzsche as a pathological symptom of nineteenth-century European culture.

There is another reason why nihilism was considered the "ultimate logical conclusion" of Western history. It is the "will to truth" or the "will to knowledge" that prompts Socratic man to seek "the truth" or "the fact" outside the apparent world in order to prove the existence and perfection of another "true world." This has been the ultimate motif and methodology of Western philosophy and theology as well as the modern sciences. Since the highest values this culture has posited so far do not have their actual or factual ground in the first place, since "we have measured the value of the world according to categories that refer to a purely fictitious world" (*WP*, 12), the "will" to prove them from a true, factual basis is no more than a fantasy, a lie. One can never find the fact of "Being" or "God" by any means that human reason could possibly provide, as Kant had finally declared in his *Critique of Pure Reason*. The concepts of "truth," "God," and all these highest values now turn against (devaluate) themselves. Modern positivist sciences logically repudiated the belief in "absolute truth" and "God" for their lack of "factual evidence," by the same "will to truth." God ends up killed by its devotees, since there is no longer any objective truth from which the "last man" could derive any meaning and value as the goal of life. Will to truth and will to knowledge then become the wills to nothingness. By rejecting any kind of truth and value in an extreme way, nihilism is completed through the history or degeneration of Western (Christian) culture.

In the face of the degeneration of the culture, the decadence of humankind, and its consequent nihilism, Nietzsche was convinced that the highest values hitherto were totally problematic. Hence, the first step of his revaluation of all values was to initiate a countermovement against the prevalent values: that is, to reverse, to invert, to subvert, to destroy the old values we have believed so far. To turn the traditional values upside down is to return to the reality of life, of what we are and where we belong originally: from Being, Truth, God, Morality, Certainty, Eternity, Reason, and Heaven to becoming, deception, individuality, immorality, change, time, sensuality, and the earth. What has been rejected or disdained, such as nature, instinct, body, desire, and passion, now should be affirmed. Most philosophers have been critics of their times, but no one like Nietzsche who wanted to be "dynamite," a philosopher with a "hammer" to destroy the whole edifice of Western ideals and values. He hammered virtually everything of his time that had long been believed as truth, from the Platonic tradition starting with Socrates down to Hegel as the mainstream tradition of Western philosophy. "I am the anti-ass *par excellence*," Nietzsche says, "*Overthrowing idols* (my word for 'ideals')—that comes closer to being part my craft," because "the *lie* of the ideal has so far been the curse on reality; on account of it, mankind itself has become mendacious and false down to its most fundamental instincts—to the point of 'worshipping the *opposite* values of those which alone would guarantee its health, its future, the lofty *right* to its future" (*EH*, "Why I Write Such Good Books," 1 and "Preface," 2); "To *reverse perspectives*: the first reason why a 'revaluation of values' is perhaps possible for me alone" (*EH*, "Why I Am so Wise," 1). However, the task of the revaluation of all values, unlike nihilism of any kind,[5] is not just to destroy or annihilate old values but to seek or create *new values*, the new values that will in the future overcome the humankind of decadence, the culture of nihilism, and the morality that has banished our "free spirit." For Nietzsche, negating and destroying the old values is the condition of saying Yes to life as it is, of being creative—"whoever wants to be a creator in good and evil, must first be a annihilator and break values" (*EH*, "Why I Am a Destiny," 2 and 4). A creator of new values, that is what Nietzsche wants to be, and he calls for the future: "The man who breaks their tables of values, the breaker, the lawbreaker; yet he is the creator" (*Z*, "Prologue," 9). Precisely, the revaluation of all values is a task that has a twofold meaning: at once destruction and creation. And the one who revalues too has a twofold role at once—as destroyer and creator, lawbreaker and legislator.[6] The latter seems to Nietzsche more important for a philosopher who is doing revaluation:

> *Genuine philosophers, however, are commanders and legislators:* they say, "*thus* it *shall* be!" They first determine the Whither and For What of man, and in so doing have at their disposal the preliminary labor of all philosophical laborers, all who have overcome the past. With a creative hand they reach for the future, and all that is and has been becomes a means for them, an instrument, a hammer. Their "knowing" is *creating*, their creating is a legislation, their will to truth is—*will to power*. (*BGE*, 136)

Nietzsche made himself very explicit here that revaluation of all values is a process of creation, "a celebration of a harvest" of new values.

> Toward *new philosophers*; there is no choice; toward spirits strong and original enough to provide the stimuli for opposite values and to revalue and invert "eternal values"; toward forerunners, toward men of the future who in the present tie the knot and constraint that forces the will of millennia upon *new* tracks. To teach man the future of man as his will, as dependent on a human will, and to prepare great ventures and over-all attempt of discipline and cultivation by way of putting an end to that gruesome dominion of nonsense and accident that has so far been called "history" . . . (BGE, 117)
>
> But all these are merely preconditions of his task: this task itself demands something different—it demands that he *create values*. (*BGE*, 136)

Therefore, he never thinks himself as a mere destroyer. The very task or mission of revaluation as creating new values opens up ways toward a future life of human beings that will enable us to redefine our existence and nature in an authentic fashion. At this point, Nietzsche's project of revaluation, contrary to nihilistic devaluation, is in fact the possible cure for nihilism.

Speaking of revaluation as creating new values, one may ask: "Does Nietzsche offer us new values?"[7] The answer is "yes." First of all, revaluation as reversed valuation has recreated values that have long been overwhelmed by our dominating tradition. Ideas such as the meaning of the earth, the ultimate affirmation of life itself, nature, instinct, body, "evil," ego, and all those that were denied and devalued now become new values in place of the old. It is from the ground of these new values that Nietzsche was able to create his new philosophical thinking.

Second of all, not only did Nietzsche re-create ancient values, he also created his own values: the method of genealogy and perspectivism, the philosophy of will to power and eternal recurrence, the idea of *Übermensch* or the man of the future, the gay science and free spirit, the anti-Christ and immoralist, the dancer and laughter, and so on. All these ideas assume new values created within the process of revaluation of all values, which is why Nietzsche believed the mission of revaluation was his destiny, a destiny to create.

Thirdly, revaluation of all values is itself a new value because it is supposed to be an ever-continuing, ever-changing, ever-renewing process. Nietzsche's revaluation is to affirm life as it is, that is, to affirm life as constant passing away and destroying, "which is the decisive feature of a Dionysian philosophy" (*EH*, "The Birth of Tragedy," 3). Why does nihilism devaluate its highest values? Because it always tries to establish something as being, as fixed value that can freeze the flux of becoming. Nihilists don't understand that the highest value they are seeking should be the "revaluation of all values" itself.

It is a constant process of revaluation of *all values*, including revaluation itself. "Revaluation of all values" is thus a contradiction: if all values ought to be revalued, what value will be left as the new value by which we are revaluing? Revaluation itself pertains to that new value, it is revaluation that finally turns into its self-contradiction, self-destruction, and self-recreation. This is the secret of Nietzsche and his understanding of becoming and life through revaluation with Dionysian spirit: to supersede or return the decadent form of life (prevailing values) to a genuine one that is itself the creative will to power, that is, the ever-new interpretation, transformation, and affirmation.

GENEALOGY: A NEW WAY OF PHILOSOPHIZING

Revaluation of all values prompted by Nietzsche's "religiosity," as we have seen, as a critique of prevalent values and creation of new values, inevitably demands a new method, a new way of looking at things (which is itself a new *interpretation*, a new *perspective*, therefore a new *value* created). Nietzsche calls it genealogy. Indeed, the word *genealogy* first appeared in his book *On the Genealogy of Morals*, but we ought not to envisage that until then he had not begun to use it, or to assume that he applied genealogy only to the study of morality. According to Nietzsche, the idea of *origin*, for which a genealogical study is launched, was triggered in his mind during his childhood.[8] Still, in the very early years of his life he had ceased to look for the origin of the evil "behind the world" and started putting historical, philological training and psychological investigation together to create a genealogical study of humanity. As he said in the Preface to *GM*: "My idea on the *origin* of our moral prejudices—for this is the subject of this polemic—received their first, brief, and provisional expression in the collection of aphorisms that bears the title *Human, All-Too-Human. A book for Free Spirits*"(*GM*, 17). If we extend the study of *origin* from morality to philosophy, religion, politics, and culture, we could easily discover that Nietzsche had looked for origin in almost every aspect of our culture by way of genealogy, though it was not yet called genealogy till the coming out of *On the Genealogy of Morals*, in which Nietzsche named his method *genealogy*.

The name of genealogy came to Nietzsche when he read Paul Ree's *Origin of the Moral Sensations* (1877). In *GM* he remarks:

> The first impulse to publish something of my hypotheses concerning the origin of morality was given me by a clear, tidy, and shrewd—also precocious—little book in which I encountered distinctly for the first time an upside-down and perverse species of genealogical hypothesis, the genuinely *English* type, that attracted me—with that power of attraction which everything contrary, everything antipodal possesses.... It was then, as I have said, that I advanced for the first

time those genealogical hypotheses to which this treatises was devoted ... (*GM*, "Preface," 4)

The British or "English-style" genealogy was a form of reasoning with the hypothesis about what causes could have led to given effects.[9] This is very close to Nietzsche's searching for origin. Yet the outcome of this British style, at least in Paul Ree's book, was, according to Nietzsche, an upside-down and perverse kind of genealogy, for it used a social-Darwinian hypothesis of the survival of the fittest that presupposes that the original mode of morality, or morality of the fittest, was the altruistic mode, that is, "selflessness," self-sacrifice, or "sympathy." Nietzsche had nothing in common with Ree and English genealogists, "proposition by proposition, conclusion to conclusion" (4) Nevertheless he began to use the name of genealogy for his own study of origin, inspired by the English-style genealogist yet in a non-English style.

Morality or the critique of morality, without doubt, was the key element of "all values" we have had hitherto, so that it deserves central genealogical concern in the task of revaluation. For Nietzsche, it is morality, or more specifically, Christian morality that has forged the entire table of values in the West: "all the forces and drives by virtue of which life and growth exist lie under the ban of morality: morality as the instinct to deny life. One must destroy morality if one is to liberate life" (*WP*, 343). Therefore, "the inquiry into the *origin of our evaluations*" (*WP*, 254), and "to what extent moral valuations hide behind all other high values"(*WP*, 2), became crucial for the task of revaluation.

> My task of preparing a moment of the highest self-examination for humanity, a great noon when it looks back and far forward, when it emerges from the dominion of accidents and priests and for the first time poses, *as a whole*, the question of Why? And For What?—this task follows of necessity from the insight that humanity is *not* all by itself on the right way, that it is by no means governed divinely, that, on the contrary, it has been precisely among its holiest value concepts that the instinct of denial, corruption, and decadence has ruled seductively. The question concerning the origin of moral values is for me a question of the first rank because it is crucial for the future of humanity. (*EH*, "Dawn," 2)

But genealogy does not confine itself merely to the limited area of morality. In fact, Nietzsche applied the method of genealogy, along with physiology and typology and others, to trace and interpret the origin of all the high values of the times, including religion, philosophy, art, science, and politics. Even in his *On the Genealogy of Morals* he did not limit his study to ethics but addressed a larger scale of philosophy and history—for instance, ascetic ideals, will to truth, etc. From his other works written and published before *On the Genealogy of Morals*, we also see that his application of genealogy was not limited to morality. His first book, *The Birth of Tragedy*, could be conceived of as an early exercise in the genealogy of philosophy and the human spirit—in terms of the birth and death and possible rebirth of ancient Greek tragedy. In his early essays in the early 1870s[10] he continued to work on genealogical studies of various subjects—truth, philosophy and metaphysics, moral values disguised by will to truth and knowledge. Most of these investigations appeared in his *Human, All-too-Human* (1878), which Nietzsche claims as the work preceding *On the Genealogy of Morals*. In his later writings, published and unpublished, on morality, religion, and metaphysics, Nietzsche still retained his genealogical method to undertake his "revaluation of all values." Thus, Nietzsche's method of genealogy was not limited to the study of the origin of morality; he believed it was equally valid in any domain of the study of humanities.

Genealogy originally refers to a "tracing of descent," or an investigation or study of family pedigrees, from which one is able to learn about one's ancestors and the origin of the family. Nietzsche borrowed the term *genealogy* from Greek antiquity,[11] also inspired by the "English genealogists," as a metaphor for his method which "attempts" to trace back the origins of those highest values such as Being, truth, goodness, and so on. Through a genealogical investigation, Nietzsche wants to determine under what condition humans devised these value judgments of good and evil, truth and error. *"And what value do they themselves possess?* Have they hitherto hindered or furthered human prosperity? Are they a sign of distress, of impoverishment, of the degeneration of life? Or is there revealed in them, on the contrary, the plenitude, force, and will of life, its courage, certainty, future?" (*GM*, 17).

Nietzsche's genealogy is against the progressive and teleological conception of history that asserts that there is an original principle or ideal running through and controlling the entire course of history. This has been the dominant form of historiography in the West, from Plato up to Hegel and modern historicism. Historians of this kind had the same mission of finding origin (*Ursprung*) as that of genealogists, but they believed that there must be an ultimate origin, such as Form, Being, God, or some other absolute principle, from which everything is generated as the unfolding manifestation and progressive completion of that original principle. Nietzsche rejects such a concept of history. Instead, his genealogical analysis tries to show that there are as many origins (*Herkunft*) as there are different families (values, cultures, lives, etc.) we can trace back, and that different origins generated different value systems from the past to the present.[12] Instead of constructing an a priori origin, a transcendent ideal, and linear totality of history, genealogy pays attention to those diverse cases of different kinds of peoples, discourses, physical conditions in different times, because all these "little things" that had been ignored so far by historians and metaphysicians could be the real *origins* of a particular value of the present. Genealogy must therefore "record the singularity of events outside of any monotonous finality; it must seek them in the most unpromising places, in what we tend to feel is without history—in sentiments, love, conscience, instincts."[13] And so Nietzsche's genealogical analysis is often associated with psychological, biological, and physiological studies.

Most historians at the time held a teleological or progressive view of history. They believed that the existing systems of thought and value were the highest accomplishment or the most advanced products of the history of progress. Nietzsche opposes this view. For him, history is not necessarily a process of continuous progress to complete an absolute ideal (Hegel) from its "primitive stage" toward the advanced or perfected stage. Rather, history is a multidimensional process of human life—domination, invasion, degeneration, decadence, etc. It is a process that shows all kinds of relationships among different forces of life—active and reactive, strong and weak, healthy and sick, etc. It is also a long story of lives that is full of surprises and accidents from which the different "families" were originated and developed. As for Nietzsche, what his genealogical investigation has revealed is in fact the opposite of what progressive historians had believed: a history of human, all-too-human degeneration, decadence, sickness, and vulgarization.

The work of historians, such as Paul Ree, is problematic also because it mistakes a certain principle, such as utilitarianism or selflessness, for the genealogical origin of morality. The ideals they used for such original principles were not causes but results or consequences of some particular genealogical origin. Further, according to a genealogical analysis, at the very beginning when the conceptions were created and used, the meanings of the words were different and heterogeneous. Why were there different meanings of the same word, for example, the word *good*? In what circumstances or for what reason were these different meanings generated and developed? How did these words finally become ultimate ideals or values? These are the questions that genealogy seeks to answer. In contrast to metaphysical philosophy and traditional history, genealogy places those words and conceptions into historical, temporal, provisional, and local contexts to decipher the various origins of their meanings. In this respect, genealogy is an efficient way to deconstruct all fixed ideals, principles, values, and meanings.

Tracing the origins and genealogies of all values is itself a process of critique which puts question marks on everything that has been absolutized, privileged, and legitimated as highest value; and this process of critique is itself a revaluation. Genealogy thus means, as Deleuze has correctly pointed out, "both the value of origin and the origin of values." For this reason genealogy as critique has its "twofold struggle"

> against those who remove values from criticism, contenting themselves with producing inventories of existing values or with criticizing things in the name of established values (the "philosophical laborers," Kant and Schopenhauer, *BGE*, 211); but also against those who criticize, or respect, values by deriving them from simple facts, from so-called "objective facts" (the utilitarians, the "scholars," *BGE* Part 6).... Nietzsche attacks both the "high" idea of foundation

which leaves values indifferent to their origin and the idea of a simple causal derivation or smooth beginning which suggests an indifferent origin for values.[14]

Genealogy became Nietzsche's new way, a powerful "hammer," a new method to overcome Kant's and Schopenhauer's shortcoming of remaining trapped in the cave of metaphysical and traditional views of values.

As critique, genealogy does not look to the origin of things for some ultimate reality or truth that we can hold on to in an ever-changing and uncertain world. On the contrary, to trace back to origins is to return from a conceptualized, petrified, and alienated world to the nature of life as it is. Origin in Nietzsche has no sense of finality or ultimatum, or any kind of metaphysical presupposition. Everything has its origin as well as its end. In the real course of life, in the world of becoming, nothing stays forever and remains unchanged, nor does a final origin or ultimate truth exist outside the flux of life. To this extent, genealogical investigating as a whole is an ever open and ever-incomplete enterprise representing and manifesting what Nietzsche called *historical spirit* or *wirkliche Historie* (*GM*, 25).

Moreover, as far as the improvement of human beings is concerned, Nietzsche applies genealogy as an instrument to diagnose the pathological symptoms of human beings. What is wrong with us? When did it happen that we humans began to degenerate and be sick? What kind of sickness and from whom have we been infected? If we don't know what problems we have and why, there will never be hope of improvement. Genealogical analysis helps us to diagnose those symptoms and to overcome them.

In summary, genealogy is the main method of Nietzsche's "revaluation of all values," and a way of his philosophizing with religiosity. It is the way to find out *who* we *really are*: who wants truth? who wills morality? who values and revalues? Before we come to the question of what truth is we should know who is asking the question. Who are we, the posers of the questions? According to Nietzsche's genealogy, only after we find answers to these questions by means of genealogy and no longer are "strangers to ourselves," are we able to overcome, "ascend," and finally liberate ourselves. This is Nietzsche's religiosity, the very motif that initiates the mission of revaluation and the ground from which the new values are created. Based on the genealogical inquiries, a possible substitution for the traditional method is experimented with (*Versuch*) and exercised.

TRUTH, KNOWLEDGE, AND MORALS

In this section, Nietzsche's notorious attack on traditional philosophy and religion will be displayed. We will see in his critique of metaphysics, "the will to truth" and knowledge, "ascetic ideal," language, and morality the primary consideration or religiosity of human existence and life. The fatal problem of this Western tradition is the negative, hostile, and pathological attitude toward

life and the world as they are. I will also show that Nietzsche's overcoming
tradition is directly an exercise of overcoming and liberating the human-all-
too-human self.

Metaphysics as a Symptom of Human Decadence

Nietzsche's task of revaluation of all values started, in his early writings, from
his critique of traditional metaphysics. He believed at the outset of his philosophical *Versuch,* as early as the 1870s, that the problems of modern culture,
the dangers of nihilism and decadence, to some extent rested on traditional
metaphysics as a systematic construction of a *true* world of Reality or Being
upon which the whole world of phenomena and appearances depends and
relies. This *true* world of metaphysics, with its accumulation of solemn names
such as Truth, God, Being, Morality, Beauty, etc., was invented to replace or
to subdue the *real* world of life, a world of appearance and becoming. Metaphysics represents precisely the type of world-interpretations that are based on
a negative tendency, that is, a hatred and denial toward existence, life, and this
world. It renounces this world and this life as something unbearable and keeps
constructing another world and another life for some ultimate redemption of
living in this condemned world. For long periods of history, such metaphysical world-interpretations have dominated the entire domain of human ideology—philosophy, theology, morality, science, and so on. According to Nietzsche,
metaphysics and its world are merely errors, because such a world has never
existed at all. In order to revaluate the values based on this metaphysical world,
in order to reach the ultimate affirmation of life, one "now has, with great
exertion of mind, to overcome metaphysics" (*HAH*, 23).

Nietzsche's first move toward overcoming metaphysics, or "overturning
Platonism" and "twisting free from it,"[15] was made in *The Birth of Tragedy.* The
title of the book might have been mistaken by some readers for a mere aesthetic study, a kind of critique of ancient Greek tragedy in terms of a form
of art. But the meaning or significance of the discussion in the book is way
beyond what could be seen from the title. It is through the historical investigation of the birth and death of Greek tragedy that "the big question mark
concerning the value of existence had thus been raised":

> What is the significance of the *tragic* myth among the Greeks of the
> best, the strongest, the most courageous period? And the tremendous
> phenomenon of the Dionysian—and, born from it, tragedy—what
> might they signify?– And again: that of which tragedy died, the Soc-
> ratism of morality, the dialectics, frugality, and cheerfulness of the
> theoretical man—how now? Might not this very Socratism be a sign
> of decline, of weariness, of infection, of the anarchical dissolution of
> the instincts? And the "Greek cheerfulness" of the later Greeks—
> merely the afterglow of the sunset? The Epicureans' resolve *against*

pessimism—a mere precaution of the afflicted? And science itself, our science—indeed, what is the significance of all science, viewed as a symptom of life? For what—worse yet, *whence* all science? How now? Is the resolve to be scientific about everything perhaps a kind of fear of, an escape from, pessimism? A subtle last resort against— *truth*? ... (*BT*, "Attempt at a Self-Criticism," 1)

Clearly, the real theme of the writing is not about the tragedy as merely an art form but as a type of life, "a pessimism of *strength*," "the *fullness* of existence," a cultural spirit or Dionysian philosophy that is fundamentally opposite to the life of decadence, of negation, of optimistic rationalism (Socratism). By interpreting Greek tragedy as a positive valuation of existence, Nietzsche found his own position and perspective, which he called, for the moment, "metaphysics of art," notwithstanding he abandoned such a term in late writings.[16] Life was presented in Greek tragedy, the greatest example of metaphysics of art, as the mysterious primordial unity of Apollinian and Dionysian duality, light and darkness, individuation and self-annihilation, dream and intoxication, joy and agony, beauty and ugliness, happiness and suffering. Such eternal contradictions of human existence and the natural world were not renounced but celebrated, affirmed, and justified by the Greeks through tragedy. Art and life finally reached perfect "oneness" in Greek tragedy: existence and the world as they are have been affirmed as works of art, and art as life itself; "as artistic energy which burst forth from nature herself" (*BT*, 2). Hence, the first thing Nietzsche has celebrated and elevated from Greek tragedy is the affirmation of a real world of life, an apparent world of uncertainty, contradiction, and fragmentation, in which lived the noblest, strongest, and most beautiful type of humanity to date—the Greeks. As Lawrence J. Hatab concluded in his paper "Apollo and Dionysus,"

> Nietzsche's attraction to the Apollonian-Dionysian dyad in early Greek culture and his later association with Dionysus (again, shorthand for the earlier dyad) are expressive of three important and interrelated Nietzschean themes: (1) an affirmation of a finite world of becoming rather than a fixed world of being; (2) an extrahuman (*übermenschlich*) element implicated in the affirmative posture of eternal recurrence; and (3) a self-consuming sense of truth that does not presume to rest or terminate in fixed, stable conditions. (Santaniello, 54)

"What I then got hold of," says Nietzsche, "something frightful and dangerous ... was *the problem of science itself*" (*BT*, "Attempt," 2). Against the tragic spirit, there had grown an "anti-Dionysian tendency" led by Socrates. "A profound *illusion* that first saw the light of the world in the person of Socrates: the unshakable faith that thought, using the thread of causality, can penetrate the deepest abysses of being, and that thought is capable not only of knowing being but even of *correcting* it" (*BT*, 15). This "sublime meta-physical illusion" revealed the fundamental secret of science, which at last caused the death of tragedy and became an instrument of Greek disintegration and degeneration. In order to reverse such metaphysical illusion and anticipate the rebirth of tragedy, Nietzsche demanded of himself *to look at science in the perspective of the artist, but at art in that of life* ("BT, Attempt," 2).

"Let us add the gravest question of all. What, seen in the perspective of *life*, is the significance of morality?" ("BT, Attempt," 4). Underneath the Platonic (Socratic) metaphysics lies another evaluation of existence: morality. Morality, accompanied with metaphysics and science, represents a hostility to life—"a furious, vengeful antipathy to life itself: for all of life is based on semblance, art, deception, points of view, and the necessity of perspectives and error." Moreover, "It was *against* morality that my instinct turned with this questionable book, long ago; it was an instinct that aligned itself with life and that discovered for itself a fundamentally opposite doctrine and valuation of life—purely artistic and *anti-Christian*. What to call it? As a philologist and man of words I baptized it, not without taking some liberty—for who could claim to know the rightful name of the Antichrist?—in the name of a Greek god: I called it Dionysian" ("BT, Attempt," 5). It is clear that *The Birth of Tragedy* is Nietzsche's starting point in his task of overturning Platonism and twisting free from it. This task as a major part of revaluation never stopped until the final years of his creative life (1889).

Now, what was wrong after all with Platonic or traditional metaphysics? Why is it an error or lie rather than a search for truth? According to Nietzsche's critique, the first problem of metaphysics is that it negates this real world of life and puts faith in the other. Metaphysics denies everything that is apparent, changeable, unstable, or uncertain, contradictory; in other words, it denies everything that originally consists of our real life and the world. A metaphysical mind cannot bear to see a world of becoming that never stops flowing, and an ironic existence that juxtaposes joy and pain, happiness and suffering as the very taste of life. Hence originated the "metaphysical need" for those who condemned this world and life as the worst curse upon man, for those who wanted to live in another world and another life. What the metaphysical need needs is a "true" world with its promise of certainty, ratio-nality, order, eternity, virtue, and happiness, in which and only in which life could be worth living. Nietzsche saw as inherent in this metaphysics a great turning away from life, the denying of life, and a sort of nihilism that invented a fictitious world based on its hatred and renunciation of this real world.

The second thing Nietzsche strongly rejects is the dualism on which the Platonic metaphysics are founded. Because the apparent world is perceived by metaphysicians as false, contradictory, and terrible, how could it be the ground for any metaphysical ideal or *true* world?

> How could *anything* originate out of its opposite? For example, truth
> out of error? Or the will to truth out of the will to deception? Or

selfless deeds out of selfishness? Or the pure sunlike gaze of the sage out of lust? Such origins are impossible; whoever dreams of them is a fool, indeed worse; the things of the highest value must have another, *peculiar* origin—they cannot be derived from this transitory, seductive, paltry world, from this turmoil of delusion and lust. Rather from the lap of Being, the intransitory, the hidden god, the "thing-in-itself"—there must be their basis, and nowhere else. (*BGE*, I, 2)

By inventing a *true* world beyond, the "primordial unity" of the apparent world and the continual flow of life have been differentiated or ruptured into dualistic opposites, namely, Being and Becoming, Reality and Appearance, Soul and Body, Certainty and Chaos, Good and Evil, Identity and Difference, Eternity and Time. Everything belonging to the system of metaphysics must be truer, better than what resides in this world and must be privileged and valued highest, while the other must be deprived and devalued. In other words, the world and the life we are living are false, evil, worthless; a metaphysical or religious beyond, instead, is what we should be longing for. Is not such dualistic metaphysics, which has dominated the Western tradition since Socrates, a symptom of degeneration, a type of nihilism that should be revalued and overcome, "for the advent of a new species of philosophers"?

> For one may doubt, first, whether there are any opposites at all, and secondly whether these popular valuations and opposite values on which the metaphysicians put their seal, are not perhaps merely foreground estimates, only provisional perspectives, perhaps even from some nook, perhaps from below, frog perspectives, as it were, to borrow an expression painters use. For all the value that the true, the truthful, the selfless may deserve, it would still be possible that a higher and more fundamental value for life might have to be ascribed to deception, selfishness, and lust. It might even be possible that what constitutes the value of these good and revered things is precisely that they are insidiously related, tied to, and involved with these wicked, seemingly opposite things—maybe even one with them in essence. (*BGE*, I, 2)

For example, metaphysics was itself originated from a "*misunderstanding of the dream*"; it is in the dream that a barbarous culture was getting to know a *second real world*. The rationality and logic actually originated from the judgment and belief at the bottom of which "lies the *sensation of the pleasurable or painful* in respect to the subject experiencing the sensation" (*HAH*, I, 5, 18).

Third, metaphysicians believe that there is a certain, unchanging Being or Reality opposite this world of appearances, and that once we get hold of it by means of metaphysics we are at home with truth. Since Being is the only identity and essence of all things, it can certainly not be changed, chosen, and multiplied. By its nature, therefore, metaphysics is necessarily arbitrary, dogmatic, absolutist, and of course unhistorical. Just as Nietzsche criticizes: "Lack of historical sense is the family failing of all philosophers; many, without being aware of it, even take the most recent manifestation of man, such as those which have arisen under the impress of certain religions, even certain political events, as the fixed form from which one has to start out. They will not learn that man has become, that the faculty of cognition has become . . . everything has become: there are *no eternal facts*, just as there are no absolute truths" (*HAH*, I/2). Moreover, if the real world is contradictory and pluralistic, how could there be any absolute "Being of beings as a whole" (Heidegger)? Or one God? Is it not an error or lie to call a particular thing or interpretation "absolute truth"?

Truths as Lies and Will to Truth as Ascetic Ideal

Now, what should be called into question is truth itself. All metaphysics, as well as science and religion, according to Nietzsche, so far have believed in truth as if it were an undoubted "fact" that could be taken for granted as the presupposition of reasoning, cognition, and judgment. This unconditional "will to truth," even in its most recent forms such as atheism, positivism, and nihilism, is still by its nature *faith in the ascetic ideal itself*—"it is the faith in a *metaphysical* value, the absolute value of *truth*, sanctioned and guaranteed by this ideal alone (it stands or falls with this ideal)" (*GM*, III, 24). It is the *metaphysical faith* in truth that has never been questioned by philosophy and science ever since, "because truth was posited as being, as God, as the highest court of appeal—because truth was not *permitted* to be a problem at all" (ibid.). Everything or every idea could be suspected and criticized except truth itself. Nietzsche has challenged this tradition precisely by interrogating truth itself.

What is truth or the truth-in-itself in which metaphysics has believed so far? In the Platonic and Christian tradition, truth is the representation of the ultimate Reality or Being that originates and presents, from somewhere beyond, the sole nature of the world and all things. The purpose of *true* knowledge is, without any doubt, to learn, to discover and communicate with this Reality or Being. Nietzsche claims that truth of this kind is an "illusion" or a lie. For Nietzsche, truth is a lie because it corresponds to nothing but a fictitious "reality" (God, Being, Good) that never existed. Based virtually on no-thing, the "man of truth" has constructed *another* world of truth in opposition to this one of appearance and becoming. "The truthful man, in the audacious and ultimate sense presupposed by the faith in science, *thereby affirms another world* than that of life, nature, and history; and insofar as he affirms this 'other world', does this not mean that he has to deny its antithesis, this world, *our* world?" (*GS*, 334). Any truth, any idea based on such metaphysical faith, such an "other world," is simply a lie, a lie invented by a type of people who were unable to stand life in this world.

Hence, knowing or knowledge is not a process of mirroring and reflecting the true reality; rather, it is the process of accommodating ourselves to the world and appropriating things to us. There is no independent or objective truth that is not anthropomorphic, that is, humanly constructed for the purpose of serving human interests. Who are these humans? In his work *On Truth and Lies in a Nonmoral Sense,* Nietzsche says that human history is minute compared to the infinite process of the universe. No one can adequately illustrate "how miserable, how shadowy and transient, how aimless and arbitrary the human intellect looks within nature. Rather, it is human, and only its possessor and begetter takes it so solemnly—as though the world's axis turned within it." This "pride" connected "with knowing and sensing lies like a blinding fog over the eyes and senses of men, thus deceiving them concerning the value of existence. For this pride contains within itself the most flattering estimation of the value of knowing. Deception is the most general effect of such pride ..." (*TL*, 1). Truth is illusory because within the illusory process of knowing we have changed the world anthropomorphically and at the same time dissimulated our ideas to some "objective," "universal," and "absolute" truths.

"Henceforth, my dear philosophers," Nietzsche says,

> let us be on guard against the dangerous old conceptual fiction that posited a "pure, will-less, painless, timeless knowing subject"; let us guard against the snares of such contradictory concepts as "pure reason," "absolute spirituality," "knowledge in itself": these always demand that we should think of an eye that is completely unthinkable, an eye turned in no particular direction, in which the active and interpreting forces, through which alone seeing becomes seeing *something*, are supposed to be lacking; these always demand of the eye an absurdity and a nonsense. There is *only* a perspective "knowing"; and the *more* eyes, different eyes, we can use to observe one thing, the more complete will our "concept" of this thing, our "objectivity," be. But to eliminate the will altogether, to suspend each and every affect, supposing we were capable of this—what would that mean but to *castrate* the intellect? (*MG*, III, 12)

There is no truth that corresponds objectively to things we confront. There are only perspectives mediated by our wills, affects, sensations, beliefs, and physical bodies which consist of our "interpreting forces," through which we open our eyes to see things we will or want to "see" and through which things come into our vision and *become* "objects" of our seeing and knowing. This is what Nietzsche called "perspectivism" and what he applied to "guard against" all kinds of metaphysics, ascetic ideals, dogmatism, foundationalism, and the like. It is not a thing-in-itself but human perspectives or interpretations that determine or justify the adequacy and "facticity" of truth. All perspectives and interpretations are conditional in accordance with the specific "space and time" and a specific type of people. To "sublimate" a perspective or interpretation to universal or absolute truth is simply to lie or to "castrate the intellect."

Language and Truth

Perhaps Michel Foucault is right that Nietzsche was "the first to reconcile the philosophical task with a radical reflection on language" (*The Order of Things*, 403). One of the most remarkable and significant contributions of Nietzsche's criticism of metaphysical truth and knowledge is his genealogical analysis of language and its constitutive function in constructing our belief in truth.

Insofar as the individual wants to preserve herself within a society of many, in the very early age of human beings "a uniformly valid and binding designation is invented for things, and this legislation of language likewise establishes the first laws of truth. For the contrast between the truth and lie arises here for the first time. The liar is a person who uses the valid designations, the words, in order to make something which is unreal appear to be real" (*TL*, 1). In other words, truth is constructed by language, that is, words, metaphors, conceptions, categories, within which "the spiritual activities of millennia is deposited" (*P*, 79).

The problem of truth in this respect rests on the problem of language, because every form of knowledge or perspective is possible only by means of language. Traditional philosophers believed that we could contemplate an object correctly, as true knowledge, with the aid of concepts (words) as representations of that object. Nietzsche opposes the representational and referential nature of language. No word or concept can picture and express reality adequately. First, we create words for things not yet known. By this process of naming we begin to discern the named not by its *essence* but by its differences or similarities to some other things known. Second, the process of naming is an artificial process of differentiation, classification, and designation in which the named becomes an *isolated* word representing only certain features that seem familiar to us. Third, whereas the world is a constant flux of appearance and becoming, words are static, standing for our will to certainty. How could a word or concept represent or mirror the nature of becoming truthfully and adequately? Fourth, "we believe that we know something about the things themselves when we speak of trees, colors, snow, and flowers; and yet we possess nothing but metaphors for things—metaphors which correspond in no way to the original entities" (*TL*, 1). Finally, we generalize and canonize the concept into truth by forgetting that we are the *"artistically creating subject"* of language; for "only by forgetting this primitive world of metaphor can one live with repose, security, and consistency" (ibid.).

In the context of these remarks, we find Nietzsche's well-known "definition" of truth:

> What then is truth? A movable host of metaphors, metonymies, and
> anthropomorphisms: in short, a sum of human relations which have

been poetically and rhetorically intensified, transferred, and embellished, and which, after long usage, seem to a people to be fixed, canonical, and binding. Truths are illusions which we have forgotten are illusions; they are metaphors that have become worn out and have been drained of sensuous force, coins which have lost their embossing and are now considered as metal and no longer as coins. (*TL*, I)

Does Nietzsche Renounce the Existence of Truth?

Many commentators argue over whether Nietzsche has renounced the existence of truth altogether.[17] I think when Nietzsche claims that truths are illusions he does not mean to reject the existence of truth in general. What he tries to do is deconstruct the metaphysical *belief* in truth as a mirroring of "reality" and as *opposite* to illusions. The entire tradition of philosophy, morality, and religion has based itself on a dualism of opposites, among them truth/illusion, being/becoming, reality/appearance, good/evil, reason/instinct, etc.; either party or category is believed to be the exclusive antagonist of the other. Nietzsche rejects such dualism. When he says that truth is lie or illusion he means that truth and untruth are ultimately identical—they are all human interpretations corresponding to nothing but human will, need, instinct, health, and everything a metaphysician would attribute to untruth or falsehood. A pure objective, indifferent, all-embracing, or metaphysical truth is not possible at all, or rather, the belief in or the will to such truth itself is an error, a lie. At the same time, the statement or sentence "truth is lie" logically implies its reverse, "lie is truth," because our life relies pretty much on lies, meaning perspectives, judgments, evaluations that have no metaphysical foundation at all. So,

> we are fundamentally inclined to claim that the falsest judgments (which include the synthetic judgments *a priori*) are the most indispensable for us; that without accepting the fictions of logic, without measuring reality against the purely invented world of the unconditional and self-identical, without a constant falsification of the world by means of numbers, man could not live—that renouncing false judgments would mean renouncing life and a denial of life. To recognize untruth as a condition of life—that certainly means resisting accustomed value feelings in a dangerous way; and a philosophy that risks this would by that token alone place itself beyond good and evil. (*BGE*, I, 4)

Nietzsche made himself very explicit here that untruth as a "condition of life" cannot be denied as untruth; it is *real;* it is truth. Therefore, the real theme for Nietzsche is not the existence of truth, but the overcoming of the dualistic metaphysics, or "to place himself beyond good and evil."

Nietzsche's theory of truth is neither metaphysical nor epistemological. He was interested neither in whether truth should be correspondent to reality nor in whether we could know such truth objectively. He is more interested in how the need for truth historically originated, why there has always been a "metaphysical need" of mankind, or simply, what the value of truth is. For Nietzsche, the strength of truth does not lie in its degree of truth-in-itself as disinterested, objective fact, but in its "character as conditions of life" (GS, 110). It is for life's sake that "our values are interpreted *into* things" (WP, 590). Therefore, the question of value is more fundamental than the question of being or certainty believed as ultimate truth. "The latter becomes serious only by presupposing that the value question has already been answered" (WP, 588).

Behind all metaphysical schemes, logical calculation, and scientific knowledge, there stand valuations or, more clearly, physiological demands and instinctive activities "for the preservation of a certain type of life"(BGE, I, 3). Truths "yield no 'being-in-itself', no criterion of 'reality', but only grades of appearance measured by the strength of the *interest* we show in an appearance"(WP, 588). In other words, truth does not correspond to any Being of beings but rather to the Will to Power as the force (strength) of life itself. We need logic and grammar to bring things under our control; we need a metaphysical world with order, necessity, and identity in favor of safety and stability; we need dreams to compensate our insatiate daily life. The *value* of truth is to release certain type of species (the metaphysician, ascetic or priest, slave, the man of decadence, etc.) from this world of life, which is construed by them as the cause of suffering, misfortune, error, and uncertainty. They therefore oppose truth to error, Being to becoming, and to the world they oppose another world, a world beyond, a *true* world. Here lies the *moral* origin of truth or the will to truth, for what they want is not "objective" truth but an ascetic ideal: a better world and a better life other than this world and this life. It is also a symptom of decadence and degeneration of mankind, a symptom called ressentiment: "the *ressentiment* of natures that are denied the true reaction, that of deeds, and compensate themselves with an imaginary revenge" (GM, I, 10). The man of such ressentiment accuses, complains, and renounces life, he wants life to become otherwise, to become truthful or virtuous and thus to correct itself and to correct appearance. He wills life to negate itself and become another life in another world, and he says No to life. This is the man *who* wills, needs, or wants truth because "truth is that kind of error without which a certain kind of living being cannot live" (WP, 493).

A Genealogical Critique of Morality

Under the disguise of will to truth hides the judgment or evaluation of life—the ascetic ideal, ressentiment, weariness and so on. The belief in truth could be deciphered as the belief in another world which indicates that this world and this life are bad, evil, and unworthy. This is exactly the *moral origin* of the will to truth, and *moral valuations* "hide behind all other high values," which are "*ways of passing sentence, negations*," and "*turning one's back on the will to existence*" (*WP*, 2). "It has gradually become clear to me", Nietzsche says, "that the moral (or immoral) intentions in every philosophy have every time constituted the real germ of life out of which the entire plant has grown ... I accordingly do not believe a 'drive to knowledge' to be the father of philosophy" (*BGE*, 6). Insofar as metaphysics and its belief in truth has its genealogical root in the development of morality, a critique of morality is a necessary and indispensable condition, "a question of the very first rank" for the overcoming of metaphysics (and religion) and for the overall task of revaluation.

Why do people believe in truth rather than *untruth*, being rather than becoming, reality rather than appearance? Since we can never prove or disprove the existence of such *opposition* (*BGE*, 2), are they not merely our interpretations or fictions we chose to impose upon the actual world? Yes, Nietzsche would say, people chose *this* rather than *that* as their true world because *this* is supposedly *good* or *better* than *that*:

> Behind all logic and its seeming sovereignty of movement, too, there stand valuations or, more clearly, physiological demands for the preservation of a certain type of life. For example, that the definite should be worth more than the indefinite, and mere appearance worth less than "truth"—such estimates might be, in spite of their regulative importance for *us*, nevertheless foreground estimates, a certain kind of *naiserie* which may be necessary for the preservation of just such beings as we are. (*GM*, 4)

Thus, every will to truth or drive for knowledge has its moral origin; and every question of *what is* indicates a request for *what ought to be*. What then is the moral origin of metaphysics? The morality Nietzsche was to criticize and negate is a type of morality, specifically the Christian morality, "that has become prevalent and predominant as morality itself—the morality of decadence" (*EH*, "Why I am a Destiny," 4).

In his *On the Genealogy of Morals* Nietzsche offered the first psychological and physiological analysis of the counterconcepts of a *noble* or *master* morality and a *herd* or *slave* morality of *ressentiment* or *bad conscience*. The later is the Judaeo-Christian morality that is the No or reverse of the former. "So that it could say No to everything on earth that represents the ascending tendency of life, to that which has turned out well, to power, to beauty, to self-affirmation, the instinct of *ressentiment*, which had here become genius, had to invent *another* world from whose point of view this affirmation of life appeared as evil, as the reprehensible as such" (*A*, 24).

The ressentiment or bad conscience, genealogically viewed, stemmed from what Nietzsche called the "reactive force" of life, which represents the negative trait of will to power. Contrary to "active force" that commands, creates, affirms, and conquers, in the world of life, "reactive force" obeys, conserves, negates, and resists and forms its negative attitude toward "active force." Life consists of these different forces: active force conquers or subdues the reactive one in order to create and affirm itself; reactive force tries to conquer, in a negative sense, or resist the active force affecting it. The interaction among different forces generates different sentiments about life. Active force loves life as its self-affirmation and self-realization, loves reactive force (enemy) as the measure of its power, loves change as its fate of creativity. On the other hand, reactive force, due to its weak and subordinate nature, resents active force (noble, master) as the cause of suffering, hates its life and itself as weak being suffering from being commanded, opposes the nature of instinct as the source of trouble. The lack of competence to make change, to dominate and to take action makes one feel ashamed of self; every move he or she reacts upon the dominant force is associated with ressentiment. The way for people of the reactive kind to balance and compensate their resentment toward life and self is to create another world that is no longer dominated by the quantum of force but by God, truth, and goodness.

Morality, originated from human ressentiment and "bad conscience" as a revolt against natural, active, and dominant instincts of life (noble or master morality), now posits "evil," "sin," and everything negative to our nature and our desires of life, posits God, truth, and good as the *enemy of life* (*TI*, 5). Life as self-affirmation and power enhancement has come to an end where the "kingdom of God," the true or moral world begins. In this world "all the forces and drives by virtue of which life and grows exist lie under the ban of morality" (*WP*, 343), because the true, the good, and the divine are perceived as the highest values superior to life. In order to retain its predominance and superiority, morality inevitably requires a rational foundation to universalize, absolutize, and legitimize itself as the only good (truth) for all that exists. Will to truth, metaphysical need, and ascetic ideal thus became the final wish, the ultimate completion of the will to deny, or the will to annihilate life.

The value of truth, both religious and metaphysical, is to preserve life in an unproductive or uncreative sense, to resist change in life, to protect weak species, to control, diminish, and eliminate the creativity of individuals and genius, to stop suffering by eliminating the force of life. For those species "of the declining, weakened, weary, condemned," of "bad conscience," "herd morality," "Nay-sayers," morality, metaphysics and religion, the good, true, and divine as values superior to life, are effective "expedients and devices" to sustain, preserve their type of life. This is indeed what Nietzsche considered the "moral origin" or value of truth. At this point, morality, metaphysics, and religion are closely connected: will to truth is *faith in the ascetic ideal itself*—it is faith in *a metaphysical* value, the absolute value of *truth*, sanctioned and guaranteed by this ideal alone (*GM*, III, 24). Hence, the overcoming of metaphysics, for Nietzsche, cannot be completed without the overcoming of the other two—morality and religion. In other words, the overcoming of metaphysics is at the same time the overcoming of the other two—it is the revaluation of *all* values.

Overcoming Metaphysics

After all, metaphysics as well as morality and religion reflect and represent a history of declining Western culture, which has been constantly losing its nobility and creativity since the "death of Greek tragedy." With the will to truth or the ascetic ideal, the history of metaphysics is precisely a course of inventing something other than or against life as becoming, change, appearance. This negative and reactive tendency or longing to get away from this world has determined at the outset that metaphysics with its ascetic ideal will arrive at the completion of nihilism, which is the ultimate sign or symptom of the decadent Western culture and the necessary outcome of modernity, "the danger of all dangers."

Metaphysics provides another (true) world of reality at the expense of this actual world of life. In the light of such an ascetic world of God, of truth, morality, and Being, human existence and the world have lost their meaning and goal. "The *will* for man and earth was lacking; behind every great human destiny there sounded as a refrain a yet greater 'in vain'... man was surrounded by a fearful *void*—he did not know how to justify, to account for, to affirm himself; he *suffered* from the problem of his meaning" (*GM*, III, 28). The meaning and truth given by metaphysics and the ascetic ideal are in fact void and illusory for they are mere inventions, fictions, and lies. Yet they are willed, no matter to what end, because

> We can no longer conceal from ourselves *what* is expressed by all that willing which has taken its direction from the ascetic ideal: this hatred of the human, and even more of the animal, and more still of the material, this horror of the senses, of reason itself, this fear of happiness and beauty, this longing to get away from all appearance, change, becoming, death, wishing, from longing itself—all this means—let us dare to grasp it—*a will to nothingness*, an aversion to life, a rebellion against the most fundamental presuppositions of life; but it is and remains a *will*! ... And, to repeat in conclusion what I said at the beginning: man would rather will *nothingness* than *not* will. (*GM*, III, 28)

And this will to nothingness is the nature of nihilism, the necessary consequence of the will to truth and metaphysics. Everything based on this metaphysical need or ascetic ideal would be nihilist—morality, religion, knowledge (science)—every longing for eternity, certainty, and the absolute would be the will to nothingness, because all these conceptions created and then believed the truths of the true world and thus negate the existence and meaning of the world we live in—"the world as it ought to be exists; this world, in which we live, is an error—this world of ours ought not exist" (*WP*, 585). The highest values hitherto to this extent are all products of such nihilistic hostility and negativity conducted by a decadent species. They need be revalued and abolished—

> Let us abolish the real world: and to be able to do this we first have to abolish the supreme value hitherto, morality.... The apparent world and the world invented by a lie—this is the antithesis. The latter has hitherto been called the "real world," "truth," "God." This is what we have to abolish. (*WP*, 461)

The key to the revaluation of all values, for Nietzsche, is to overcome metaphysics and its accompanying morality and religion. This is also the essential step toward the overcoming of nihilism and human liberation as affirmation of life.

A series of debates have been going on for quite some time among Nietzsche scholars: Is Nietzsche a metaphysician? If his thought cannot fit into the category of metaphysics, is he a nihilist? I think Nietzsche is neither a metaphysician as Heidegger would insist, nor a nihilist as Danto would argue. First of all, according to Nietzsche, metaphysics itself is nihilistic because of its otherworldliness, and so Nietzsche would not categorize himself as a metaphysician, because to be a metaphysician for him is tantamount to being a nihilist, while he was searching to transcend metaphysics, and thus, nihilism. Second of all, unlike most philosophers in history, Nietzsche is much less interested in asking what Being or Reality or Truth are than in questioning the concept of Being, Reality, or Truth itself.[18] Nietzsche did not inquire into what Being is in its essence, but thought the whole tradition of metaphysical belief, indeed the very concept of Being, was problematic. After he critiqued and deconstructed metaphysics, he had no interest in setting up another metaphysics but rather in surpassing it to the height of freedom and affirmation of life. In this respect, what Nietzsche fought against was not a particular kind of metaphysics, morality, and religion, but the whole tradition, idea, and nature of metaphysics. Furthermore, he did not confine himself to criticizing concrete virtues or ideas of goodness, as most moral philosophers did, but focused on overcoming the very idea of morality as a whole. He did not want to reinterpret any particular Christian idea but to be an anti-Christ. For him, it is these ideas that actually created our culture of decadence. In the course of Western history, the form of society, the pattern of life, the custom of people, etc. are changing, but the fact of decadence has not been changed since the time of Socrates. Why? Because the very ideas of metaphysics, morality, and religion themselves have not been changed. Nietzsche did not wish to quarrel about which religious belief was valid as opposed to another, but rather thought religious belief itself should be "brought into question." Therefore, what Nietzsche really wanted to do was to overcome the tradition itself—metaphysics itself, morality itself, and religion itself.

One may argue, as John Richardson did in his *Nietzsche's System*, that Nietzsche's very use of grammar and concepts inevitably roots him within the metaphysical tradition, "for the very need for expression in language subverts anyone's effort to state an antimetaphysical lesson" (5). That is to say, by using a language that is in its very structure metaphysical, Nietzsche lands himself in the same trap from which he wishes to free everyone. Such an argument is not necessarily valid, for it would not only make it impossible for opposition to be taken to metaphysics within language, the possibility of which is obvious and invoked and understood frequently, but would make the whole issue of negation in general logically odd. Language allows us to use propositional negations, such as "there is no such thing as x," without thereby committing us to a belief in x; it also allows us to viably negate a putative entity, as in for instance "there is no such thing as what you say x is." To insist that Nietzsche cannot escape the tradition of metaphysics because he is necessarily involved in a language that has traditionally been employed to construct metaphysical systems, indeed some have argued that it is in its very structural exigencies metaphysical, would commit us to an untenably strong version of correspondence, a strong version that even those commentators who insist that Nietzsche is a metaphysician do not hold. If they did hold such theories, why not say, in addition to "Nietzsche's supposed antimetaphysics is metaphysical," "Nietzsche's antichrist is Christian," "Nietzsche's overcoming of nihilism is nihilist," and so forth? In fact Danto and even Nishitani Kenji have espoused the latter view, but such an exegesis accepts and employs the same type of suspicion of what Nietzsche says that Nietzsche directs to other philosophers. If these commentators believe it is valid for Nietzsche to entertain suspicions of what other philosophers posit with respect to metaphysics, indeed turn that very suspicion on Nietzsche himself, then they tacitly accept Nietzsche's method of calling into question metaphysical beliefs, while at the same time deny him the capability to make antimetaphysical or antinihilistic statements. The respective appraisals of Nietzsche by commentators such as Richardson, Danto, and Nishitani then are not really coherent, for they make it impossible for us to accept not only Nietzsche's position, but also his method, a method furthermore to which they do not have any explicit objections. If negation is possible in a language, then, it would seem, negation of the facets and implications of the language in use is also possible within that language. In this vein, I tend to side more with the postmodernist take on Nietzsche's relationship to metaphysics, that of Derrida and Deleuze, as opposed to the views that Nietzsche must be a metaphysician exemplified in the readings of Heidegger and Richardson.

It may be more apt to argue whether Nietzsche succeeded in his effort of overcoming metaphysics and nihilism, rather than whether Nietzsche is a metaphysician or not. Nietzsche's denial of the existence of any fixed, absolute truth is implied in what he critiques as the will to truth, which he believes is merely a symptom of a decadent, ascetic, and nihilistic denial of life. What Nietzsche really desired to carry out is his experiment of overcoming them, not recreating them. This is what Sara Kofman speaks of as "the radical novelty and originality of Nietzsche" (121), for so far in history he is one of the first philosophers who have made such an effort. Only after we have overcome those dominant ideas are we able to stand still in the soul of the grand earth and begin to create our "grand style of life," as Zarathustra would call it. This life and this world should now be restored or recovered or recreated as the foundation of what Nietzsche called "the philosophy of the future." Here again, we see how a religiosity, a longing for liberating and affirming life, bursts as passionate "dynamite" for all Nietzsche's critique of tradition and all Nietzsche's creation of "new values."

THE WORLD OF APPEARANCES AND THE WILL TO POWER

In the following sections, I will focus more on the other part of Nietzsche's project of "revaluation of all values," the part in which he creates new values. Particularly in this section, I attempt to explain Nietzsche's view of the world as appearance and the will to power in relation to his inner religiosity.

Once the metaphysical world comes to an end, once nihilism completes itself in the course of the dominance of metaphysics, morality, and religion, once "God is dead," what shall we moderns do in such a circumstance: recreate another metaphysics, rescue the dead God, keep ourselves entrapped in this all-too-decadent humanity, or revaluate all prevalent values, overcome metaphysics and nihilism, and seek human liberation? Nietzsche's answer is easy to find. He said as early as *Human All-Too-Human*:

> Let us for once accept the validity of the skeptical point of departure: if there were no other, metaphysical world and all explanations of the only world known to us drawn from metaphysics were useless to us, in what light would we then regard men and things? . . . For the historical probability is that one day mankind will very possibly become in general and on the whole *skeptical* in this matter; thus the question becomes: what shape will human society then assume under the influence of such an attitude of mind? Perhaps the *scientific demonstration* of any kind of metaphysical world is already so *difficult* that mankind will never again be free of a mistrust of it. And if one has a mistrust of metaphysics the results are by and large the same as if it had been directly refuted and one no longer had the *right* to believe in it. The historical question in regard to an unmetaphysical attitude of mind on the part of mankind remains the same in both cases. (*HAH*, 21)

There is no way to go back to any kind of metaphysical world. The question now is, "In what light would we regard men and things?" Since the metaphysical world is an unreal, invented one, then which world is real, is really for us or the people of the future? Nietzsche put the effort of his experiment (*Versuch*) with an "unmetaphysical attitude" on a new kind of interpretation of the world: the world of appearance and will to power.

The world is *appearance* (*Schein*) or *mere appearance*. For Nietzsche appearance is no longer something degraded, distorted, erroneous, and thus opposed to the higher Being. Nor is it a mere attempt to demonstrate that Being is Becoming against Platonic metaphysics, as Heidegger would like to suggest, for any metaphysical distinction between a true and an illusory (apparent) world of becoming is only a symptom of the decline of life (*TI*, IV). And again, "The true world—we have abolished. What world has remained? The apparent one perhaps? But no! *With the true world we have also abolished the apparent one*" (*TI*, V). So it is important to know that the term *appearance* here is devoid of a contrary, an *opposite* and is something beyond the Platonic duality:

> What is "appearance" for me now? Certainly not the opposite of some essence: what could I say about any essence except to name the attributes of its appearance! Certainly not a dead mask that one could put on an unknown *x* or remove from it. (*GS*, 54)

There is therefore only one world or the "oneness" of the apparent world (*TI*, III, 2). The world is what appears and is appearing without any thing behind it, without any transcendental Being beyond it. Everything simply appears and relates to everything else and thus constitutes the world of appearances. In other words, this world appears simply as everything that appears and as the relationship among these appearances; nothing else could be more essential, truer or better than this *one* that appears. Things as a whole are in fact everything that appears, everything that appears is in fact things as a whole. Things appear from nothing but appearances, things are appearances simply because they appear. What Nietzsche meant by "oneness," "primordial unity," or "wholeness" is not an arbitrary Being nor a Nature asserted against many and differences but a nonduality in which the Platonic duality seems to have been dismissed altogether.

Nietzsche pictures the world of appearances as a world of becoming, change, contradiction, multiplicity, and even chaos. Things appear, become, and change, things disappear, are destroyed and annihilated. Nothing stays permanent, certain, and fixed, all is in the flux of becoming; this is what Nietzsche has in mind as the sole necessity of the apparent world. The world of appearances is indeed a constant or perpetual flow of appearing and disappearing, becoming and passing away, in which nothing can be possibly fixed, structured, endured as Being, Reality, and certainty. Hence, "The total character of the world," Nietzsche writes, "is in all eternity chaos—in the sense not of a lack of necessity but of a lack of order, arrangement, form, beauty, wisdom, and whatever other names there are for our aesthetic anthropomorphisms" (*GS*, 109).

There are at least two meanings we can give to Nietzsche's idea of appearance. First, he employed the term, mostly in his notes, to explain the actual world as appearance and becoming. He perhaps had the intention to experiment with a new *Weltanschauung* in place of traditional metaphysics, but this intention was never fulfilled and was kept "silent" in his unpublished notes. This is perhaps why in his published texts Nietzsche is often hesitant to fabricate the concept of "universe" or "cosmos" beyond the concerns of life and human beings. What he talked most about with confidence is the second meaning: the world of appearance as the world of life, or more specifically, the world of human life. The second meaning seems to be more important and explicitly expressed in Nietzsche's philosophy, which addresses itself entirely to the problems of human life and human liberation.

"Appearance is an arranged and simplified world, in which our practical instincts have been at work; it is perfectly true for *us*; that is to say, we live, we are able to live in it" (*WP*, 568). Nietzsche likewise contends that there is no world-in-itself that is apart from our condition of living in it and our perceptions and perspectives. The apparent world is essentially the world of relationships between "things and humankind," people and people, society and individual, nature and culture, actions and reactions, etc. Appearance appears under certain conditions and relationships and thus has a differing aspect from every point of view. Things appear to and for us inasmuch as we see, smell, touch, want, and interpret them under certain conditions and perspectives. We appear as human beings inasmuch as we act. Hence, it is our perspectives and actions that decide the character of the appearances. Thus, on the one hand, as the world of life, appearances represent the actual world in which we animals live, suffer, enjoy, create, perish, are born, and die; it is a flux of life. On the other hand, appearances represent "the world seen, felt, interpreted as thus and thus so that organic life may preserve itself in this perspective of interpretation" (*WP*, 678).

According to what do we perceive the world of appearances? Under what condition do we interpret things? Nietzsche suggests that the apparent world is "a world viewed according to values; ordered, selected according to values" (*WP*, 567). It is value and evaluation under the condition and demand of a certain kind of life that decides or is chosen to determine our perspectives and the character of appearances, because "there would be no life at all if not on the basis of perspective estimates and appearances" (*BGE*, 34). And what drives us to estimate, evaluate, interpret, and thus live or form a certain type of life? The will to power. According to Nietzsche, in every event or appearance, of course in this world of life, "a *will to power* is operating" (ibid.).

Will to power (*Wille zur Macht*) is a notion Nietzsche created and so attempted, hypothetically and genealogically, to use in order to explain or revaluate "the essence" of our instinctive life, the flux of becoming, and the apparent world. What does Nietzsche mean by will to power? Why will to power? Why not will, as Schopenhauer puts it?

In opposition to the traditional view of the will, which in effect turns it into a metaphysical substance or ultimate cause and source of all that exists, Nietzsche conceives of it as "something *complicated*, something that is a unity only as a word":

> [I]t is precisely in this one word that the popular prejudice lurks, which has defeated the always inadequate caution of philosophers. So let us for once be more cautious, let us be "unphilosophical": let us say that in all willing there is, first, a plurality of sensations, namely, the sensation of the state "*away from which*," the sensation of the state "*towards which*," the sensation of this "*from*" and "*towards*" themselves, and then also an accompanying muscular sensation, which, even without our putting into motion "arms and legs," being its action by force of habit as soon as we "will" anything.
>
> Therefore, just as sensations (and indeed many kinds of sensations) are to be recognized as ingredients of the will, so, secondly, should thinking also: in every act of the will there is a ruling thought—let us not imagine it possible to sever this thought from the "willing," as if any will would then remain over!
>
> Third, the will is not only a complex of sensation and thinking, but it is above all an *affect*, and specifically the affect of the command. That which is termed "freedom of the will" is essentially the affect of superiority in relation to him who must obey: "I am free, 'he' must obey"—this consciousness is inherent in every will; and equally so the straining of the attention, the straight look that fixes itself exclusively on one aim, the unconditional evaluation that "this and nothing else is necessary now" . . . and whatever else is necessary belongs to the position of the commander. (*BGE*, I, 19)

Here Nietzsche explicitly points out that will as a fundamental element of human life is not merely sensations and thinking, but "above all" an affect of a command and obedience. "'Freedom of the will'—that is the exercising volition who commands and at the same time identifies himself with the executor of the order—who, as such, enjoys also the triumph over obstacles, but thinks within himself that it was really his will itself that overcame them" (ibid.). This specific will, the affect of a command, the sensation and feeling of this "freedom" to discharge its strength, is the *one* basic form of the will, which is called by Nietzsche "will to power."

Power designates force, not any kind of natural, physical force, but the force driven by the will toward (*zur*) the demonstration or release of this force. "A quantum of force is equivalent to a quantum of drive, will, effect—more, it is nothing other than precisely this very driving, willing, effecting" (*GM*, I, 13). Hereby, to the concept of "force" an inner will *must be* attributed, and only this kind of force Nietzsche designates as "will to power" (cf. *WP*, 619).

Will to power, the power thus desired, should be understood as the essential force of life, everything that becomes, appears, commands and obeys, grows and declines, is in fact a spectacle of will to power: "A living thing seeks above all to *discharge* its strength—life itself is *will to power*" (*GM*, I, 13). Power cannot be perceived as entity, reality, being, or thing, as something already existing as a "goal" to which the will wills, for example, political privilege, wealth, social status, etc., but as a dynamic life force of becoming, forming or creating, overcoming, which does not have any goal because it is its goal itself.

There are at least two basic kinds of force: active force and reactive force. Each appears or creates a type of life, the ascending life or the decadent life. The distinction of these forces is the very core of Nietzsche's notion of will to power. Commanding, dominating, conquering, creating, possessing, and appropriating are characteristics of active force. The active force seeks the enhancement of life, enjoys the triumph over obstacles and resistance, imposes and creates forms and rules by exploiting circumstances, transforms the existing order and condition of life into a new height, etc. People who possess and exercise such force are superior, noble, and masterful; they act as creators, legislators, geniuses, and conquerors and feel good about themselves and their lives. On the contrary, obedience, adaptation, weakness, negativity, and decadence are qualities of reactive force. People who exercise such force are an inferior and dominated species who direct their will to power toward another direction—resisting creativity, individuality, transgression in order to save or preserve their life. Being violated, oppressed, suffering, unfree, they are uncertain of and feel contempt for themselves. The struggle and interaction between these two forces are above all the dynamic sources of life and the world of appearance and becoming.

The nature and relationship of these two forces, or two types of will to power, seem to be crucial with respect to the origin and development of almost all aspects of our lives and our world, since will to power, as the essence of life, as life itself, is operating in every event that appears or comes into being. It is this bipolarity of will to power that forms the basis from which the method and experiment of genealogy receives its definition. Nietzsche selects the term *will to power* as the genealogical element rather than metaphysical Being or anything similar, as a demand for method rather than absolute truth, to find or trace the origins of different types of life. Why will to power? Nietzsche gives an explicit answer in *Beyond Good and Evil*, section 36:

> Suppose nothing else were "given" as real except our world of desires and passions, and we could not get down, or up, to any other "reality" besides the reality of our drives—for thinking is merely a relation of these drives to each other: is it not permitted to make the experiment and to ask the question whether this "given" would not be *sufficient* for also understanding on the basis of this kind of thing the so-called mechanistic (or "material") world? I mean ... as holding

the same rank of reality as our affect—as a more primitive form of the world of affects in which everything still lies contained in a powerful unity before it undergoes ramifications and developments in the organic process (and, as is only fair, also becomes tender and weaker)—as a kind of instinctive life in which all organic functions are still synthetically intertwined along with self-regulation, assimilation, nourishment, excretion, and metabolism—as a pre-form of life.

In the end not only is it permitted to make this experiment; the conscience of *method* demands it. Not to assume several kinds of causality until the experiment of making do with a single one has been pushed to its utmost limit.... In short, one has to risk the hypothesis whether will does not affect will wherever "effects" are recognized—and whether all mechanical occurrences are not, insofar as a force is active in them, will force, effects of will.

Suppose, finally, we succeeded in explaining our entire instinctive life as the development and ramification of *one* basic form of the will—namely, of the will to power, as *my* proposition has it; suppose all organic functions could be traced back to this will to power and one could also find in it the solution of the problem of procreation and nourishment—it is *one* problem—then one would have gained the right to determine all efficient force univocally as—*will to power*. The world viewed from inside, the world defined and determined according to its "intelligible character"—it would be "will to power" and nothing else.

One could mistake these words easily as some kind of metaphysical assertion. Yet what Nietzsche attempts to say here is just the opposite. First, he is proposing the novel perspective or method of his genealogical experiment on what was original, "given," and "pre-formed" of the world of "affects" and "organic process." When he says empathetically at the outset, "suppose," he makes clear that he is making an experimental hypothesis because "the conscience of method demands it." Second, he wants to apply the term *will to power* to be the primitive form of force which "undergoes ramifications and developments in the organic process." Will to power is not construed as an external reality or metaphysical entity but as the genealogical essence of our world of desires and passions, or the "intelligible character" of the world,[19] from which all forces or efficient forces of organic functions could be traced. Finally, will to power is a perspective or interpretation of the world only *viewed* "from inside" and *defined* according to its "intelligible character."[20]

The "intelligible character" interpreted and reinterpreted forms and transforms the world of appearances. What determines our interpretation? Will to power, Nietzsche replies, and "nothing else." The will to power that works as appropriation, commanding and overcoming, is at the same time the action of interpretation through which we impose our perspective and project forms upon things and different species we are encountering. Things appear differently in different ways of interpretation. This is why the world as will to power has no such things as "fact," "objective truth," or "absolute reality." There are only interpretations. So, not only is the will to power his interpretation of the nature of the world and the essence of life, according to Nietzsche, but will to power is itself interpretation. To this extent, Nietzsche makes another proposition "which really *ought to be* established now":

> [T]he cause of the origin of a thing and its eventual utility, its actual employment and place in a system of purposes, lie worlds apart; whatever exists, having somehow come into being, is again and again reinterpreted to new ends, taken over, transformed, and redirected by some power superior to it; all events in the organic world are a subduing, a *becoming master*, and all subduing and becoming master involves a fresh interpretation, an adaptation through which any previous "meaning" and "purpose" are necessarily obscured or even obliterated. (*GM*, II,12)

Thus, the will to power as the essence of life is conceived as the "essential priority of the spontaneous, aggressive, expansive, form-giving forces that give new interpretations and directions," although the reactive force follows after and denies it (ibid., and *BGE*, 22, 23).

Interpretation, seen by Nietzsche as will to power, means that human life is indeed a constant process of interpreting and reinterpreting; there is no dogmatic meaning or fixed truth of life and the world. On the other hand, interpretation as life force is not something that relies on "text" (hermeneutics), nor on literary criticism or deconstruction of the constructed meaning of signs (postmodernism); it is instinctive action or direct praxis of life itself. It creates and preserves, constructs and destructs signs, senses, and texts in order to claim its power of life. Again, it is no "matter of fact," no "text," but only "interpretation" (*BGE*, 22).

For all these reasons Nietzsche can say that there is no disinterested or objective interpretation that is not associated with evaluation; in other words, will to power evaluates as long as it interprets. All the values created, preserved, affirmed, and denied so far are the results of evaluation and revaluation. Different values represent a different quantum of will to power. Will to power manifested as active force creates new values and affirms them, while, in contrast, reactive force conserves the old and rejects or denies new values. Hence, there is no universal, common value or good but only different evaluations and hierarchies of values. For Nietzsche, the will to power he wants to promote, value, and enhance is firmly the active, aristocratic, or noble type that has been repressed, corrupted, and lost and thus needs to be revalued in today's culture. Finally, *the will to power* is herein *the attempt at a revaluation of all values*—"in this formulation a countermovement finds expression, regarding both principle and task; a movement that in some future will take the place of this perfect nihilism" (*WP*, "Preface," 4).

Life and its world of appearance, thus defined and pictured according to will to power, are by all means the constant flux of self-overcoming (*Selbstüberwindung*). As will to power is the unexhausted procreative will of life, Zarathustra says, "[L]ife itself confided this secret to me: 'Behold,' it said, 'I am *that which must always overcome itself.*'" "Whatever I create and however much I love it—soon I must oppose it and my love; thus my will wills it" (*Z*, II, "On Self-overcoming"). Nietzsche again and again claims that truth, being, good and evil that are not transitory "do not exist," for the will to power as the "*instinct of freedom*" can never be fixed in any of those categories and conceptions; it must overcome itself over and over. "And whoever must be a creator in good and evil, verily, he must first be an annihilator and break values. Thus the highest evil belongs to the highest goodness: but this is creative" (ibid.).

This is Nietzsche's world of appearances with its nature as will to power. It is *this* world of becoming, chaos, change, impermanence, difference, suffering, and happiness: "[T]his world, eternally imperfect, the image of an eternal contradiction, an imperfect image—a drunken joy for its imperfect creator: thus the world once appeared to me" (*Z*, I, "On the Afterworldly"). In this world, Nietzsche has plunged into the never-ending creation of new values, forged the meaning of earth, and anticipated the coming of the *Übermensch* or over-man. On this world, Nietzsche rests his religiosity, or his new "hope" for the recovery and liberation of present decadent humanity by affirming the world as appearances and will to power.

RELIGIOSITY: LIBERATION AS LIFE AFFIRMATION

Now let us enter Nietzsche's world and observe his religiosity—liberation as life affirmation. After he launched his attack on the "old truth" and "idols," Nietzsche tells us, "[W]hat we get hold of is no longer anything questionable but rather decisions. I am the first to hold in my hands the measure for 'truths'; I am the first who is *able* to decide.... And in all seriousness nobody before me knew the right way, the way up; it is only beginning with me that there are hopes again, tasks, ways that can be prescribed for the future—*I am he that brings these glad tidings*" (*EH*, "TI," 1). The whole project of revaluation of all values, to which Nietzsche had devoted his life and blood, is designed explicitly and implicitly to reach the shore of "our sea," an "open sea" of liberation: to deliver or elevate "the type of man" from the course of decadence, or in his own words, "the last thing *I* should promise would be to 'improve' mankind" (ibid., "Preface," 2).

What is the human-all-too-human problem? Why has the human race been sick and decadent and why does it need to be "improved?" How did all these highest or "decadent" values based on nothingness or nihilism prevail and triumph over life itself? What is wrong with us? "Man has been educated by his errors," Nietzsche replies,

> First, he always saw himself incompletely; second, he endowed himself with fictitious attributes; third, he placed himself in a false order of rank in relation to animals and nature; fourth, he invented ever new tables of goods and always accepted them for a time as eternal and unconditional: as a result of this, now one and now another human impulse and state held first place and was ennobled because it was esteemed so highly. If we removed the effects of these four errors, we should also remove humanity, humanness, and "human dignity." (GS, 115)

As the effect of these errors, human beings lost their will to power as active and creative force, as elevation, enhancement, and strength of life, and became reactive, weak, "virtuous"—"the domestic animal, the herd animal, the sick human animal—the Christian" (A, 3).

Humankind, therefore, is something that shall be overcome. The problem Nietzsche poses now "is not what shall succeed mankind in the sequence of living beings (man is an *end*), but what type of man shall be *bred*, shall be *willed*, for being higher in value, worthier of life, more certain of a future." This higher type of human being, "is, in relation to mankind as a whole, a kind of *Übermensch*" (A, 3, 4).

At the beginning of *Thus Spoke Zarathustra*, Zarathustra proclaims himself as the teacher of the over-man: "I *teach you the over-man*. Man is something that shall be overcome" (Prologue, 3). Seeing that God is dead and remains dead, it is the mission of Zarathustra to "bring men a gift," which is in his words—"God died: now we want the over-man to live" (IV, "On the Higher Man," 2).

Übermensch in Nietzsche's writings does not mean "superman," as we have seen in English novels and movies. Walter Kaufmann correctly pointed out that Nietzsche's conception depends on the associations of the word *über*, over.[21] It refers, in a metaphorical way, to the one who has overcome and will keep overcoming himself or herself as human in the customary sense. Humankind, no matter of what type—sick, decadent, noble, low, higher, least, small, and great—is after all something that must be overcome; this is the essence of over-man, "the greatest reality" that we shall look up to and play within. *Über* is excess and "cross over," over every limit or bar that the human-all-too-human set up for itself by the knowledge of good and evil, so that the "instinct of freedom" and will to power as creative force can reach their super-exuberance and ultimate ecstasy. *Über* also stands for the height, a higher or highest state of a liberated perspective. From "6000 feet beyond man and time" one sees, laughs, dances, and celebrates the life that some people used to blame. *Übermensch* thus is no longer *mensch* or human being but the human being who has been overcome, or the man who is *over*. Now listen to the teacher Zarathustra again:

> Behold, I teach you the over-man. The over-man is the meaning of the earth. Let your will say: the over-man *shall be* the meaning of the earth! I beseech you, my brothers, *remain faithful to the earth*, and do not believe those who speak to you of otherworldly hopes! Poison-mixers are they, whether they know it or not. Despisers of life are they, decaying and poisoned themselves, of whom the earth is weary: so let them go.
>
> Once the sin against God was the greatest sin; but God died, and these sinners died with him. To sin against the earth is now the most dreadful thing, and to esteem the entrails of the unknowable higher than the meaning of the earth. (*Z*, "Prologue," 3)

The meaning of the earth is revealed after the overcoming of human being whose head was buried in the sand of heavenly things and otherworldly values, which have lured the human mind away from its body and made us "more ape than any ape" (ibid.). The "over-man" shows itself as the meaning of the earth by destroying these values and returning back to the body, to instinct, to the earth, to life and happiness, "that it may give the earth a meaning, a human meaning" (*Z*, I, "On the Gift-giving Virtue," 2). That is to say, the human being that must be overcome is the human being of "that world," "that dehumanized inhuman world which is heavenly nothing"(*Z*, I, "On the Afterworldly"). Thus, the overcoming of dehumanized humanity is virtually and simultaneously the returning and becoming the real humanity and the "over-man," who is the meaning of the earth.

Humankind as such, Zarathustra says,

> is a rope, tied between beast and over-man—a rope over an abyss. A dangerous across, a dangerous on-the-way, a dangerous shuddering and stopping.
>
> What is great in man is that he is a bridge and not an end: what can be loved in man is that he is an *overture* and a *going under*....
>
> I love those who do not first seek behind the stars for a reason to go under and be a sacrifice, but who sacrifice themselves for the earth, that the earth may some day become the over-man's ... (*Z*, "Prologue," 4)

Nietzsche's returning is not to preserve life but to create the meaning of one's existence, so it is crossing *over*, an endless self-overcoming and transforming. "And because it requires height, it requires steps and contradiction among the steps and the climbers. Life wants to climb and to overcome itself climbing" (*Z*, II, "On the Tarantulas"). Crossing over the steps of contradiction, climbing and going under, returning and overcoming, destroying and creating, living and dying. Whoever takes such steps will be the "chosen people," and out of them there shall grow the "over-man." "Verily, the earth shall yet become a site of recovery. And even now a new fragrance surrounds it, bringing salvation—and a new hope" (Z, I, "On the Gift-giving Virtue," 2).

"Man is the rope between beast and *Übermensch*." We should not miss the meaning implied: the "over-man" is a part of the rope, or the very possibility of that humanity. Nietzsche never in his writings characterizes over-man as something transcendent or super, as some kind of substitute for the dead God. On the contrary, he envisages "over-man" as the realization or manifestation of the essence of life, as the people who have overcome and liberated themselves by themselves. Hence, we ought not to seek "over-man" outside ourselves and our world. We are in fact the creator of "over-man" and the liberator of "over-man" from the prison of man himself. "To be yourself," to "recreate yourself" and "become who you are," this is how one reaches "the other shore" of "over-man."

> Once one said God when one looked upon distant seas; but now I have taught you to say: over-man.
>
> God is a conjecture; but I desire that your conjectures should not reach beyond your creative will. Could you *create* a god? Then do not speak to me of any gods. But you could well create the over-man. Perhaps not you yourselves, my brothers. But into fathers and forefathers of the over-man you could re-create yourselves: and let be your best creation . . .
>
> Creation—that is the great redemption from suffering, and life's growing light. But that the creator may be, suffering is needed and much change. Indeed, there must be much bitter dying in your life, you creators. Thus are you advocates and justifiers of all impermanence. To be the child who is newly born, the creator must also want to be the mother who gives birth and pangs of the birth giver . . . (Z, II, "Upon the Blessed Isles")

We shall become creators of our new hope and new self, which Nietzsche also called "new born," "child," and "over-man." We shall be fathers and mothers of ourselves and shall be the children we give birth to. This must be our destiny or fate, because we are the bearers of life and advocates and justifiers of our own transformation and liberation. For this Zarathustra tells the parable of the three metamorphoses: how the spirit transforms itself into a camel; and the camel, a lion; and the lion, finally, a child. The camel designates the tamed animal who yet knows nothing about what it really wants except taking acorns and the grass of knowledge, and for the sake of the truth, wanting to be well loaded. The second metamorphosis occurs in the loneliest desert: "[H]ere the spirit becomes a lion who would conquer his freedom and be master in his own desert". The lion, for the first time, says "No" to the dragon whose name is "Thou shalt," to values thousands of years old. The lion once loved "thou shalt" as most sacred: "[N]ow he must find illusion and caprice even in the most sacred, that freedom from his love may become his prey: the lion is needed for such prey."

However, to create new values—that even the lion cannot yet do. The spirit needs still another metamorphosis in order to complete itself—the child, who is the overcoming of the lion. "But say, my brothers, what can the child do that even the lion could not do? Why must the preying lion still become a child? The child is innocence and forgetting, a new beginning, a game, a self-propelled wheel, a first movement, a sacred 'Yes'" (Z, I, "On the Three Metamorphoses").

A sacred Yes, the child born out of the pangs of birth and baptized by the fire of revaluation of all values, symbolizes the ultimate affirmation of life as liberation, as *Übermensch* and the meaning of the earth. Saying Yes to everything that used to be banned by religion, morality, and metaphysics demonstrates the strongest will to power of the child over the lion. This sacred Yes, this ultimate affirmation, is what Nietzsche wants to achieve through all his painful yet creative life. All the ideals, metaphors, modes he has applied in his writing, creator, *Übermensch*, artist, philosopher, child, aristocrat, noble, master, dancer, laughter, etc., are different expressions and ways of this Yes-saying type of humanity and type of life.

Of course, we shall never forget that this is also the ultimate meaning of Nietzsche's concept of the "Dionysian," the Greek god with whom Nietzsche kept company from beginning to end. When he talks about his *Zarathustra* in *Ecce Homo* (1888) he says:

> My concept of the "Dionysian" here became a *supreme deed*; measured against that, all the rest of human activity seems poor and relative.... Let any one add up the spirit and good nature of all great souls: all of them together would not be capable of producing even one of Zarathustra's discourses.... In every word he contradicts, this most Yes-saying of all spirits; in him all opposites are blended into a new unity.... Here man has been overcome at every moment; the concept of the "over-man" has here become the greatest reality— whatever was so far considered great in man lies beneath him at an infinite distance.... *But that is the concept of Dionysian himself*... how the spirit who bears the heaviest fate, a fatality of a task, can nevertheless be the lightest and most transcendent—Zarathustra is a dancer—how he that has the hardest, most terrible insight into reality, that has thought the "most abysmal idea," nevertheless does not consider it an objection to existence, not even to its eternal recurrence—but rather one reason more for being himself the eternal Yes to all things, "the tremendous, unbounded saying Yes and Amen".— "into all abysses I still carry the blessings of my saying Yes".—*But this is the concept of Dionysus once again.* (EH, "Z," 6)

Now let us look at the idea of the "eternal recurrence of the same" (*der Ewigen Wiederkunft des Gleichen*), the most abysmal and difficult thought that Zarathustra wants to teach in association with the teaching of the *Übermensch*.[22] As Nietzsche has claimed, the fundamental conception of *Thus Spoke Zarathustra* is by all means the idea of eternal recurrence. "This highest formula of affirmation that is all attainable, belongs in August 1881: it was penned on a sheet with the notation underneath, '6000 feet beyond man and time'. That day I was walking through the woods along the lake of Silvaplana; at a powerful pyramidal rock not far from Surlei I stopped. It was then that this idea came to me" (*EH*, "Z," 1). From then on, for the rest of his life, he went his way in the most luminous brightness of this extraordinary experience.

In *The Gay Science*, section 341, Nietzsche, for the first time, introduced his idea of eternal recurrence.

> *The greatest weight.*—What, if some day a demon were to steal after you into your loneliest loneliness and say to you: "This life as you now live it and have lived it, you will have to live once more and innumerable times more; and there will be nothing new in it, but every pain and every joy and every thought and sigh and everything unutterably small or great in your life will have to return to you, all in the same succession and sequence—even this spider and this moonlight between the trees, and even this moment and I myself. The eternal hourglass of existence is turned upside down again and again, and you with it, speck of dust!"
>
> Would you not throw yourself down and gnash your teeth and curse the demon who spoke thus? Or have you once experienced a tremendous moment when you would have answered him: "You are a god and never have I heard anything more divine." If this thought gained possession of you, it would change you as you are or perhaps crush you. The question in each and every thing, "Do you desire this once more and innumerable times more?" would lie upon your action as the greatest weight. Or how well disposed would you have to become to yourself and to life *to crave nothing more fervently* than this ultimate eternal confirmation and seal?

What does Nietzsche mean by this? The story seems to be simple, but it contains incredible richness and the power of Nietzsche's spirit. Many have probed the riddle of the idea. It has been explored in terms of metaphysics (Heidegger), cosmology (Danto), psychology (Soll), scientific hypotheses (Kaufmann), moral responsibility (Kundera), and myth (Magnus).[23] Most seem to agree that it is the ultimate formula of life affirmation,[24] as Nietzsche has said clearly in the first place. But this formula of life affirmation needs to be understood as an act of "ultimate concern," that is, an act embodying Nietzsche's unique brand of religiosity. Why after all should one end up with *craving nothing more fervently* than eternal recurrence? Why is the idea entitled "the greatest weight" (*Das Grösste Schwergewicht*), which "would change you as you are or perhaps crush you?" Why did Nietzsche call eternal recurrence a "selective principle" (*WP*, 1058), "the great cultivating idea" (*WP*, 1053, 1056) and "a prophecy" (*WP*, 1057)? I think none of these approaches or "strategies" applied so far solves this riddle completely, because the notion of eternal recurrence surpasses all these ordinary and normative levels of perspective to a level of "religiosity" or a sole faith that experiences, affirms, and celebrates life as divine and sacred. Only if one reaches this level of affirmation and experience can he or she get a better picture of this spirit.

The passage begins with "what ... if," and we understood it may not be a narration of any sort of factual report. In fact, the language used here is hypothetical as well as symbolic and metaphorical. Nothing should be taken literally or factually.

A demon, not a god, a sage, or a philosopher, conveys the message to you about the truth of life that you never heard of, not into your happiness but into your loneliest loneliness. There could be only joy or happiness that wants to last forever and there is only God who can send his promises for our heavenly future. But *what if* it is at the moment you are suffering, alone, *what if* the demon tells the truth of this life? "This life," only this life as you have lived it and live now, will recur eternally, says the demon. Can anyone imagine anything more terrifying, horrible, cruel, unbearable, and destructive than this? *What if* one was told in the most miserable moment of life that it would happen again and again? Is it not the greatest weight in the world of life? Is it not the most rigorous test of one's strength of affirming life? Is anyone strong enough to take life as eternal recurrence, as if?

"Alas, man recurs eternally! The small man recurs eternally!" (*Z*, III, "The Convalescent," 2) Even Zarathustra cannot always put up with it.

> Naked I had once seen both, the greatest man and the smallest man: all-too-similar to each other, even the greatest all-too-human. All-too-small, the greatest!—that was my disgust with man. And the eternal recurrence even of the smallest—that was my disgust with all existence. Alas! Nausea! Nausea! Nausea! (ibid.)

Zarathustra's nausea is occasioned by the absurdity of this most ridiculous idea of eternal recurrence. It is absurd because it seems contradict Zarathustra's other teachings: If everything recurs why should we bother to will, to act, to overcome, to create? If the smallest will recur, then in what sense should we climb so hard toward greatness? If everything recurs infinitely, why does Nietzsche set up the task to revaluate all values? Why the *Übermensch*? And worst of all, what if this absurdity, this nausea, will recur eternally?

To confirm such absurdity with nausea!? Life is itself absurd because it is an eternal flux of becoming, chaos, contradiction, creation and destruction, coming-to-be and passing away. All ideas such as the will to power, the

Übermensch, revaluation, Dionysus, and tragedy are hence absurd or paradoxical by their nature. Traditional philosophy or metaphysics has been fighting to
eliminate this absurdity at the expense of negating *this life* and *this world*.
Nietzsche, in contrast, wants to affirm it and welcome its eternal coming back.
To this extent, the teaching of eternal recurrence does not contradict other
teachings. In fact it speaks of will to power, the over-man and revaluation by
pushing, hypothetically, the absurdity to the extreme: *What if* you were told
that life is absurd?; *What if* you were told that self-overcoming would be
impossible inasmuch as even the smallest you tried to overcome would recur?;
What if all your striving for enhancing life and creating new values is virtually
in vain since there is nothing new in the "eternal recurrence of the same"?;
Would you still do it and say Yes to what you are doing? Is it not the ultimate
test for the "quanta" and quality of the will to power? Is it not the absolute
affirmation of life as eternal self-overcoming, self-becoming, and self-creating?
Why not! It is by the affirmation of absurdity and the absurd affirmation of
life that the active will to power, the revaluation of all values, and the
Übermensch are at work.

For Nietzsche, the demon's whisper is not a matter of claiming what life
is, nor a matter of looking for some "metaphysical comfort" and taking
"revenge" against time. It is about a sacred decision, a divine affirmation, an
unconditional saying Yes to life as it is and it has been. It is an ultimate trial
of a person: Would you gnash your teeth and curse the demon, as most people
would do, or say: "Yes, I want my life just like this, no matter how it is, *once
more* and countless times, with all its joy and pain, wisdom and absurdity, gaiety
and terror!"? It is a decision that shows one's greatest courage, confidence,
esteem, and faith in life, for nothing else would be heavier and more terrible
than this. More significantly, it is a crucial moment of spiritual transformation
and liberation. Once one says Yes to the demon, he or she attains "enlightenment" and nothing will stop him or her from becoming an over-man, a
drunken god Dionysus, laughing, singing, dancing, and celebrating life eternally. Just as Laurence Lampert writes,

> [I]nasmuch as they carry forward the ark of values created by the
> wisest, Zarathustra's victory over the spirit of gravity will mean that,
> with time, their opinions will be those shaped by the truth of eternal
> return. In this way, the selective thought of eternal return is "the
> great cultivating idea" (*WP*, 1056; 1053), for it cultivates a human
> stance toward life and beings and encourages the nurture of a love
> of life; in that love, the new people of mankind will experience its
> ennoblement and enhancement. (*Nietzsche's Teachings*, 168)

It is in this "great cultivating idea" of eternal recurrence that I have found
Nietzsche's religious or spiritual perspective, which has been hidden or invis-
ible from most of his readers. The very meaning of the idea of eternal recurrence is to live and to affirm, to say Yes to life religiously and fervently, and

to recognize this demon's words as the most godlike and divine one has ever heard. Saying Yes or affirming life as such has nothing in common with passive acceptance of traumatic sufferings such as hunger, terror, injustice, oppression, etc., which we encounter in life everyday. With an affirmative attitude toward life, instead of "bad conscience" or resentment, one raises a positive will to power to confront and overcome whatever happened in his or her life, one is able to take responsibility for his or her own liberation from suffering for whatever reason. In this love and courage of affirmation, "the new people" of humankind that Nietzsche expected to see will gain its ennoblement and enhancement. What this idea of eternal recurrence intended to elicit is much more like a "religious" commitment, an ultimate enlightenment and spiritual liberation, than merely a philosophical interrogation of *what* life *is* or is supposed to be. Whatever the nature of one's life, whatever has happened in one's life, one sees and affirms it as the life worth living, one must believe it as his or her own divine destiny, and love this destiny (*amor fati*) ecstatically. From his early years to the end of his life, this is the tremendous moment and ultimate sea to which all Nietzsche's thinking was directed.[25] It is with such religiosity that Nietzsche stands six thousand feet above sea level and much higher above human-all-too-human beings.

CHAPTER 4

AN INTERPLAY BETWEEN ZHUANGZI
AND NIETZSCHE

Nietzsche knew little about Chinese thought, though he had some acquaintance with Indian Buddhism and Hindu culture,[1] certainly enough to prompt his disparagement of them. Nietzsche conceived Buddhism as the highest mode of nihilism and pessimism (*WP*, 55, 154; *A*, 20). He also very briefly mentioned the Chinese tradition as an Oriental example of the overall decadence of the human race (*A*, 32; *WP*, 129), without any awareness of the fact that there was also a "fortunate accident" and "exception" in Chinese history as in Greek history. Perhaps, Nietzsche would have perfectly agreed with this if he had, by "accident," read Zhuangzi, or such Chinese Buddhist schools as, for example, Tiantai, Huayan, or Chan Buddhism. In any case, whatever small acquaintance Nietzsche had with Chinese culture, Zhuangzi had no idea at all of the West (Europe). His thought was initiated entirely from his own life experience and the cultural environment of ancient China. With such a vast separation in time and cultural context, is it possible to bring Zhuangzi and Nietzsche together and come up with an interplay of their texts? There is not much difficulty even from the surface to see how different they are in light of their cultural backgrounds and their philosophical works. My concern here is: How much affinity or commensurability could be there between the two obviously different thinkers?

Some have already recognized the affinity between these two philosophers. Joan Stambaugh, in her article "The Other Nietzsche," suggests that Eastern mystical experience, such as Chan experience, may have been the hidden or the other Nietzsche we have largely neglected in the scholarly literature: the mystic poet and "the poetic mystic." At the end of the article she surprisingly remarks:

> Apart from the reference to Dogen, this essay has not made an explicit comparison of Nietzsche with Eastern thought. It has attempted to select some strains of Nietzsche's thought that are most consonant with an Eastern temper of experience and to let the reader reach his own conclusions about parallels and affinities. The fact that

Nietzsche's own understanding of Eastern thought was pretty well mutilated by the influence of Schopenhauer does not facilitate seeing or understanding these affinities. In particular, Buddhism gets lumped together with Christianity and both pronounced "religions of exhaustion." Temperamentally, Nietzsche was perhaps closest to Laozi and Zhuangzi with his rejection of the metaphysical background and his understanding of the world as play. (*Nietzsche and Asian Thought*, 30)

Yet she provides little argument or articulation of this suggestive observation. She also misses certain fundamental affinities between Nietzsche and Zhuangzi. Other than J. Stambaugh and scholars who did some partial comparisons such as Graham Parkes, Zhou Guoping, and Roger Ames, Chen Gu-ying is the first Chinese scholar who did a brief comparative study of Zhuangzi and Nietzsche. But since he focused superficially on their literary and stylistic affinities, he avoided a discussion of major philosophical themes of metaphysics, language, knowledge, and morality in the works of Zhuangzi and Nietzsche. Thus, he failed to make visible the profound philosophical insights and affinities of the two philosophers.

In this chapter I intend to undertake a sustained analysis of less obvious affinities and differences between Zhuangzi and Nietzsche. By interplay and cross-reading of their texts, looking at basic philosophical issues, such as language, knowledge, morality, nature, and human life, in each as well as their ultimate concerns, I hope this comparative study will illustrate what I see as their shared religiosity.

GOBLET WORDS AND DIONYSIAN DITHYRAMB

Zhuangzi and Nietzsche are explicit in claiming that human language has constructed and determined human ways of thinking and living. They would agree that language is not, as many people have believed, the "proper" representation of the "thing" it represents. Nor is it an *adequation* to *nomos*, to the thing-in-itself, or to Being. Words are only signs and metaphors used by human beings to describe and appropriate things and to communicate with each other. Both Zhuangzi and Nietzsche concluded that there is no way to reach reality through common language, invented as it is by human consciousness and human appropriation.

Daoism has always been suspicious of the adequacy of language. Dao, as the nature of the world, cannot be daoed or spoken of; thus said Laozi, the founder of Daoism. According to Laozi, Dao is the origin of the world as well as of human language, so it is impossible to define the origin by the outcome of the origin. Since the whole cosmos is created from the Dao as nothingness or nonbeing (*wu*), how can we find any word that will correspond to such *wu*? If there is no word that can properly correspond to the origin and the nature of the world, why should we rely on words or language to pursue the Dao? We do get help from language to discern things and ideas, but more often we confuse words with reality or attach ourselves to language as if it reveals the absolute truth to us. Language can in fact be one of the greatest hindrances in apprehending Dao, something that must be subdued and overcome.

As the greatest successor of Laozi, Zhuangzi continues to investigate the problem of language in his more sophisticated and radical way. Words are signs that can only signify partial traits of the signified. When we point at an animal and signify it as "horse," we believe without second thought that the name "horse," which Nietzsche would say is a metaphor, is the proper representation of the thing we called "horse" in-itself. Then we begin to define what "horse" is with many different definitions, and every definition we give simply puts one more layer, one more sign to the original one. Within the frame of language we cannot get to the point at which the signifier and the signified, or the name and the reality coincide: "horse" is not *horse*, "horse is not horse" is not *horse* either; "Dao" is not *Dao*, neither is "Dao is not Dao." Language could never lead one to the truth or Dao; instead, it could trap us in an infinite game of language. This is exactly what Nietzsche called "the seduction of words" (*BGE*, 20). People could hardly resist such seduction, driven by their desire for appropriation, their "will to power" and their fixed mind (*chengxin*). They have turned the language game into wars for truth, for Dao, for the "ascetic ideal" and for "civilization." Serious disasters result from the serious pursuit for truth, which is indeed an empty word, a humanly fabricated sign or metaphor. Zhuangzi, before Nietzsche, had realized that language is one of the major problems of human beings. Zhuangzi says in "*Qi Wu-lun*" section 3:

> Words are not blowing breath. Words have worded, but what a word worded is never determined. Have words indeed worded? Have words never worded? If words are distinguished from the peeps of baby birds, is there indeed a distinction? Is there no distinction? Whence does Dao withdraw while "true" and "false" come to the fore? Whence is worded hidden while "right" and "wrong" are sounded? Whence can Dao be absent while it goes? Whence can worded be disfavored while it is wording? Dao is always hidden by limited knowledge, worded is always covered by the words of glory and luxury. This is why there are full of "rights" and "wrongs" among Confucians and Moists, they all make their own "wrong" "right" and other's "right" "wrong." There is no way to affirm what they deny and deny what they affirm, so better be enlightened.

The problem with language here is that words fragment and differentiate the unity of nature (Dao). The word is applied and later believed the *only* "proper" representation, no longer corresponding to fragment and difference but to the universal truth or the Being of beings. How does this work?

How can we ever stop arguing about "right" and "wrong" within the trap of language? " 'Right' is an infinity, 'wrong' is an infinity as well" (ibid.). Because there is no difference between the two, they are all just words and form only opinions, so why should we cling to them? "Therefore better be enlightened" (ibid.). "Be enlightened" (*yiming*, 以明) means to realize the limitation of language, to overcome the fixation of words, letting nature shine by its own light and appearance *through* our mind.

Nietzsche's position on language is similar to Zhuangzi's. He is skeptical that language can represent the true nature of things. Words are signs and metaphors that we invented to express those things we don't know. "We set up a word at the point at which our ignorance begins, at which we can see no further, e.g., the word 'I,' the word 'do,' the word 'suffer':—these are perhaps the horizon of our knowledge, but not 'truths' " (*WP*, 482). We have to deal with language all the time; it does not mean that we are getting truths, nor that word represents thing-in-itself. We cannot stand the world of appearances and becoming as will to power, so we bury our head in the sand of language to imagine another world of stability, certainty and security. Nietzsche says in *Human all-too-Human*:

> The significance of language for the evolution of culture lies in this, that mankind set up in language a separate world beside the other world, a place it took to be so firmly set that, standing upon it, it could lift the rest of the world off its hinges and make itself master of it. To the extent that man has for long ages believed in the concepts and names of things as in *aeternae veritates* he has appropriated to himself that pride by which he raised himself above the animal: he really thought that in language he possessed knowledge of the world. The sculptor of language was not so modest as to believe that he was only giving things designations, he conceived rather that with words he was expressing supreme knowledge of things; language is, in fact the first stage of the occupation with science. Here, too, it is the *belief that the truth has been found* out of which the mightiest sources of energy have flowed. A great deal later—only now—it dawns on men that in their belief in language they have propagated a tremendous error. ("Of First and Last Things," 11)

Here is the tremendous error of those who have forgotten that truths are merely words composed of metaphors, symbols, and tropes based essentially upon analogy and dissimulation. Ironically, they have believed that language and its formation (grammar) reflect exactly the nature and structure of the thing-in-itself, from which a fictitious "other world" of abstract meaning and conceptual universality derives. For Nietzsche, if we cannot break through the problem of language we will never be able to overcome metaphysics and the ascetic will to truth.

Now, the problem Zhuangzi and Nietzsche have to encounter is how to overcome the limitation and fixation of language by using language. It is obviously impossible to accomplish the task by means of the traditional use of language. Thus, Zhuangzi and Nietzsche, two great masters of language, have created and played in their texts with unique ways of *speaking* language, their new language that speaks for its own creation and destruction.

The goblet words (*zhiyan*), as I elaborated in chapter 2, the words that can never be filled and that overflowed with their ever-multiplying and trans-figuring senses, are what Zhuangzi has created and experimented with in his writing. If the world of life appears paradoxical and contradictory, as Nietzsche would put it, the best or appropriate language to "imitate" this world must be paradoxical language, or goblet words. Speaking goblet words manifests the constant flow of the "Heraclitian flux" into which a person stepped, which *is* and *is not* the same water synchronically and paradoxically. Goblet words speak a continuing play of language in which creating and destroying, construction and deconstruction, individuation and self-annihilation are not opposites but one "dice throw" of *chongyan* (dual words). The formula of such "dual words" makes the paradoxical statements that "A is A" and "A is non-A" or "non-A is A" at the same time, or asks the double question "Is A A?" and "Is A not A?" or "Is non-A not A?" Zhuangzi, by playing with goblet words, means to show his readers that language is not truth or law of reality but one of the limited, deceitful, and unreliable tools on which humans are doomed to rely for their life. Nietzsche would have commented at this point that Zhuangzi's goblet words demonstrate distinctively the impossibility of a logically certain, identical, and absolutely asserted truth presented by language. On the other hand, Zhuangzi suggests that at the bottom of all human argument or dispute, there is no difference between thesis and antithesis, right and wrong: both *are* and *are not* valid, adequate, "okay" (*ke*, 可). This does not mean that any claim can be arbitrarily made without regard to its relation to what is "true," for indeed Zhuangzi himself is trying to tell us something "true" about language, how it functions, and what its limitations are. What it does mean is that every claim as regards the nature of things (*welun*, 物论) is subject to the incom-pleteness and inadequacy of language to provide us with any permanently "right view" given the ever-changing flux of life and reality. This is a view Nietzsche also holds, as he asks: "Why should we squander our lives in arguing words when "life is no argument?" (*GS*, III, 121). Why do we have to speak a truth (Dao) that cannot be spoken? Let us speak goblet words, speak lan-guage itself, just as the sun rises and sets every day by itself, which says nothing, which says everything (*Zhuangzi*, 2/27).

Another aspect of goblet words is *yuyan*, as we have seen in the precious chapter, which is allegorical, metaphorical, and indirect language used often in the book of Zhuangzi. Like Nietzsche, Zhuangzi's book is composed of allegories, aphorisms, anecdotes, dialogues, and poems. Instead of formulating discursive and polemic argument, or forming a systematic doctrine or a "metaphysical" edifice, Zhuangzi frequently tells stories, makes jokes, creates myths and folk tales, as one of the first fiction writers in Chinese history. Concepts generated from metaphors are still metaphors but are displaced, repressed, forgotten, or simply dead. From their writing style and their use of metaphorical and figurative language, we are well informed that for Zhuangzi and Nietzsche, returning to metaphorical language is to revive the vitality and truthfulness of language. In doing so Zhuangzi and Nietzsche have inaugurated, apart from the mainstream of traditional philosophy, "a type of philosophy which deliberately uses metaphors, at the risk of being confused with poetry." Speaking in metaphors makes it possible for language to find its very original art of naming and most natural form of expression.[2]

"Goblet words" may well be rendered as a metaphor of Nietzsche's way of speaking language, especially Zarathustra's discourse, which was described by Nietzsche as such: "In every word he contradicts, this most Yes-saying of all spirits; in him all opposites are blended into a new unity" (*EH*, "Z," 6). He called such discourse "Dionysian dithyramb": "What language will such a spirit speak when he speaks to himself? The language of the *dithyramb*. I am the inventor of the dithyramb" (ibid., 7), which originated from the Greek choral hymn for Dionysus. Now language speaks dithyrambically: "Epigrams trembling with passion, eloquence become music, lightning bolts hurled forward into hitherto unfathomed futures. The most powerful capacity for metaphor that has existed so far is poor and mere child's play compared with this return of language to the nature of imagery" (ibid., 6).

Zhuangzi would use another metaphor for such Dionysian dithyramb or music—*tianlai*, or the sound of heaven. Beyond the sounds of man and earth, which are played accordingly by either their determined instrument or their fixed shape, the sound of heaven plays without a fixed mind or premeditated "goal." It simply is "blowing on the ten thousand differences, letting go all by itself spontaneously, making different sounds naturally without obeying any ruler" (2/1).[3] Language thus liberates itself from the fixation of designation or signified (truth), from the battlefield of "rights" and "wrongs," and becomes the wind of nature (*tianlai*) or Dionysian dithyramb from which "we hear nothing but the accents of an exuberant, triumphant life in which all things, whether good or evil, are deified" (*BT*, 3). A language beyond itself, "the language without words" now comes into play and opens up as well infinite space for free dancing and wandering.

TRUTH, KNOWLEDGE, AND INTERPRETATION

Humankind has celebrated its gift of rationality and consciousness since Confucius and Socrates, who discovered that human dominance over the physical and animal world lies in the capacity of *knowing* and *reasoning* about the truth of things. By means of learning, reasoning, and thinking, one is supposed to possess the knowledge of truth that corresponds exactly to the reality of the world (thing-in-itself or the Being of beings). Pursuing knowledge and acting accordingly are believed to be the guaranteed way toward a true, moral, and beautiful life. Both Zhuangzi and Nietzsche reject such belief.

Truth refers traditionally to the knowledge that corresponds objectively and properly to the reality or thing-in-itself—God, Dao, Being, the Good, etc. Zhuangzi and Nietzsche have made their point clear that human knowledge or *wulun* is but limited and perspectival opinions and interpretations which can only carry some temporal and provisional meaning or reference. Knowledge is a product of human-all-too-human aspirations for appropriating things (*zheng*) and convincing others (*bian*), which reflects on our social and moral relationships. What we have done so far in the name of knowledge is to separate our rationale from the whole course of knowing and living, to separate a particular thing—actually an opinion of this thing—from the primordial unity of the world and, ironically, turn it into the only representation of the whole world. And even worse, after we have formed our knowledge or opinion we forgot it was our invention and estranged ourselves into believers in and slaves of it, prostrating ourselves before what we have created and henceforth waging wars against ourselves as original interpreters, creators, and legislators. Knowledge, especially the beliefs in metaphysics, theology, and even the sciences, is therefore something that confuses and devastates us; it is a symptom of decadent cultures and weary minds.

In chapter 2, Zhuangzi made a very vivid description of this:

> Big knowledge is broad and idle; small knowledge is detailed and hasty; big words are arrogant and imposing; small words are garrulous and quarrelsome. [With these] man is haunted by spirits while he sleeps, and irritated while he is awake; every time he encounters the external world his mind struggles, perhaps being panicked, perhaps plotting a conspiracy, perhaps hiding some secrets. Small fears are worrisome and sorrow; big fears are agitating and stunned; he sets up devices in order to create rights and wrongs; he insists on his fixed ideas in order to overpower others. Thus he decays like fall and winter day by day. He drowns in what he has done and can never turn back. His mind is getting darker and darker when he becomes older and older. Such a dying mind cannot be recovered. Joy, anger, sorrow, delight, worry, regret, fickleness, dissipation, disguise, insolence, all come out like music from emptiness or mushroom from dampness, replacing each other day and night on the fore. No one knows where they sprout from. Enough! Enough! Having these [troubles] in man's mind morning and evening, this is what his life all about! (2/2, Watson, 37–38)[4]

For Nietzsche, knowledge is what appeals to sick people. "What do they really want? At least to *represent* justice, love, wisdom, superiority—that is the ambition of the 'lowest', the sick. And how skillful such an ambition makes

them!" (*GM*, III, 14). "Gradually, the human brain became full of such judgments and convictions, and a ferment, struggle, and lust for power developed
in this tangle. Not only utility and delight but every kind of impulse took
sides in this fight about 'truths' " (*GS*, 110). Underneath the love of knowledge
there is "profound *nausea*," hatred of life and "the will to nothingness"—all
that makes one say No to life. "Psychologically, too, science rests on the same
foundation as the ascetic ideal: a certain *impoverishment of life* is a presupposition of both of them" (*GM*, III, 25).

Therefore, all kinds of ideals hitherto, from Confucianism, Moism, Platonism, and Christianity to democracy, socialism, and science, are not truths
but only interpretations (opinions) based upon different types of people whose
perspectives have been differently formed. These opinions become illusions
and lies when people universalize, categorize, and absolutize their own interpretations in place of the real world of life. This is why arguments of right
and wrong, the will to truth and knowledge, the belief in God and metaphysics are called into question and laughed at by both Zhuangzi and Nietzsche;
they are something that must be overcome.

The awareness that knowledge is temporal, provisional, and elusive is the
starting point of overcoming the common or traditional notions of knowledge
in both Zhuangzi and Nietzsche. There is no knowledge or truth in general
but only *one's* interpretation or opinion on things that one has encountered
under certain circumstances in one's relation to the other. It is impossible to
reach the finality and justification of an exclusive standard or arbiter that will
decide what is right. In this respect the knowledge of right and wrong is
"infinite"; how could a finite being not be pathetic in tracing or exhausting
the "infinite" (Zhuangzi, 3/1)? Inasmuch as the standard or thing-in-itself
cannot be found, different opinions or interpretations are *equally* mere opinions or interpretations. This is what Zhuangzi called *Qi Wu-lun*, equalizing or
identifying opinions, and what Nietzsche called perspectivism. As soon as one
realizes that knowledge is simply our interpretations or opinions, the gate to
overcome it opens up to one. And as soon as one enters this gate, one sees
also the different approaches of Zhuangzi and Nietzsche.

According to Zhuangzi, there is a kind of genuine knowledge (*zhenzhi*,
真知) beyond common and rational opinions, possessed by those enlightened
and liberated minds: *zhenren* (真人, true person), *zhiren* (至人, completed
person), *shenren* (神人, spiritual person). Three steps are set up by Zhuangzi
to attain genuine knowledge. The first step is to *know* the limits and borders
of knowledge in order to equalize (*qi*) or "level out" all opinions of rights
and wrongs and be free from endless arguing. The second step is to *know* how
to *stop* knowing what cannot be known. According to Zhuangzi's mythical
exposition, our ancestors used to know this perfectly, so that they never were
bothered by the hopeless pursuit after knowledge; they never wasted their lives
in trying to know something outside their knowledge (2/4). For knowledge
is composed of opinions which separate, isolate, and distort things, so that the
more we know the more layers of hindrance accumulate and the more distant

we are from the nature of things. "To know where to stop knowing what cannot be known, this is perfect" (2/5; 23/4). The third step is to *know not* at all. An enlightened mind (*yiming*) empties everything within, reaches the ultimate stage of the genuine knowledge which is the knowledge without knowledge, not even a least opinion that would obstruct or interrupt it from embracing nature and life completely. Only great sages can obtain such knowledge through Daoist cultivation:

> Yen Hui said, "I'm improving!"
>
> Confucius said, "What do you mean by that?"
>
> "I've forgotten rites and music!"
>
> "That's good. But you still haven't got it."
>
> Another day, the two met again and Yen Hui said, "I'm improving!"
>
> "What do you mean by that?"
>
> "I've forgotten goodness and righteousness!"
>
> "That's good. But you still haven't got it."
>
> Another day, the two met again and Yen Hui said, "I'm improving!"
>
> "What do you mean by that?"
>
> "I have sat-forgetting (*zuo-wang*)."
>
> Confucius looked startled and said, "What does 'sit-forgetting' refer to?"
>
> Yen Hui said, "I smash up my limbs and body, drive out intelligence, cast off forms, get rid of knowledge, and make myself identical with the Grand Transparency [of nature], This is what I called 'sit-forgetting.'"
>
> Confucius said, "Once you're identical [with nature], you must be free from any prejudice! Once you're transforming [with nature], you must be free from any fixation! What a worthy man you have become now! Even I'd like to be your follower." (6/9, Watson, 90–91)

In addition to this state of sitting-forgetting, the ideas of "fasting-the-mind" (4/1), "losing-self" (2/1), "perfect integrity" (*caiquan*, 才全, 5/4), "staying-in-the-middle" (*shouzhong*, 守中, 2/3), and "walking both ways" (*liangxing*, 两行, 2/4) are all meant to express this genuine knowledge. Having cast off all biases one merges oneself with Dao, or vice versa, Dao merges itself with one. Without intentional strife (*wuwei*) everything will transform and complete itself; without using knowledge (*wuyong*) the utility of things will function perfectly by itself. In other words, to embrace all functions or utilities by not using or utilizing them; this is what Zhuangzi called "being enlightened" and throughness of One (*yiming* and *tong*, 2/4).

Nietzsche's position on knowledge is somewhat more complex than that of Zhuangzi. He would have agreed in many respects with Zhuangzi's idea of overcoming knowledge. For example, when he talks about "the mastery of the knowledge drive" in Greek philosophy, he says, "If we are ever to achieve a culture, unheard-of artistic powers will be needed in order to break the unlimited knowledge drive, in order to produce unity once again. *Philosophy reveals its highest worth when it concentrates the unlimited knowledge drive and subdues it to unity*" (*P*, 30). He might see the Greek philosopher whom he admires as the great master of the knowledge drive, just like ancient Chinese sages who know when to stop knowing. But in principle, Nietzsche's solution of overcoming knowledge is very different from Zhuangzi's.

"Truths cannot be recognized. Everything which is knowable is illusion" (*TL*, 187). This assertion by Nietzsche echoes Zhuangzi's claim that every truth is "illusion," "error," or "lie" with no real distinction whatsoever between true and false, right and wrong. But unlike Zhuangzi, Nietzsche has no desire to cultivate disinterest or a pure state of mind to replace illusions. Quite the opposite, since truths are illusions constructed by the herd consciousness and designed for a hostile and finally destructive relationship to life, we must remove thoroughly the belief in truth as the most delusory mask of human sickness and decadence. While Zhuangzi teaches us to transcend all knowledge and opinions, Nietzsche urges us to reverse the truth *back* to the real world of appearance. His criticism hence focuses on how to recover original human nature, such as instinct, affect, the body, and sexuality, which have been so far negated under the names of truth, knowledge, reason, and God. Lie, illusion, error are *truer* than truths.

Nietzsche's ideal substitute for truth and knowledge is art. "How is it that art is only possible as a lie?"

> When they are closed, my eyes perceive countless changing images within themselves. Imagination produces these images, and I know that they do not correspond to reality. Thus I believe in them only as images, and not as realities.
>
> Surfaces, forms.
>
> Art includes the delight of awakening belief by means of surfaces. But one is not really deceived! [If one were] then art would cease to be.
>
> Art works through deception—yet one which does not deceive us.
>
> What is the source of the pleasure we take in deception which we have already tried, in an illusion which is always recognized as illusion?
>
> Thus art treats *illusion as illusion*; therefore it does not wish to deceive; it *is true*. (*TL*, 184; cf. *GS*, 59; 107)

We do not know anything more than surfaces; we cannot penetrate the appearances to the core of things-in-themselves, for there is no such core whatsoever. All is interpretation designed for the service of a certain type of life we are living. When we become artists who treat illusion as illusion, lies as lies, we enter the threshold of free interpretation and creation which is Nietzsche's noble way of active life or *true* life. "Our salvation lies not in *knowing*, but in *creating*! Our greatness lies in the highest illusions, in the noblest emotion" (*P*, 84). For Nietzsche, only those cowardly persons are afraid of mistakes and errors; they cannot take life as it is so that they need to *know* the truth on which they can lean.

The value of truth is thus reversed: truths are illusions; illusions are truths. And thus we return to life as it is, a type of life that has been denied for millennia. At this point Nietzsche meets Zhuangzi again: life is a kind of art—"a mocking, light, fleeting, divinely untroubled, divinely artificial art that, like a pure flame, licks into unclouded skies.... There are few things we now know too well, we knowing ones: oh, how we now learn to forget well, and to be good at *not* knowing, as artists" (*GS*, "Preface for the Second Edition," 3).

Zhuangzi would likely have trouble celebrating with Nietzsche the world of illusions. Reversing truth and error would not help one to unleash the struggle between opinions and interpretations. It could lead one to a never-ending argument about your truth and my truth, your illusion and my illusion, or whose truth is illusion, whose illusion is truth. If there is no truth but illusion, why should we prefer artistic interpretation to that of Christianity and Platonism? Noble tragedy to mass romanticism? Is it not "man's music" that is way below the music of heaven "six thousands feet above sea level"?

Nietzsche would have likely replied that he loved war and victory. Life could be made degenerate by certain interpretations; yet life could also be enhanced and transformed by active and creative interpretations. Is not ecstatic celebration of destruction and creation preferable to the stillness of no-mind and just sitting-forgetting? For false judgments and illusions are indispensable conditions of life. Would not renouncing them mean renouncing life?

"Oh!" Zhuangzi would have responded, "Heaven has bestowed life to you, but you'd rather finish it by arguing whether whiteness and solidity are different, I hope you would not end up as my friend Huishi" (cf. 2/4, 5/6).

REVALUATION AND DEVALUATION: BEYOND GOOD AND EVIL

What if it is my fate that I have to wage the war of revaluation of all values; that I stand in opposition to the mendaciousness of millennia (*EH*, "Why I am a Destiny," 1)? Nietzsche thus continues:

And we are fundamentally inclined to claim that the falsest judgments (which include the synthetic judgments *a priori*) are the most indispensable for us . . . that renouncing false judgments would mean renouncing life and a denial of life. To recognize untruth as a condition of life—that certainly means resisting accustomed value feelings in a dangerous way; and a philosophy that risks this would by that token alone place itself beyond good and evil. (*BGE*, 4)

Zhuangzi certainly would like to take this risk with Nietzsche. They both relentlessly criticized prevalent morality and values. First of all, if there is no metaphysical reality and no absolute truth, then no categorical imperative or original goodness (*ren, yi*) can be discovered. Second, morality originated and evolved genealogically on account of certain social and psychological demands for stability, order, and the preservation of certain type of life. Both Zhuangzi and Nietzsche seemed to share the presupposition that in the early societies, those Olympian gods, pre-Yao Chinese, and tragic age Greeks, knew nothing about morality and did not bar themselves from spontaneous or instinctive activities. At some later point during the course of history morality came into existence.

Emperor Yao and Shun (ca. 2,200 BCE), the great ancestors of Confucian tradition, according to Zhuangzi, were responsible for the creation of morality in China. According to Zhuangzi, Yao and Shun were the earliest rulers who governed the nation by inventing the moral principle of *ren* and *yi* (benevolence and righteousness) based on Yao's loving heart and "good conscience." Nietzsche, on the other hand, argues that morality as it has been till now was actually invented by the herd or slaves with their "bad conscience," representing their hatred or ressentiment toward themselves, their masters, and life in this world.

In spite of their different conceptions of the origins of morality, they agreed that the origin and development of morality was a sign of degeneration and a symptom of decadence, though their pictures of human degeneration were somewhat different. This does not mean, of course, that Zhuangzi and Nietzsche envisioned societies without "mores," that is to say, societies without any patterns of social conduct or interaction. When Zhuangzi and Nietzsche critique morality, they are critiquing "fixed moral doctrines," in the case of the former Confucian and the latter Christian, which they felt stifle the creative dynamism that allows cultures to grow and develop. Zhuangzi sadly commented that after Yao and Shun, Chinese culture had lost its genuineness and harmony and had undergone catastrophic decline and disintegration. The world and people began to split under these moral categories; moral value and the interests they represented began to manipulate human action, and finally different opinions fought each other for the authority of interpreting what *renyi* or morality was. In Nietzsche's eyes, the decadence of European culture began when Socratic rationalism and Christian morality began to prevail and dominate Europe. An original species, who was born to be master and whose "work is an instinctive creation and imposition of forms" (*GM*, II,

18), had then been domesticated, castrated, and eventually extinguished by herd morality or the ascetic ideal. After all,

> That this ideal acquired such power and ruled over men as imperiously as we find it in history, especially wherever the civilization and taming of man has been carried through, expresses a great fact: the *sickliness* of the type of man we have had hitherto, or at least of the tamed man . . . (*GM*, III, 13)

Fourthly, since morality is only "a kind of provisional formulation, an interpretation and psychological misunderstanding of something whose real nature could not for a long time be understood or described *as it really was*—a mere word inserted into an old *gap* in human knowledge" (ibid.), it cannot be some universal or absolute "mandate of heaven" and "categorical imperative" as Confucius and Kant put it. So both Nietzsche and Zhuangzi agree that there are only plural, different, and changing moral systems brought into existence by different types of people for different "utilities" or purposes during different times. And this plurality of human-all-too-human morality eventually catalyzes the disaster of social chaos and self-dispersion (Zhuangzi), and the advent of nihilism and "the death of God" (Nietzsche). So the final conclusion about morality for both Zhuangzi and Nietzsche is obviously the same: unless we overcome morality and the worldview it embodies, we can never liberate ourselves from alienation and our enslavement to herd consciousness.

In the task of the *revaluation of all highest values* lies Nietzsche's sole presumption to cure human sickliness and decadence. The notorious names he called himself, such as "immoralist," "anti-Christ," "destroyer," "creator," and "Dionysus," make explicit his stand against traditional values and his decision to create new values, the twofold mission of revaluation. By this approach Nietzsche has chosen to cope with the traditional values in ways fundamentally at odds with Zhuangzi's.

Notwithstanding that Nietzsche kept using the phrase "beyond good and evil" and called himself an "immoralist," what he meant by them seemed more about negating and overturning old values rather than going "beyond" them. He says,

> Fundamentally, my term *immoralist* involves two negations. For one, I negate a type of man that has so far been considered supreme: the good, the benevolent, the beneficent. And then I negate a type of morality that has become prevalent and predominant as morality itself—the morality of decadence or, more concretely, *Christian morality*. (*EH*, "Why I Am a Destiny," 4)

Indeed, the term *beyond* in Nietzsche's usage refers more often to a state of liberty that results from being a "destroyer," "legislator," "revaluator," or "creator." "Beyond good and evil" can very easily be understood as merely "beyond" Christian morality. He does try harder to replace "good" by "evil," soul by body, slave morality by master morality than to renounce morality completely.

Compared to Nietzsche, Zhuangzi is a radical immoralist who denies the need for moral values totally, and tries to devaluate rather than revaluate all values. All values are fabricated by humans, they are human opinions driven by various purposes, which do nothing but interrupt and violate the natural course of things. Zhuangzi has no intent to justify any particular moral teaching and evaluate any evaluation made by any particular school. What he negates is neither Confucian nor Moist morality but all moral values. A liberated person must be a real "immoralist" who acts completely in accordance with no moral obligation but instead with one's own nature, which is an immediate manifestation of "heaven and earth." An ideal society too must act according to its spontaneous dynamism, because contesting moral doctrines can lead only to exactly that, contest, and it is contest that is precisely the most destructive thing for any society. Morality is but a problem or symptom of a sort of desperate and troublesome life and people, and it deserves to be overcome:

> When the springs dry up and the fish are left stranded on the ground, they spew each other with moisture and wet each other down with spit—but wouldn't it be much better if they could forget each other back in the rivers and lakes. Instead of praising the good emperor Yao and condemning evil dictator Jie, it would be much better if one could forget both and stay amidst Dao. (6/2, Watson, 80)

If fish left water they would die no matter how "good" and "moral" they were to each other; if we left our natural life for the sake of a moral doctrine we would perish sooner or later in the same way. To this extent we can say that Zhuangzi is a more radical immoralist than Nietzsche.

Nietzsche's revaluation, as I have mentioned before, is to enhance life through constant self-overcoming, transforming, and annihilating. "Whoever wants to be a creator in good and evil, must first be an annihilator and break values. Thus the highest evil belongs to the greatest goodness: but this is— being creative" (*EH*, "Why I Am a Destiny," 2). And this is what is really meant by "beyond good and evil." In the process of continual destruction and creation there can never be any constant good and evil. Striving for the process of destroying and creating values is thereby the nature of Nietzsche's task of revaluation.

In contrast, Zhuangzi's devaluation is neither reversing nor creating values but removing them from our mind along with all controversial opinions so that they can no longer interfere or interrupt the actual course of nature. Zhuangzi emphatically and deliberately cultivates the idea of *wuwei* (doing nothing or non-doing), *ziran* (self-so or spontaneity, also nature), *wuyong* (useless or no-to-use), and *xujing* (虚静, void and still), as *daos* (ways) of reaching the harmony of nature and life. So Zhuangzi's devaluation is more of an inward transformation of one's mind and perspective rather than the action (*wei*) of changing, destroying, and creating things. To create as well as to destroy for Zhuangzi means no more than to cause trouble and generate disharmony in life. No values need to be created for an instinctive, natural, and free life.

It is very hard to reconcile the two masters at this particular point. For Zhuangzi, Nietzsche's revaluation maintains its task of overcoming morality within the territory of human-all-too-human evaluation, which may be effective in criticizing and destroying traditional values but may not be capable of crossing over "beyond good and evil." Every time a value is reversed or created all you have done is have the old table of values changed and another kind of artificial system imposed. Yet the confrontation, the antinomy of "good" and "evil," remains unsolved. In the same way, Nietzsche's passion for creativity seems to Zhuangzi problematic as well. Unless revaluation at last devalues itself and really goes beyond "good and evil," no creativity or freedom can be achieved.

Nietzsche would likely have accused Zhuangzi of being passive and nihilistic at this point. If life is interpretation and evaluation why shouldn't we affirm it? True revaluation still causes trouble and suffering, but it also brings joy and the harvest of creativity. What if life is contradiction, confrontation, and will to power; what if life is to fight, conquer and suffer; why should we be afraid to affirm and live it? My "beyond good and evil," Nietzsche might say, does not mean "beyond life"; it suggests instead "the affirmation of passing away *and destroying*, which is the decisive feature of Dionysian philosophy; saying Yes to opposition and war" (*EH*, "The Birth of Tragedy," 3). Not to affirm life in this way is to be no different than those ascetic priests or Confucian saints.

This kind of disagreement seems to have no end. But when we notice what Zhuangzi and Nietzsche try to protect and revive we see that the difference between revaluation and devaluation is not as great as it appears. The ultimate concerns of Zhuangzi and Nietzsche are very similar, no matter how different their approaches may seem. Both philosophers are destined or determined to overcome the all-too-human and to return to and ultimately affirm the nature of life as it is. "Man is something that must be overcome," just as language, knowledge, belief in truth and all highest values, must be overcome with him, not because these ideas could or could not find a cogent or perfect proof for themselves but because they are "slanders of nature." Zhuangzi couldn't agree more when Nietzsche speaks thus:

> I find those people disagreeable in whom every natural inclination immediately becomes a sickness, something that disfigures them or is downright infamous: it is *they* that have seduced us to hold that man's inclinations and instincts are evil. *They* are the cause of our great injustice against our nature, there are enough people who *might*

well entrust themselves to their instincts with grace and without care; but they do not, from fear of this imagined "evil character" of nature. That is why we find so little nobility among men; for it will always be the mark of nobility that one feels no fear of oneself, expects nothing infamous of oneself, flies without scruples where we feel like flying, we freeborn birds. Wherever we may come there will always be freedom and sunlight around us. (*GS*, 294)

It is these "people" who say or think natural instincts are "evil," Zhuangzi would claim, not nature itself, which makes no moral distinctions. Once we have removed all moral evaluations we stand right at the middle of the earth and heaven and dance with ten thousand things.

NATURE AS PRIMAL UNITY

Such terms as "nature," "*tiandi*" (heaven and earth), "world," and "Dao" which appear in Zhuangzi's and Nietzsche's works have no reference to any metaphysical reality or being. Neither of them admits any transcendent "Lord" nor Being behind, above, or *prior* to the apparent world in which we are living. Zhuangzi stated many times in his writing that we should not even ask what that "Lord" or "Dao" was, if we were never able to *know* whether it exists or not. Nietzsche, in a similar antimetaphysical posture, accuses metaphysics of negating this world in favor of fictitious or imaginary ones. It is true that both Zhuangzi and Nietzsche have no intention of constructing a new system of metaphysics by their critique. But it is also true that they have no intention of denying this world as a natural unity while they reject traditional metaphysics.

Two kinds of interpretations of Nietzsche and Zhuangzi exist with regard to their worldviews. One construes each as a metaphysician because he does talk about the world as a whole; the other counts each as a relativist, skeptic, and even nihilist because of their objection to metaphysics.[5] I think both interpretations have evidence to support their arguments but at the price of missing something essential. The major contribution the two great thinkers made is that they have created a new way, or as we now like to call it "strategy," "paradigm," and "discourse" of philosophizing which apparently paralyzes or de-valorizes customary conceptions. They are antimetaphysicians in the sense that they reject metaphysics, which subjectively divides or differentiates the world into a dualistic, either/or system and then absolutizes one abstraction out of it as Being. And they are skeptics and relativists trying to undermine such traditional beliefs in metaphysical truth whose real essence is to negate and say "No" to this life and this world (Nietzsche) or to devastate nature (Zhuangzi). Nevertheless, they seem to know that being skeptical or antimetaphysical could still be metaphysical if one struggles within the old metaphysical schemes of a metaphysical world. More profoundly, they have indicated, explicitly and implicitly, that skepticism, relativism, and finally nihilism are precisely the inevitable consequences of metaphysics.

In the *Book of Zhuangzi*, the best friend of Zhuangzi was Huishi, one of the most prestigious sophists of the time. Every conversation ended with Huishi being mocked, ridiculed, and educated by Zhuangzi. At the end of the book his comment on Huishi is thus recorded:

> Huishi tried to introduce a more magnanimous view of the world and to enlighten the sophists. The sophists of the world were happily delighted by his arguments, such as "an egg has feathers"; "a chicken has three legs" ... "eyes do not see" ... "T square is not right-angled"; "compass cannot make circle" ... "the shadow of a flying bird never moves" ... "white dog is black".... Cut away half of a pole one foot long everyday, and at the end of ten thousand generations there will still be some left. Sophists who join Huishi arguing like this will have no result till the end of their days.... What a pity—that Huishi abused and dissipated his talents without achieving any virtuality (*de*), chasing after ten-thousand things without returning to [the root]. What he did is trying to exhaust sound by speaking loud or to race against his shadow. How sad! (33/8)

Zhuangzi insists that there is no way to reach anywhere by merely being skeptical and making endless arguments based on language, logic, and knowledge. A person of Dao should cross over or clean up all these relative opinions and arguments in order to see, to touch, and to live the genuineness of nature.

In his *Gay Science* and *On Truth and Lies in a Nonmoral Sense*, Nietzsche too speaks of skepticism:

> When a philosopher suggests these days that he is not a skeptic ... everybody is annoyed.... It is as if at his rejection of skepticism they heard some evil.... For skepticism is the most spiritual expression of a certain complex physiological condition that in ordinary language is called nervous exhaustion and sickliness; it always develops when races or classes that have long been separated are crossed suddenly and decisively. In the new generation that, as it were, has inherited in its blood diverse standards and values, everything is unrest, disturbance, doubt, attempt; the best forces have an inhibiting effect, the very virtues do not allow each other to grow and become strong; balance, a center of gravity, and perpendicular poise are lacking in body and soul. But what becomes sickest and degenerates most in such hybrids is the *will*: they no longer know independence of decisions and the intrepid sense of pleasure in willing—they doubt the "freedom of the will" even in their dreams. (*GS*, 208)

But how is *skepticism* possible? It appears to be the truly *ascetic* stand-point of thought. For it does not believe in belief and thereby destroys everything that prospers by means of belief. (*TL*, 177)

None of these attributions, neither "metaphysician," "relativist," "skeptic," nor "nihilist" can fairly be made of Zhuangzi or Nietzsche. We can easily find something similar in their writings for they are still using human language and living in the same world as all of us do. It is always wrong to jump to conclusions too soon without carefully examining the nuances and tricks of the words they actually use. They are something else. They have tried to draw different pictures of the world from those we are used to seeing, they try to communicate the world in which they religiously lived and affirmed.

The affinity of the pictures of the world that Zhuangzi and Nietzsche have is not so hard to locate. They both confirm that this world, the world of our everyday life, is the only *real* world; the nature of this world lies is not its metaphysical or religious underpinning but what it *appears* to be and becomes as it is (*ziran*). Dao is no-thing (*wu*) and hence everything (*wu-wu*, *wudao*) that exists and dies, appears and disappears everywhere, all by itself. Anything *prior* or foundational that we have so far conceived is either illusory or suspicious; it could do no more than conceal the real nature of the world. Nietzsche was worried that the term *appearance* could suggest "Reality" or "Form" *prior* to his "apparent world." I think he might have been very happy to see how Zhuangzi's term *ziran* could work more adequately than "appearance."

Zhuangzi and Nietzsche both see the world as a flux of changing and becoming and therefore see it as chaotic, accidental, and unable to be fixed by any language, doctrine, or laws. For Zhuangzi, *ziran* never stops changing and transforming itself (*zihua*)—from nothingness to becoming, from birth to death, from construction to destruction, from darkness to light, and from void to fullness. Nowhere and nothing can be designated or hypostatized as the final root or Lord of the world origin or creator. In chapter 17, *Autumn Floods*, North Sea Ruo tells the Lord of the River,

> Ten-thousand-things are equal, [you cannot judge] which is short which is long. Dao has no beginning and end, things live and die, there is no completion that can be gotten hold of; now empty now full, there is no form that can be occupied. The years cannot be restored, time cannot be stopped; decay, growth, fullness and empti-ness, now end now begin. Thus I talk about the "trace" of Dao and the "necessity" of ten-thousand-things. Things are becomings, either violently or at ease they alter by every movement and shift in every moment. Does it matter that one should or shouldn't do anything about this? Everything has its intrinsic tendency of self-transforma-tion (*zihua*)! (27/1, Watson, 182)

Within the flow of *zihua* or self-transformation everything will fulfill its destiny as good with no extra effort, help, and "will to power" required: "[D]o nothing and everything will be done." *Ziran* as such seems to be rather more chaotic than systematic and unitary; any effort trying to "correct" it will cause the "death" of *ziran*, like what had been done to the Emperor Chaos in Zhuangzi's parable:

> The emperor of the South Sea was called Shu [Swift], the emperor of the North Sea was called Hu [Sudden], and the emperor of the central region was called Hun-tun [Chaos]. Shu and Hu from time to time came together in the territory of Hun-tun, and Hun-tun treated them very generously. Shu and Hu discussed how they could repay his kindness. "All men," they said, "have seven openings of organs so they can see, hear, eat, and breathe. But Hun-tun alone doesn't have any. Let's trying boring him some!"
>
> Everyday they bored another hole, and the seventh day Hun-tun died. (7/6)

Nietzsche has a very similar picture of the world when he insists that everything is becoming, which indicates the primacy of change, transformation, and metamorphosis. Nietzsche would likely emphasize something more in addition to Zhuangzi's notion of spontaneity or *ziran*—the notion of will to power, the active force of will to power. *Wuwei* would very likely sound too passive or reactive to him, because what he is calling for is not the recognition of transformation in nature but creative, noble, and aggressive transformation of the self. This might be seen as another major difference between the two: Zhuangzi's *wuwei* of *ziran* seems more conservative and adaptive than Nietzsche's *ziran* of will to power, which commands, imposes, transgresses, appropriates, and overcomes. Nevertheless, Zhuangzi's *wuwei* of *ziran* could be conceived of as just as radical as Nietzsche's will to power. First of all, *ziran* as self-so and self-transformation affirms the changing nature of things, which is the precondition of the will to power. Every thing things, that is, becomes or creates (*ran*, 然) what it is not by any predetermined Being or True Lord but itself. Second, the word *transformation* (*hua*) in Chinese and Zhuangzi's use is sometimes "*sheng*," which literally means produce, give birth, and grow, but can also be extended to creation and creativity. Zhuangzi, as well as Laozi, sees the world or Dao as an ever-new, ever-productive or creative (*shengsheng*, 生生) process, so to do nothing about or against this process is what indeed is meant by *wuwei*. Let our instincts of sensuality, creativity, and the will to power flourish exuberantly as the spontaneous dynamic of our life and our self-transformation. Thirdly, if self-adaptation (*zishi*, 自适) is to adapt self to the nature of self-transformation or self-overcoming, as Nietzsche puts it, then it can be as radical as the concept of appropriation or *Ereignis*. To adapt oneself to *ziran* is to yield completely to the flux of creation (*sheng*) and transformation, or to say Yes and affirm life unconditionally. Finally, Zhuangzi does not worship any idol nor does he oppose any fixed principle and regulation; there is only the self-transformation of nature, which in fact creates itself endlessly.

Another invaluable idea the two philosophers initiated in a very similar fashion is their special understanding of unity. Speaking of unity or the world as a whole often makes people wonder whether it has something to do with traditional metaphysics, especially for those who are overwhelmed by postmodern or deconstructionist criticism. Yet both of them advocate the concept of unity or Oneness as an indispensable part of their perspectives of the world.

One or Oneness (*yi*) is often used by Zhuangzi to refer to Dao, *ziran*, and the highest perspective of Dao—"From the perspective of Dao everything is seen as One." The world (*tian*) of Dao or *ziran* is One because ten-thousand-things are becomings (*sheng*) in a constant (*chang*, 常) process of impermanence (*wuchang*, 无常). In the same respect, the ten-thousand-things transform, and in this transformation are the totality of Oneness; they are equally drops of the flowing stream; they are identically parts of permeating air (*qi*, 气). There is nothing in this Oneness that should be privileged or marginalized, for all of its elements are dependent on each other as inseparable ones of the One. Difference itself originates from differences; difference becomes difference only amidst relation to others. Therefore, One is also the relation which makes everything come to be and become different. From the perspective of relationship one sees the Oneness of all things.

Thereby, the One that Zhuangzi talked about is not a homogeneous unity but a heterogeneous One of differences and multiplicity, which makes things equal by connecting them (*qi, tong*, 同) through differences, unifies multiplicity, and makes everything display its own becoming. Inasmuch as all things are different they are equally the same and one; inasmuch as all things are equally same and one they are able to create and transform differently all by themselves. This is what Zhuangzi called the "chaos," "harmony," and "throughness" of the world (*tianjun, tianni, tiandao, daotong*, 大通, etc.); this is the music of heaven (*tianlai*) Zhuangzi enjoyed with a liberated mind.

The highest perspective is to look at things from the state of Dao or *ziran*, that is the perspective of One (*yi*). Ordinary people limit their perspectives to different things as an only One and a close-minded self, so they prefer profit to deficit, fame to disgrace, beauty to ugliness, good to evil, and finally life to death. They only see the differentiation of things but fail to see the constantly changing nature of everything. Thus, they always attach themselves to ephemeral things and convince themselves that the things they attach themselves to are ultimate, just like the fool trying to pick up the foam of a tide without embracing the ocean. They divide the world of *ziran* into different categories and human-all-too-human values. Dao is no longer through; it is blocked and stops flowing. The One of differences now becomes "vicious," exclusive differences; the harmonious chaos now becomes devastating chaos;

the world falls into endless war between the privileged and the marginalized, between different groups of people, and also between different individuals. These consequences could have well been prevented if we had reached Zhuangzi's perspective of Dao-throughs-as-One from which everything different is equally seen as one and the same:

> Things all must have that which is *so* (*ran*); things all must have that which is *okay* (*ke*). There is nothing that is not *so*; there is nothing that is not *okay*. For this reason you see the differences between a little stalk and great pillar; a leper and the beauty Xi-shi; things ribald or shady and things grotesque or strange. Dao throughs as One. Their differentiation is their completion; their completion is their dissipation. Out of completion and dissipation things return to throughness as one. (2/4)

By reaching this spirit of clearing and throughness, one becomes a true or genuine person who "treats what he prefers as one, deals with what is not favorable as one. His Oneness is One; his not-oneness is also One" (6/1).

As early as his first book, *The Birth of Tragedy*, Nietzsche began to interpret the tragic world view, which he always praised and celebrated, as the synthesis of two divine forces, Dionysian and Apolinian, the dark force of destruction and the bright force of individuation. The two were conceived of by pre-Socratic Greeks as the "primitive unity" that contains the difference and contradiction between annihilation and individuation, dream and intoxication, death and life, joy and suffering. This primitive unity of two ever-contradicting and reconciling original forces is the essence of Greek tragedy and the tragic spirit of that time. Later, Nietzsche overcame the still too Hegelian duality of the two deities and established Dionysus alone as the only tragic unity of the world. The primal unity or Dionysus aims no longer to resolve or reconcile the eternal and original contradictions of existence and life but to affirm them as such, as the nature of the world of becoming and appearance.

In his *Ecce Homo*, Nietzsche restated through the voice of Zarathustra the idea he voiced at the outset:

> I walk among men as among the fragments of the future—that future which I envisage. And this is all my creating and striving, that I create and carry together into One what is fragment and riddle and dreadful accident. (*EH*, "Z," 8)

The idea of this Dionysian unity is also implied in Nietzsche's developed principle of the will to power as the essence of life and the world. The will to power is the dynamic force that determines what becomes and appears in the world. Everything becomes what it is supposed to be as a manifestation of the will to power. On the other hand, will to power is itself different and multiple forces, such as active and reactive, creative and conservative. Therefore, the will to power is simultaneously one and many, difference and identity, unity and multiplicity. Deleuze has commented:

> We should not ask whether, in the final analysis, the will to power is unitary or multiple—this would show a general misunderstanding of Nietzsche's philosophy. The will to power is plastic, inseparable from each case in which it is determined; just as the eternal return is being, but being which is affirmed of becoming, the will to power is unitary, but unity which is affirmed of multiplicity. The Monism of the will to power is inseparable from a pluralist typology. (Deleuze, 86, cf. 22–24)

Even though Deleuze's interpretation has some metaphysical flavor, he is still one of the few commentators who really who has taken into account Nietzsche's thoughts on unity and difference.

The inseparability of one and many, unity and difference is essential in both Zhuangzi's and Nietzsche's vision of the world. And, I would like to argue, it is their emphasis on such inseparability that has distinguished them from both traditional metaphysics and skepticism or relativism. First, they have overcome the dualistic view of the world that is the fundamental presupposition of metaphysics. Second, the oneness or unity in both philosophers is not static Being but difference per se. It is the unity of multiplicity, plurality, and different types of transformation. Third, the unity is an ever-changing, transforming, and impermanent process of becoming that cannot fit in any metaphysical or onto-theological category. Fourth, apart from individual differences there is no unity, hence everything or every different individual is the manifestation of the whole or unity. Every process of becoming, creation, and annihilation realizes the whole world of *ziran*, Dao, and will to power. Finally, the world as such is thus affirmed: say Yes not only to individual things and happenings but to all of them, to life and the world as a whole. Is this metaphysics? Or is it not? Is it skepticism? Or is it not? Is it relativism? Or is it not?

I believe that both Zhuangzi and Nietzsche would laugh at these questions: Does it matter? Could any of these names make the world different or our life worth living? Why can we not forget them for a while to see what is really going on in and outside of ourselves? What we try not to do is create another name, conception, or –ism in addition to the many-all-too-many of them, but to sweep them from our minds. Let nature be *ziran* that works, appears, becomes, sings, dissipates, from its own origin of nothingness (*wu*) and no-nothingness (*wuwu*, Dionysus). In this way, the two philosophers may have striking differences with different perspectives and values to some extent, but their religiosity or ultimate concern with returning to the root or nature of our life is surprisingly similar. By reading their works superficially and sometime literally, one would easily assert that Zhuangzi and Nietzsche have little in common: the will to power versus *wuwei*; creativity versus *ziran*;

becoming versus *wu* and Dao; difference versus Oneness and identity; chaos versus harmony; appropriation versus adaptation; anthropological versus naturalistic perspectives; and so on. Some might see these superficial oppositions as reflective of so-called Western and Chinese cultures: dynamic versus obsolete; creative versus conservative; aggressive versus retrospective; commanding versus obedient; individualist versus collectivist. Even Nietzsche more than once mentioned Chinese culture as if it were merely an oriental version of decayed Christian culture or European nihilism. He himself has been misunderstood in the same way, and even made use of as a pioneering thinker of Nazism. In the same vein one could argue that these oppositions explain why China lost the Opium War in 1880s and why she fell "backward" in the era of industrialization.

I am suspicious about such comparisons. My study of both philosophers does not provide much evidence to support such claims. Quite the contrary, if I am right, the superficial and literal contradictions shown in terminologies or words sometime can connote and convey very similar perspectives, let alone the fact that two philosophers were great players of language games. We will find that Zhuangzi is as radical and as liberal as Nietzsche and as any other philosopher, if we follow Zhuangzi carefully and look into the depth of what he really suggested by his goblet words, such as *wuwu*; *wuwei*. After all, both Zhuangzi and Nietzsche proposed new perspectives of the world and nature in which human beings can ultimately enjoy living in a spontaneous, creative, and healthy life world.

TRUE PERSON AND *ÜBERMENSCH*: LIVING IN THE WORLD

When asked: "What is heaven (*tian*)? What is human?" North Sea Ruo replied: "Horses and oxen have four feet—this is called heaven; Putting a halter on the horse's head and piercing the ox's nose—this is called human" (17/1). According to Zhuangzi, human beings originally were part of nature (*tian*) and came into being by natural transformation (*wuhua*, 物化). It might not be so bad if we used the resources bestowed by nature, such as riding horses and driving oxen, without harming them or devastating nature. Yet things become ugly if humans put halters on their own heads and ropes in their pierced noses. This is, unfortunately, what the position of humans was in Zhuangzi's time.

Just as Nietzsche loves ancient Greece, Zhuangzi is nostalgic about an earlier time when people enjoyed their peaceful and spontaneous lives. But with the development of so-called civilization, with the inventions of politics, morality, knowledge, and technology, human beings began to lose their identity with nature. The oneness of the world fell apart, the original harmony of chaos and differences evolved into jostlings and wars. Apart from nature and fixed by all those artificial opinions and normative regulations, human life became confusion:

Once a man receives this fixed bodily form, he refuses to transform himself [with the nature of becoming] waiting for the end. Struggling and clashing with things, he always hustles himself into action and nothing can stop him. Is he not pathetic? Sweating and laboring to the end of his days and never seeing his accomplishment, utterly exhausting himself and never knowing where to return to his home—is this not a sorrow? What good is that if there is no death? When body decays and the mind follows it—is this not a greater sorrow? Is human life supposed to be this messy? How could I be the only messy one, and others not? (2/2)

"Do you hear? Do you hear, O Zarathustra?" "The cry is for you. It calls you: Come, come, come! It is time! It is high time!" (Z, IV, "The Cry for Distress"). Zarathustra has heard it and agreed. "The earth" he said, "has a skin, and this skin has diseases. One of these diseases, for example, is called 'man'" (Z, II, "On Great Events"). For the sake of "the meaning of the earth" and a healthy life, both Nietzsche and Zhuangzi found the solution through their diagnosis: "Man is something that must be overcome!" Human is human's own denial and fetter of freedom. Human nature and freedom cannot be regained or obtained until men and women have overcome themselves. Zhuangzi and Nietzsche not only have provided the most acute criticism and profound diagnosis of the problems of humanity but also prescriptions to cure them. All the projects we have studied above regarding language, metaphysics, knowledge, and the revaluation and devaluation of all values, are designed by both philosophers precisely for the purpose of this self-overcoming and self-liberating. Yet there are still further ways to human self-overcoming, especially in the *Book of Zhuangzi*, that are worth mentioning.

In the Daoist tradition, *wuwei* is not literally understood as non-doing, non-action, or non-effort, but as an ultimate state of Dao in reference to either the reality of the universe or of spirituality. Since we humans have split away from Dao for so long, regaining our spontaneity and instinct is not an easy task. It requires enormous courage and effort to practice and fulfill such a task. To reach the state of *wuwei* one should do (*wei*) a lot of work, or as Wu Kuang-ming put it, one has to try hard to be "not-trying." This doing, practicing, or trying is called *xiu* or *xiu-yang* in Chinese, meaning perfecting self or self-cultivation. Going through this practice (*gongfu*, 功夫) of *xiu* (修) is the only path for the accomplishment of self-overcoming. Zhuangzi has created some special ways of *xiu* which are very influential in Chinese culture because they can be applied both spiritually and practically. The whole work of Zhuangzi, the seven inner chapters, can be understood as the Dao of *xiu* which leads to the ultimate state of transformation or self-overcoming.

The first chapter, *Xiao Yao You*, sets up the model of the state of ultimate liberation and freedom on which all the following chapters and discussions revolve and toward which all practice and cultivation are deliberately oriented.

The ultimate state of freedom (*tong*, 通) is the state of independence or non-reliance (*wudai*) on things and opinions. Monstrous Bird Kun-peng can go thousands of miles with one stroke of its wings and keep flying for months, yet it depends on an enormous amount of air, wind, and food to support its distant journey. It is distant (*yao*) enough yet lacks the grace of the easy and free (*xiao*). The cicada and the little dove, who laugh at Kun-peng's size and the distance it must go, may well enjoy their easy going life (*xiao*) in a small yard, yet they could never even imagine the sight and perspective that Kun-peng created from the distance. If we realized that both Kun-peng and the little birds are equally limited and dependent, we would not attach to either of them the only truth. When we end the discrimination or distinction between big and small, far and near, good and evil, life and death, we will no longer be dependent on anything that is limited and relative. Our spirit will thus amount to the state of *xiaoyaoyou* or freedom.

> If one had mounted the nature of heaven and earth, ridden the changes of its six breaths, and thus danced with the boundless, then what would he have had to depend on? Therefore it says that Perfect Man has no self; the Spiritual Man has no merit, the Sage has no name. (1/1)

To be a person of *xiaoyaoyou* is to be one with *ziran* and to dance with the rhythm and flow of life in an absolute affirmative state of mind. This is very similar to Nietzsche's Dionysian spirit, the ultimate will to power, which says Yes to life as it is. However, Nietzsche's Dao of achieving this state is somehow different. His self-overcoming is achieved through being stronger, through being master or commander, noble or great, creator and legislator, this is to say, to be Kun-peng. Zhuangzi might comment that there is no object and authoritarian standard to determine what is really strong or big and what is the opposite. All these are just relative attributes in accordance with certain circumstances and perspectives. The strong could be weak when compared to something stronger. To be a master one may become a slave because he relies on the servants' obedience. The stage of being master has not yet surpassed the stage of dependence, which is why Nietzsche finally prefers the image of the child as the symbol of liberation, an image that is often forgotten or overlooked by his readers.

Qi Wu-Lun, the second chapter, is the key step toward the mind of *wudai*. Beyond his brilliant reflection on the problems of knowledge, language, morality, and nature or Dao, which we have discussed previously, Zhuangzi has proposed the concept of *sangwo* (losing-self or forgetting-self) as a form of practicing Dao. All the problems in our life, our arguments, and competitions, have something to do with the human obsession with the self. All the biases and fetters we have had, knowledge, language, and morality, are created by our consciousness of self as well. Only if the self is overcome and forgotten are we able to make our mind transparent, through, and enlightened (*yiming*), accepting all the differences without prejudices or differentiation. For the purpose of overcoming self, one should try to forget language and the ideas of right and wrong, which is called "guyi"(滑疑) a state of mind that remains uncertain and ambiguous—this is the real light of heaven and what the sage steers by (2/4). Then one must always try to ease the tension between rights and wrongs, take no position on either side, this is called "liangxing," meaning "walking both ways" or "both will do" (2/4). Then one ought to refrain from politics, not seek profit, not defy necessary harm, and not even pursue Dao deliberately or forcibly. Self will be forgotten or dead sooner or later through these means of practice, and one will become one with nature and be dissolved entirely in the flux of becoming. This is perhaps the implication of that famous story of his butterfly dream:

> Once Zhuang Zhou dreamt he was a butterfly, a butterfly flitting and fluttering around, happy with himself and doing as he pleased. He didn't know he was Zhuang Zhou. Suddenly he woke up and there he was, solid and unmistakable Zhuang Zhou. He couldn't help wondering whether it was his dream of Zhuang Zhou being a butterfly or the butterfly's dream of its being Zhuang Zhou. There must be a distinction between Zhou and butterfly! This [distinction] is called the transformation of things. (2/7, Watson, 49)

The next chapter, Yang Sheng Zhu (养生主) or the Way of Caring for Life, is about how to keep in good health. To follow nature is the best way of keeping oneself in good health: "Life is limited, yet knowledge has no end. Chasing the unlimited by the limited is harmful.... If you do good, stay away from fame. If you do bad, stay away from illegal things. Follow the central pulse and let [qi] through veins, that can protect body, complete life, stay healthy, and die at the right time" (3/1). Nietzsche too cares about the physical condition of the human body but he stresses more the strength a body has in its struggle for power, while Zhuangzi concentrates on letting the body work by and for itself with no human interruption. Life is the most precious gift from heaven and we have no reason not to complete it. The story of cook Ding provides the best metaphor or example of the way of completing life.[6] If one follows nature spontaneously, the ox will be cut without extra effort and the knife (body) will not be broken. After Ding has explained, the duke says: "Excellent! I have heard cook Ding's words and learned the way of keeping in good health" (3/2).

Chapter 4, Ren Jian Shi or the Human World, deals with the way of living in a society. In Zhuangzi's vision, society was corrupted a long time ago ever since rulers began worrying about governance and created rituals, norms, titles (ming), and laws to regulate people. Full of bad lords and greedy people, society became more and more a dangerous place to survive. Zhuangzi does not attempt to present any remedy for changing the social reality, nor does he intend to suggest that we should renounce our social lives.[7] What he is concerned with is how to live well and happy *in* the world, especially in a corrupted society.

Many in history, who had devoted their lives to saving the world from decadence, either failed or aggravated the situation, because they ought against what they had not overcome inside themselves. Therefore, Zhuangzi teaches us that if you want to help others help yourself first; if you want society to be just be yourself first. "Perfect yourself before perfecting others! When you're not even sure what you've got in yourself, how do you have time to bother about what some tyrant is doing?" (4/1).

Xinzhai, 心斋, or mind fasting, is the practical way of perfecting oneself:

> Yanhui said: "I dare to ask what *xinzhai* is."
>
> Confucius said: "Unify your will as such! Listen with your heart instead of your ears; then listen with your breath (*Qi*) instead of your heart! Let ears stop listening and let heart stop reflecting. Breath is what is vacant (*xu*) that embraces [but can never be occupied by] things. It is Dao that favors vacancy. Being vacant is *xinzhai*".
>
> Yanhui said: "Before I heard this, I was certain that I was Hui. But now having learned this, there is no more Hui. Can this be called vacancy?"
>
> "Exactly! I now tell you: if you are able to play even in a tyrant's cage without any perception of fame or success; if you are able to sing when he can listen and keep silence when he cannot; if you are able to have no prejudice nor plot, keep your mind in the house of One and live with what cannot be avoided, you will be close to success." (4/1, Watson, 58)

With a vacant mind one is able to live well under all kinds of circumstances and get along with all kinds of people. Different from escapists and ascetics who renounce life in reality, Zhuangzi does not teach us to escape even from bad times or situations, which are conceived as what cannot be avoided (*budeyi*, 不得已). We are to fast our minds cultivating them to the state of Dao, enabling ourselves to "let mind move freely among things and keep the body nurtured within what cannot be avoided" (4/2).

Another capability one should learn to practice is to "use the useless." "People only know how to use the useful but don't know the use of the useless" (4/4). Therefore, they all want to be useful and run after things that are useful at the expense of harming themselves. There are always useless trees that keep alive from the carpenters who cut only the trees that can be *used*; the handicapped can stay away from battlefields and complete their lives. Unlike Nietzsche, Zhuangzi would rather keep himself disengaged from any kind of competition than try hard to be a hero, a master, or someone who dominates and controls others.

The person who can live thus in the world is the person capable of being "*De Chong Fu*" (chapter 5), or "Virtue Adequate and Conformable," and the person capable of following "*Da Zong Shi*" (大宗师, chapter 6), or "Great Principal Model." With a vacant mind which no longer knows a distinction between right and wrong, good and evil, I and the other, big and small, finally life and death, one attains ultimate enlightenment and freedom and becomes a person of Dao or true person (6/1) who affirms and embraces everything that becomes, appears, changes, decays, and dies in this world and this life. Finally, this type of person can always do best with no special effort in any position she or he is destined to have, such as a peasant, an artisan, a poet, a cook, a scholar, a hermit, a minister, or a king, an emperor. After the completion of self-overcoming and transformation, everybody is king and emperor herself, or at least, capable of being a sage inside and king outside (chapter 7, *Ying Di Wang*, 应帝王, or "Fit for Emperors and Kings"). This is what Zhuangzi would have defined as the "over-man."

Compared to Zhuangzi, Nietzsche did not provide detailed ways of self-overcoming and self-transforming. His teaching is more conceptual, more philosophical than practical. Revaluation, genealogy, psychology, and typology are his hammers of philosophizing. Scattered among them, though, there are some suggestions for practice here and there. Perhaps it is because, as he has confessed, "I am too inquisitive, too questionable, too exuberant to stand for any gross answer" (*EH*, "Why I Am so Clever," 9). Perhaps he considers his thinking merely an experiment, a signpost for future mankind. Perhaps he insists that everybody should try her way all by herself. Perhaps,

> By many ways, in many ways, I reached my truth: it was not on one ladder that I climbed to the height where my eyes roam over my distance. And it was only reluctantly that I ever inquired about the way: that always offended my taste. I preferred to question and try out the ways themselves.
>
> A trying and questioning was my every move; and verily, one must also learn to answer such questioning. That, however, is my taste—not good, not bad, but *my* taste of which I am no longer ashamed and which I have no wish to hide.
>
> "This is *my* way; where is yours?"—thus I answered those who asked me "the way." For *the* way—that does not exist.
>
> Thus spoke Zarathustra. (*Z*, III, "On the Spirit of Gravity," 2)

However, the general requirement or orientation for a self-overcoming practice is not lacking in Nietzsche: to twist free from traditional values; to go back to one's instinct and body; to be master, noble, and destroyer; to be yourself and a creator of yourself; to be a child—"and above all I learn to stand and walk and run and jump and climb and dance" (ibid.). At first glance these do not look compatible with Zhuangzi's teaching and opposites seem at once to appear: for example, passion versus vacancy, competition versus disengagement, the master who commands versus the sage who embraces, being self versus losing self, frenzy versus ease, etc. Perhaps such distinctions are inappropriate if we maintain a dualistic, either/or mode of thinking here. They may be contradictions but may not contradict each other; they may be different but may create a similar spirit. If we change our perspectives from the customary one, perhaps we can ascend from them to the height of this affirmation of life.

ZIRAN AND FREEDOM: LIFE AFFIRMATION

The ultimate concern for both Zhuangzi and Nietzsche is to liberate humans from the human-all-too-human boundaries of their freedom through various ways of overcoming and cultivation. Both have used the metaphor of the child to describe the person who reaches the ultimate state of liberation—the true person and *Übermensch*.

Zhuangzi's true person has the following traits: she does not rebel against want, does not show off success, and does not deliberate about her doings; thus, she cannot be frightened by height nor drawn by water nor burnt by fire; she has no discrimination against either life or death, letting it come and go as natural course of transformation; her mind forgets, her face calms, her forehead widens, she is chilly like autumn and balmy like spring; her delight and fury go along with the four seasons; she can fly like Kun-peng thousands of miles up in the air and be carefree like little birds easing down to the field; she is perfectly one with heaven and earth, she *is* heaven and earth (6/1).

On the other hand, Nietzsche describes his ideal of the *Übermensch* as follows:

> The word "over-man", as the designation of a type of supreme achievement, as opposed to "modern" men, to "good" men, to Christian and other nihilists—a word that in the mouth of a Zarathustra, the annihilator of morality, becomes a very pensive word—has been understood almost everywhere with the utmost innocence in the sense of those very values whose opposite Zarathustra was meant to represent—that is, as an "idealistic" type of a higher kind of man, half "saint," half "genius." (*EH*, "Why I Write Such Good Books," 1)

The *Übermensch* is the person who has overcome him or herself as an alienated human-all-too-human being; she puts behind every highest value and creates his or her new values merely by following his or her instinct of freedom and his or her will to power; she is an immoralist and goes beyond good and evil; he is strong physically and mentally and capable of destroying and creating; she is a Dionysian artist who enjoys, affirms, and says Yes to everything and becomes and dies in the world of appearances; she laughs, dances, ascends high, and goes under ecstatically as a drunken god; and after all, she is "the meaning of the earth."

Now, from this highest stage of human liberation, looking back over those aforementioned discrepancies between Zhuangzi and Nietzsche, we have found that they are no longer as incompatible as they once seemed. Both Zhuangzi's devaluation and Nietzsche's revaluation are aimed at returning humankind back to its true nature. They both advocate instinct and spontaneous activities beyond good and evil and all human-made boundaries. Zhuangzi favors disengagement from human competition because he thinks this is the best way to overcome competition, which is conceived as the real victory of all competition. On the other hand, Nietzsche often talks about innocence and the child as the highest state of self-overcoming in which all fighting will be over.

By the same token, Zhuangzi's notion of "non-self" could be seen, on the one hand, as a way to achieve the genuine self by forgetting the artificial self. All we normally call the "self" is either a conception or an image that is imposed upon us by authoritarian traditions and ideologies. Only if we overcome or forget such a self can we discover our real nature. On the other hand, Zhuangzi's forgetfulness of self is the way to regain the sovereignty of a genuine self. Such a self never compromises with rulers and the crowd of marketplaces, but creates a free and unique individual who can even swim in filthy water without being contaminated. Nietzsche seems to have a similar sense of the self. He remarks in Zarathustra's teaching on the *Übermensch*: "I love him whose soul is overfull so that he forgets himself, and all things are in him: thus all things spell his going under" ("Prologue," 4). Put together, non-self is genuine self and genuine self is non-self, because for both philosophers, becoming oneself is to be one with nature.

Some readers may wonder if Zhuangzi is at root a cold-blooded ascetic unable even to mourn at his wife's funeral. The story may sound outrageous at the outset, but not after Zhuangzi explained himself: Zhuangzi's wife died. When Huizi went to convey his condolence, he found Zhuangzi sitting with his legs sprawled out, pounding on a tub and singing. "You lived with her, she brought up your children and grew old," said Huizi, "it should be enough simply not to weep at her death. But pounding on a tub and singing—this is going too far, isn't it?"

> Zhuangzi said, "You are wrong. When she first died, do you think I didn't grieve like anyone else? But I looked back to her origin but saw no birth, not only did I see no birth but no form either, not only did I see no form but no breath (*qi*) either. It was in the midst of the chaos of wonder and mystery that a change took place and a breath was risen; then a change of the breath brought forms into being; then a change of forms brought my wife's birth. Today there was another change and she died. It is just like the progression of the four seasons. Now she is going to lie down peacefully in a vast hall [of nature]. If I were to follow after her bawling and sobbing, it

would show that I don't understand anything about the nature of life. So I stopped." (18/2, Watson, 191–92)

What we learn from this story is Zhuangzi's celebration of the natural process of becoming and transformation and his overcoming of the opposition between life and death. I see in him, rather, the Dionysian frenzy or tragic spirit that Nietzsche came to celebrate. Moreover, Zhuangzi did not ask us to eliminate human desires, but rather to restrain them so that we can regain our suppressed spontaneity and naturalness. A true person, therefore, sets free her passions and affections as part of her nature, and lets sorrow and joy display themselves along with the four seasons.

From the appearance of the words *true person* and *Übermensch* we may get the impression that *Übermensch* seems more aggressive and transcendent,[8] while true person sounds more down to earth and spontaneous. I do not think such a conclusion is cogent. As I mentioned before, Zhuangzi's "returning" and Nietzsche's "overcoming" are neither contradictory nor opposite but compatible and reciprocal, for the true person and the *Übermensch* are the persons who have returned to their nature and thus have overcome the unnatural humanity. So returning is overcoming and vice versa; they are not heading in opposite directions but one: to be "the meaning of the earth" or "one with heaven and earth," and ultimately, to reach the state of liberation and freedom which lies in an unconditional, childlike, Dionysian affirmation of life as it is. Returning is overcoming. Liberation is affirmation. Liberation or freedom is not a negation of this world nor a rejection of life and nature. It is, rather, a divine affirmation and a sacred saying Yes to this world and this life. What is this world? What is this life? What is it that Zhuangzi and Nietzsche want to affirm?

It is this world, the earth covered by blue heaven and lighted by sun, the natural world in which all species are breeding, that must be affirmed, as well as instinct, body, will to power, and everything spontaneous. To be natural and spontaneous is to open up oneself completely to nature with no human regulation whatsoever. What should be overcome are not sensual desires, passions, and affection, but human-all-too-human ressentiment which has tried by all means to suppress everything spontaneous in us. To be one with heaven and earth (*ziran*), to be one with the flux of becoming (Dionysus), that is freedom and liberation for Zhuangzi and Nietzsche.

It is this life, no matter how terrible, how difficult, how tragic it is, that must be affirmed. People tend to appreciate life when it is happy and blame it when it is difficult, which is why they often end up exhausted in seeking to preserve happiness and prevent hardship. Zhuangzi suggests that life changes are an infinite process of becoming which no one can grasp rationally. This process is called *ming* or fate. A true person never bothers to know what or why fate is as it is, but simply accepts and affirms what is happening to her. Nor does she have any preference for what fate or destiny brings to her, even with the situation of life and death. Like Zhuangzi, Nietzsche's affirmation of life is ultimately tested by his love of fate—*Amor Fati*—and the idea of eternal recurrence. Everything that happens in one's life should be affirmed and willed to happen again, once more, and numerous times more. With such an affirmative mind, one is able to say: "All days shall be holy to me" (*Z*, II, "The Dancing Song") and becomes a free dancer, wanderer, laughter, and creator of himself.

FURTHER REFLECTIONS ON DIFFERENCES BETWEEN ZHUANGZI AND NIETZSCHE

The affinities between Zhuangzi and Nietzsche have been elaborated upon throughout this chapter, from their criticism of metaphysics, religion, knowledge, language, and morality, to their creative work on how to overcome these obstacles and liberate the human spirit. Such affinity in what seems freest, healthiest, strongest, and most genuine is remarkable in two thinkers so far removed from each other in time. We can hardly imagine how close the spirit of their work is when we contemplate their distance in time and space.

With this final recognition of their affinities let me recapitulate some major points of difference in conjunction with what have been discussed above.

1. Chen Guying has made it quite clear: "Although the philosophies of these two thinkers have much in common, they were articulated from utterly different cultural and social backgrounds. Nietzsche's philosophy is shaped against the background of the convergence of the tragic spirit of the Greeks and the Judeo-Christian culture; Zhuangzi's philosophy, on the other hand, critiques the constraints imposed on human nature by artificially contrived clan-based moral and political systems, seeking as it does freedom for the human spirit" (*Nietzsche and Asian Thought*, 128).
2. Although both Zhuangzi and Nietzsche held a nondualistic view of oneness and differences, harmony and chaos, their emphasis in understanding the world is different. Zhuangzi stresses more the *Oneness* of the differences and the *harmony* of the chaos and thinks that to attain this oneness and harmony is the way (Dao) of liberation. Nietzsche stresses more the *differences* of Oneness and the *chaos* of harmony, which are the nature of the world as becoming, as the exercise of will to power. He prefers Heraclitus's war as legitimate contestation for the exaltation and transformation of one's existence, whereas Zhuangzi chooses to forget about competition to obtain the ultimate serenity of one's mind.
3. Both have a strong naturalistic tendency in understanding the relation of human beings to nature yet with different focal points. Zhuangzi is more focused on *ziran*, seeing it as the foundation of this relationship. A person should be the person of *ziran* who follows and never tries to do anything against the nature of "heaven and earth." Nietzsche seems focused more on the human world: human beings are the creator and legislator of things

through their interpretation and evaluation animated by their will to power. This is why Zhuangzi's liberation is expressed as "losing self or man and returning to *ziran*" while Nietzsche expresses it as "overcoming self" in the sense of enhancing the creative nature of "being self."

4. Regarding social ideas, Zhuangzi prefers a natural order to a civilized society. We do not need morality to love our parents, we do not need politics to direct superiors how to treat subordinates, for without any artificial human effort (*wuwei*) nature always does everything for us. On the other hand, Nietzsche prefers a society ruled by strong aristocrats to the idea of a "state" or democratic society conceived of as a result of human decadence. But I do not think there is a "Zhuangzian egalitarianism which contrasts with Nietzsche's promotion of an 'order of rank' " (Chen Gu-ying, 128). Zhuangzi is not an egalitarian; his term *qi* (equalize and identify) does not signify the social idea of equality. He might accept some kind of "order of rank" in the form of society when he discusses different classes of people such as sages, emperors, ministers, farmers, even handicaps, etc. He seems to be in favor of a society in which the social and political "order of rank" is adopted as a natural division of roles based on natural differences among things and species, rather than on the competition of the will to power that leads to the establishment of a civil society. However, he certainly does not think that one's social rank or status would mean much in terms of his or her spiritual liberation. Many sages or true persons described in the Book of Zhuangzi are from lower social classes and even physically disabled, all should be seen as equals as far as liberation is concerned.

5. Both philosophers reject dogmatism and absolutism and advocate pluralism and perspectivism. However, Zhuangzi promotes his method of *qi wu-lun* or equalizing the opinions of things, emphasizing the limitation and relativity among all perspectives and interpretations, which should be overcome or forgotten at the ultimate state of Dao perspective or throughness. Nietzsche characterizes his perspectivism with the idea of "order of rank," which is determined by the quantum of will to power that a particular perspective has manifested. The result is quite ironic. Zhuangzi dances with great ease with all the differences he encounters, by disengaging himself from passing judgment on them; Nietzsche goes to the mountain with Zarathustra's solitude because he cannot bear the "herd" and its sick, lowly perspectives.

6. Their ways toward freedom and affirmation are different. Zhuangzi teaches us to disengage ourselves from ordinary competition and argument as much as possible in order to return to the harmony and oneness of *ziran*, while Nietzsche encourages us to wage war against all dominant values and create new ones. The most exciting realization is that they have taken apparently different, even opposite, ways and arrived at the very similar state of liberation as affirmation.

7. They both have their own problems. Nietzsche's critique of tradition and modernity is very powerful and rhetorical and his revaluation also makes

sense for the self-transformation of a fixed-minded person. But the creative part of his mission is somewhat weak and remains abstract compared to his work of destroying. Dionysus, over-man, eternal recurrence, will to power, are but mystic and spiritual ideals, which cannot help people to deal with their lives in a concrete way. They are too artistic, poetic, philosophical, and religious to be understood by ordinary people who face serious problems. Ironically, it is easy for such thinkers to be misunderstood and even misled into unintended directions, just as the Nazis appropriated Nietzsche during their reign. On the other hand, Zhuangzi was skillful at deconstructing opinions and language, but he preferred disengagement from the critique of social problems, seeking instead to address personal freedom. Though he expected everyone would be liberated through existential transformation, he did not provide specific alternatives to help people who were oppressed and suffered at the hands of an unjust political structure or corrupt ruler. His teaching is designed for individual or existential experience and for spiritual liberation in a somewhat mystical way; unfortunately it shows very little concern for any kind of social practice or mass transformation. This is why Zhuangzi never was taken serious account of by any dynasty in the history of China. His influence remains great only in marginalized groups, such as artists, poets, retired officials, and among some Buddhist schools, especially the Chan school, and hermits.

Nevertheless, the philosophies of Nietzsche and Zhuangzi, each with its original insight and profound religiosity, are inspiring and valuable both intellectually and practically. Nietzsche's influence in this century is evident, just as interest in Zhuangzi increases both in China today and in various countries around the world. Zhuangzi and Nietzsche have provided two grand styles of life which evoke the creative possibility of shaping our lives in an affirmative and spiritual way. This Zhuangzi and Nietzsche would applaud as ultimate human liberation and the affirmation of life.

CHAPTER 5

CONVERGING NEW WORLDS: ZHUANGZI, NIETZSCHE, AND CONTEMPORARY PHILOSOPHY

In this chapter I want to analyze and explore the possible implications and contributions of my present project for the contemporary study of philosophy. As seen in the preceding chapters, the two philosophers I have compared seemed to have many familiar concerns that coincide with themes discussed by some postmodern thinkers, such as Foucault, Deleuze, and Derrida. There is no question about Nietzsche's significant impact on the rise of postmodernism and specifically poststructuralism. What about Zhuangzi? Can his philosophy or writing, passed on for about twenty-four hundred years, be relevant in the context of postmodernity? My answer is "yes." And I will indicate that both Zhuangzi and Nietzsche, as I read them, can be relevant not only in terms of postmodernist criticism of traditional philosophy but also in terms of a possible philosophy of the future. On the other hand, I would also like to show how my interpretation will help scholars in China who study Nietzsche, Zhuangzi, or both to have access to a new way of reading their works. Having so long struggled with either colonialist oppression or communist dictatorship in the last century, Chinese intellectuals have focused exclusively on how to surmount the political and economic crisis even in the field of philosophy. Zhuangzi and Nietzsche have been two of the many victims of this exclusivity. I will give a picture of Zhuangzi and Nietzsche somewhat different from that of my Chinese colleagues. At the same time, an attempt will be made in this chapter to show how my interpretation will open up a new dimension for my Western colleagues to understand Zhuangzi's philosophy and its actual influence on configurations and transformations of Chinese culture. Finally, I will conclude this study with a reiteration of my concept of "religiosity" and a further explanation of its relation to the field of both philosophical and religious studies, with Zhuangzi's and Nietzsche's philosophies as special cases of this philosophical religiosity.

AFFIRMATION AFTER DECONSTRUCTION:
ZHUANGZI AND NIETZSCHE CHALLENGE
POSTMODERN SOLUTIONS

Much has been written about Nietzsche's influence on the intellectual movement named "postmodernism." The term *postmodernism* here broadly refers to
a multidimensional and polystylistic philosophic trend, arising after World War
II, which, led by French poststructuralist "new philosophers" and other literary critics, questions and criticizes the philosophical tradition of modernity
that had been theretofore seen as the apex of Western thought. There can be
no question that Nietzsche appears at crucial points in the development of
some of the postmodern thinkers such as Foucault, Deleuze, Derrida, and
Lyotard, who credited Nietzsche with being the first champion against a
modernity based on Renaissance and Enlightenment-inspired ideas. They
discovered in Nietzsche's writings "the systematic mistrust as concerns the
entirety of metaphysics, the formal vision of philosophical discourse, the
concept of the philosopher-artist, the rhetorical and philological questions put
to the history of philosophy, the suspiciousness concerning the values of truth
('a well applied convention'), of meaning and Being, of the 'meaning of Being,'
the attention to the economic phenomena of force and of the difference of
forces, etc."[1] Pursuing these themes originally addressed by Nietzsche, postmodern thinkers have tried to respond to the present epoch, after the death
of God and all other absolute truths and values. Here in this section, I would
like to contrast Nietzsche and Zhuangzi to a few of the postmodern thinkers,
particularly Derrida, one of the most influential thinkers of poststructuralism
or deconstructionism. They are representatives of poststructuralism and postmodernism, I should make this clear, but not the only representatives of
postmodernism. Therefore, when I use the term *postmodernism* or *postmodernist*
I am referring only to these few thinkers.

One of the central motifs of poststructuralism is to put an end to the
logocentric tendencies of metaphysical thinking, the thinking constructed for
and centered on the determination of the truth of Being as "presence," and
the logical and metaphysical thinking which supported this determination that
dominated the history of Western philosophy. The crucial point poststructuralist thinkers have found to denounce or reject in metaphysics has been radical
reflection upon the nature of language and interpretation.[2] Derrida substitutes
the term *logocentrism* for metaphysics in order to emphasize that the dependence on *logos*, a "transcendental signified," is what has characterized the
Western tradition of metaphysics. Western philosophy used to believe that signs
such as "Idea," "God," "Being," or "Truth" corresponded to the transcendental
signified or "ultimate reality." To interpret a sign was therefore to interpret its
meaning in accordance with the signified as the fixed truth of presence. Such
a tradition, as Foucault remarks, causes the repression and even the death of
interpretation.[3]

The main method or strategy Derrida and the like employ is deconstruction, through which is demonstrated the "undecidability" (Derrida), "spatiality," or "locality" (Foucault) of the meaning of signs we used to believe was absolute. For Derrida, the structure of logocentrism is constructed by a philosophical binarism or what Nietzsche dubbed as "oppositional thinking" (*BGE*, 2). Within binary oppositions such as intelligible/sensible, true/false, speech/writing, literal/figurative, masculine/feminine, present/absent, etc., a hierarchical order of subordination was established. Derrida takes deconstruction as the task of breaking through such a hierarchical order to show that the "privileged" pole of any such opposition cannot be independent of the other for its identity and presence. A metaphysical Being of presence is impossible since "the signified concept is never present in and of itself, in a sufficient presence that would refer only to itself." According to Derrida, "[E]very concept is inscribed in a chain or in a system within which it refers to the other, to other concepts, by means of the systematic play of differences."[4] This deconstructive play is called by Derrida "*differance*," a term that stands for an operation and effect of both "differing" (spacing) and "deferring" (temporizing) the movement and relation of signifier and signified, self and other. Instead of the traditional or logocentric belief in a homogeneous, absolute, static, and determined or fixed truth of presence, Derrida and his contemporaries disclosed the undecidability, heterogeneity, the *differance* of signs to dismantle binary or oppositional thinking. Through deconstructive reading of texts and the play of signs, all oppositions are reversed, displaced, and finally erased, borders of opposing terms are overrun. As Madan Sarup describes,

> The deconstructor's method often consists of deliberately inverting traditional oppositions and making the play of hitherto invisible concepts that reside in the unnamed gap between oppositional terms. In the move from hermeneutics and semiotics to deconstruction, there is a shift of focus from identities to differences, unities to fragmentations, ontology to philosophy of language, epistemology to rhetoric, presence to absence. (54)

All the "privileged" categories in the history of Western philosophy, such as "subject," "consciousness," "history," "unity," "humanity," and so forth, are put into question by postmodern thinkers. A play of signifiers and interpretations freed from the constraints of truth or logos is now made feasible. "The life of interpretation," as Foucault remarks, "is to believe that there is nothing but interpretation."[5]

Alan D. Shrift, in his *Nietzsche's French Legacy*, has shown how close is the relation of Nietzsche to some of the leading figures of postmodernism: Derrida, Foucault, Deleuze, Lyotard, Kofman. Almost all the themes these thinkers brought up and developed were first addressed by Nietzsche, Shrift says.

Nietzsche's critique of truth, his emphasis on interpretation and the differential relations of power and knowledge, and his attention to questions of style in philosophical discourse have become central motifs within the works of the poststructuralists, who have developed these Nietzschean themes in a number of ways: by attending to questions of language, power, and desire in ways that emphasize the context in which meaning is produced while making problematic all universal truth and meaning claims; by challenging the assumptions that give rise to binary, oppositional thinking, often opting to affirm that which occupies a position of subordination within a different network; by questioning the figure of the human subject, challenging the assumptions of autonomy and transparent self-consciousness while situating the subject as a complex intersection of discursive, libidinal, and social forces and practices; by resisting the impulse toward claims of universality and unity, preferring instead to acknowledge difference and fragmentation. (6–7)

My interpretation of Nietzsche endorses Shrift's observation on Nietzsche's relation to postmodernism.

What about Zhuangzi? Does he have anything to do with this? By reading Zhuangzi carefully we will have little problem seeing affinities between postmodern critics and Zhuangzi. According to my reading, Zhuangzi could have been the first Chinese "deconstructionist" in terms of his challenge to metaphysics, language, logic, morality, self, and anything authoritarian and hierarchically categorical. And his stylistic writing and "goblet" language may be seen as an early endeavor to "deconstruct" the distinction between philosophy and literature, true and false, "this and that." My comparative study of Nietzsche and Zhuangzi indicates that it is quite possible to treat Zhuangzi's thought as an ancient and foreign ally of Western postmodernism. Many have acknowledged that some other traditions outside Western philosophy, such as Buddhism and Daoism, rejected metaphysical kinds of thinking long ago. My study shows that the effort to think in ways other than within metaphysical logocentrism is not only a "Western matter" but also a part of Asian thought, though it has been marginalized and even sometimes deprived of its voice in history.

A. C. Graham found Laozi's concept of reversal (*fan*) to be parallel to Derrida's project of deconstruction. He says,

The affinity of Laozi and Derrida is that both use reversal to deconstruct chains in which A is traditionally preferred to B, and in breaking down the dichotomy offers us a glimpse of another line which runs athwart it—for Laozi the Way, for Derrida the Trace. Both use a language which already escapes the opposition "logic/poetry," a language in which contradictory statements do not cancel out, because if made in the appropriate sequence or combination they set you in the true direction. (*Disputers of the Tao*, 227)

Although there are different contexts and motifs between the two philosophical traditions, then, the affinity between Laozi, Zhuangzi, and Derrida is undeniable for Graham.

Other modern thinkers also have found through comparative study "essential similarities" between Zhuangzi and Derrida.[6] Chen Chung-ying undertook a comparison between the notions of Dao and Derrida's *différance* and concluded that the Dao as ineffable, as the interaction of *wu* (is not) and *you* (is) and therefore as self-transformation, coincides with Derrida's *différance*. Chien Chi-hui, for basically the same reason as Chen, claims that Zhuangzi's Dao is as deconstructive a maneuver as Derrida's "trace." Michelle Yeh has gone so far as to say, "[W]ith the exception of the difference in emphasis, Zhuangzi and Derrida make essentially the same statement" (115). Most of these scholars have emphasized the similarities between Zhuangzi and Derrida with respect to their metaphysical skepticism, deconstructive strategy, playful style toward the traditional understanding of language, knowledge, and morality. As Mark Berkson has concluded,

> There are important similarities in how Zhuangzi and Derrida approach language; both of them share a similar *negative* project. They both point out the relativistic, arbitrary elements in language. Both employ apophatic language in order to dismantle the rationalist project and undermine the reader's confidence in the ability of language to carry or convey stable meaning or absolute reality. They both use a variety of techniques to unravel other positions, poke holes in arguments, and show the absurdity of certain claims. Both advocate approaches that will put the reader or listener in a certain state of mind—skeptical, receptive to paradox, open to acceptance of both sides of binary opposites. (120)

There is thus ample evidence that we can find in Zhuangzi's writings elements of resonance with the postmodern conversation. Yet the most distinct theme that affiliates Zhuangzi to postmodernism is his attempt to undermine beliefs in any absolute or metaphysical truth, putative truths that are in fact constructed, maintained, and authorized by human language knowledge and evaluation. Zhuangzi tried to warn us that it is the metaphysical intention that enslaved or alienated human beings, especially stifling their spontaneity and their harmony with the natural world. His attack on language, knowledge, and morality all aim at the deconstruction or destruction of the metaphysical delusion of a "True Lord," just as Derrida's thought is meant to undermine the logocentric truth of a universal presence in the West. However, the aforementioned scholars, to a large extent, still see Zhuangzi as a metaphysician who, along with Laozi, held the Dao to be an ontological Being. Zhang

Long-xi, for example, even states that Zhuangzi suffered from the same kind of logocentrism that actually formed the mainstream of Western philosophy (394–95). My reading of Zhuangzi attributes no metaphysical intention to him. On the contrary, overcoming or deconstructing metaphysical truth is for Zhuangzi a necessary and crucial condition for liberation. This is what Zhuangzi had started as "postmodern critique" long before the modern era began.

The differences between Zhuangzi and postmodernism have also been discussed and explored in the recent comparative studies mentioned above. Zhuangzi differs from Derrida in that he does not merely restrict himself to the project of deconstruction, but presses on toward positive and affirmative self-transformation and liberation, while Derrida remains in the closed, academic world of language, text, writing, and interpretation. Zhuangzi's critique of language, knowledge, and morality does not aim to achieve a radical skepticism, relativism, or nihilism but attempts to reach at a higher state of consciousness, what I have called "religiosity." At this point, as Mark Berkson remarks, "Zhuangzi would see Derrida as still fettered by text, unable to be freed ... out of the new prison in which he has found himself after deconstructing the old one" (121).

I want to stress in detail one additional point with respect to Zhuangzi's special treatment of language. He deconstructs both the signified and signifier (*zhi*, 指, *ming*, 名, *suozhi*, 所指, *sou-ming*, 所名). In responding to his contemporary sophists who laid emphasis on the strict differences between the signifier and signified, in their context the abstract (general) noun and the concrete (modified) noun, Zhuangzi said:

> To use the finger (*zhi*) to indicate that that finger is not a finger is
> not as good as using a non-finger to indicate that it is not a finger;
> to use a horse to indicate that a horse is not a horse is not as good
> as using a non-horse to indicate that it is not a horse. (2/4)

Here "finger" and "horse" refer to a signifier or a name, which for sophists is never in accord with the signified or named. This sentence can be deciphered thus, to use a finger or horse (*zhi*, signifier or name) to indicate the finger or horse (*suozhi*, signified or named) is not as good as using a non-finger or non-horse (*feizhi*, 非指, non-signifier or non-name) to indicate that a finger or horse (signified) is not a finger or horse (signifier). For Zhuangzi, since an absolute identity between finger as signifier and finger as signified could never exist, it is better to stop playing the two off of one another and instead use a non-signifier (*buyong*) of signifier to "signify" this non-identity or *différance*, thus achieving a thorough deconstruction of language. When one reaches this state of making no-use of the signifier and signified, according to Zhuangzi, one is able to break through the biases of language to the world of nature that contains no separation or distinction among things. One is then able to speak or play freely with no fixations about signifier and signified—"heaven and earth are one finger, ten-thousand-things are one horse" (2/4).

In the system of language, according to Derrida, there are only signifiers because every signified is merely another signifier; the signified is inscribed or carried by the signifier. So eventually the problem of the signified switches itself, after Derridean deconstruction, to the problem of signifier, because "truth," "Being," "God," etc. are all only signifiers. Inverting the opposites or switching the position of the formerly privileged signifier cannot free one from Platonic logocentrism entirely. In fact, the way Derrida talks about *differance*, trace, text, and writing gives one the nagging impression that his tone sounds metaphysical. For example, after having declared that everything is and has been writing, he says, "[W]e know this is a priori, but only now and with a knowledge that is *not knowledge at all*" (*Of Grammatology*, 159). This inversion of opposites, though construed as "neutral deconstruction," slides into a clinging or obsession with the other side of the opposites. Zhuangzi called such obsessive minds who wanted to abstract and privilege one thing into *only one* or *a priori* the minds of "three in the morning":

> What do I mean by "three in the morning"? When the monkey trainer was handing out acorns, he said, "You get three in the morning and four at night." This made all the monkeys furious. "Well, then," he said, "you get four in the morning and three at night." The monkeys were all delighted. There was no difference made at all in both words and reality, and yet the monkeys responded with joy and anger. This is what [the mind of] "three in the morning" is. (2/4, Watson, 41)

Hence, Zhuangzi (as well as Nietzsche) would not at all be contented were only the fictitious signified deconstructed. Within the prison of language one could be oppressed by either the signified or signifier. For Zhuangzi and Nietzsche, the danger of becoming logocentric cannot be removed thoroughly until both signifier and signified as well as the opposition of both are deconstructed. In this respect, we can say that Zhuangzi's critique and deconstruction is different and more radical than that of Derrida. Therefore, my study of Zhuangzi's philosophy may contribute a possible alternative on how to free ourselves from the hegemony or tyranny of logocentrism.

To recapitulate, it is a mistake to conceive of either Nietzsche or Zhuangzi as fully in line with the concerns and goals of deconstructionism. There are some quintessential differences, as far as my investigation is concerned, between Nietzsche, Zhuangzi, and Derridean thinkers. First of all, although these thinkers have made great contributions in resisting and even destroying the hegemony of Platonic metaphysics and thus opening the doors of emancipation, they do not seem to have made much substantial progress regarding an attainment of emancipation within the "postmodern condition." Zhuangzi and

Nietzsche, on the other hand, never put aside their ultimate concern with human liberation as life affirmation. It seems to me that what postmodern thinkers have developed or radicalized from Nietzsche is only a part of his project of the "revaluation of all values," that part which critiqued metaphysics, language, truth, and morality. The other part of Nietzsche, the part wherein he tried to create new values and to celebrate life by overcoming the kind of "humanity" forged by a tradition of decadence and nihilism, was somehow overlooked. My interpretation of both Nietzsche and Zhuangzi can help to make explicit the point that to deconstruct or destroy the prevalent values and customary systems, for Nietzsche and Zhuangzi, is only one significant and necessary stage on the path to a higher state of liberation or "free spirit." It is this project of affirmation that distinguishes Nietzsche's and Zhuangzi's thought from postmodernist thinking.

Second, it is true that Nietzsche and Zhuangzi were among the first who connected the philosophical task with a reflection on language; but, contrasted with Derrida and others, they did not consider the question of language as "the single most important question confronting the contemporary *episteme*";[7] they did not constrain their critique and revaluation just within the realm of language. Language has in fact constructed logocentric or metaphysical truth, but the philosophical project, for Nietzsche and Zhuangzi, ought to go further. If the meaning of language or the chain of signifiers is never determined and definite in its own right, then what is that which has made or constructed language as such? Language is not transcendental or some autonomous structure that works by and for itself; on the contrary, language itself is constructed and altered incessantly along with the circumstances of human life. For Nietzsche, language is an expression of a different type of will to power that appropriates, interprets, and creates; for Zhuangzi, language often occurred to be associated with human desire for competition that constructs different discourses. The overcoming of metaphysics cannot be accomplished just within the territory of language. Thus, in contrast to Derrida's notion of the trace of the perpetual movement of *differance*, Nietzsche and Zhuangzi expanded their critique of language, which has been constructing, repressing, and alienating human life, to a radical critique of morality, knowledge, politics, and other aspects of human cultures. Furthermore, while Derrida focuses on how to free signs or signifiers from the constraints of truth as presence, Nietzsche and Zhuangzi were concerned with the emancipation of human beings from the constraints and oppression of their own product, language.

Third, for the purpose of putting an end to any reference to universal, absolute, monolithic truth, postmodernism radically promotes the ideas of difference, heterogeneity, fragmentation, undecidability, and so on. According to Zhuangzi, radicalizing difference could bear the same consequence as absolutism because absolutism does not indeed represent any uniform truth that exists on its own, but always is one among different opinions that has become privileged, dominant, and absolutized. Whatever is absolute according to Zhuangzi is a difference that has become absolutized in terms of value. To

realize difference can open up one's mind, but to become attached to difference can also close one's mind by causing it to resist differences previously
privileged and causing it to obsess about one's own difference. Therefore,
Zhuangzi maintains that in order to affirm a world of differences we ought
to realize the "sameness" or "Oneness" of differences and "equalize," even
"identify" (qi), them from the perspective of Dao, as I have discussed in chapter
2. On the other hand, Nietzsche too emphasizes that an affirmative Dionysian
spirit does not denounce, reject, or attempt to escape but embraces and dances
with differences and contradictions. As Derrida himself recognizes, for
Nietzsche, "the same, precisely, is *differance* (with an *a*) as the displaced and
equivocal passage of one different thing to another, from one term of an
opposition to the other ... on the basis of this unfolding of the same as *differance*, we see announced the sameness of *differance* and repetition in the
eternal return."[8] To see differences through their "Oneness" and "sameness"
and to see "Oneness" and "sameness" through differences, as Zhuangzi suggested, can help to build a pluralistic and dynamic world, which allows every
different individual to develop as freely as any other. The process of deconstruction is not merely the freeing of one pole of binary or oppositional
thinking from subordination, but the freeing of the human individual to subordinate, to play with differences as befits their living circumstances. The
tyranny of difference is no more emancipatory than the tyranny of the absolute; what is required for human liberation is the elimination of any kind of
tyranny.

Fourth, there is a clear line distinguishing Nietzsche's and Zhuangzi's
affirmative philosophy from being the kind of nihilism that casts a shadow
over some postmodern thinkers, a nihilism afraid of commitment. The former
attacks and deconstructs metaphysical thinking in order to justify its saying
Yes to life, while the latter does so in order to justify its extreme skepticism
and relativism, which avoid saying Yes to anything. The former requires
courage and resolution to decide one's own destiny in action in a world
revealed as indeterminate, chaotic, and ever changing; the latter remains evasive,
irresolute, and distrustful, as if any affirmative decision would call back some
kind of logocentrism. For Nietzsche, the disclosure of differences, contradictions, and contingencies enables one to become a master, legislator, and creator
and to overcome one's self in a constant process of evaluation. I think this is
what Nietzsche expects to occur after the death of God and the death of
"man" as Subject (Foucault); this is what Nietzsche means by the *Übermensch*
as the "meaning of the earth" and as "active live force of the will to power."
For Zhuangzi, after one is emancipated from metaphysical thinking and the
self constructed by contending opinions, one returns to or rejoins the spontaneous world of *ziran*, being free (*xiaoyaoyou*) in a way that follows and affirms
every step of one's self-transformation (*zihua*).

It seems to me that its lack of resolution, its rejection of any solution to
interpretive problems, makes postmodern thinking artificially invincible and
inapplicable. Artificially invincible in the sense that it never takes a stance and

position of its own that would leave it open to criticism, to differences. This could be dangerous since anything invincible can become as authoritarian, repressive, and exclusive as traditional logocentrism or metaphysical truth. Inapplicable in the sense that, due to its refusal to commit to anything, it can hardly offer any positive alternative to what it opposes. It could not be applied to any actual or concrete situation in life, in which evaluation and choice among alternatives is always necessary. Deconstruction is an academic enterprise, not a philosophy of life, not a philosophy that has implications for human living. At this point, my interpretation emphasizing Zhuangzi and Nietzsche's religiosity, the ultimate affirmation of life and the part that some postmodern Nietzscheans have overlooked, provides a possible way to overcome the above mentioned shortcomings of the postmodern project.

THE LIBERATION OF THOUGHT: ZHUANGZI AND NIETZSCHE IN CONTEMPORARY CHINA

In this section I intend to illustrate how my project will contribute to the studies of Zhuangzi and Nietzsche in contemporary China. As I stated at the outset of this study, Zhuangzi's philosophy has attracted Chinese intellectuals and students as one of the most precious heritages of Chinese culture for more than two thousand years. Today, as people awaken from the communist sleep, they have begun to look back to their own cultural traditions, which were almost washed away during Mao's reign in the revolution. In order to move the nation from a "modernized" into a postmodern context, although they are sometimes overwhelmed by more urgent desires for economic reform and improvement, there has been since the late seventies an urgent aspiration for Chinese to recover and revive their own traditional treasures for the sake of resisting and replacing the existing communist ideology. On the other hand, some Chinese are still enthusiastic about ideas from Western culture other than Marxism and communism, especially the ideas of democracy, individualism, and liberalism, which seem to them absent in indigenous Chinese traditions. Along with this, Nietzsche is perhaps among the few most popular Western thinkers in China. Knowing his name is almost a standard measure of high education. On account of their unusual popularity and influence in China, I will first undertake a brief summary on how and what Chinese scholars have known about Zhuangzi and Nietzsche.

The study of Zhuangzi in China first began in the fourth century BCE, even before the *Book of Zhuangzi* was completed. Most of the *Outer* and *Miscellaneous Chapters*, written by his followers, were indeed the first cluster of interpretations of Zhuangzi's thought. According to Liu Xiao-gan's study, at least three schools of Zhuangzi's followers presented their different interpretations in the *Book of Zhuangzi*, the *Outer* and *Miscellaneous Chapters*. The first one Liu calls the "Transmitter school" (*shu Zhuang pai*) and assigns to them chapters 17–27 and 32. Their thought closely resembles and sometimes expands on that of the *Inner Chapters*. The second group he calls the "Huang-

Lao" or "Yellow Emperor and Laozi" school of the late Warring States period and perhaps early Han Dynasty, to whom chapters 12–16, 33, and the latter part of 11 are ascribed. These Huang-Lao writers synthesize Zhuangzi's Confucian and Legalist ideas based on Emperor Huang and Laozi's teachings of "*tiandao*" or the "Dao of Heaven." The third is the "School of No Sovereign" or "Anarchists" (*wu jun pai,* 无君派), to which chapters 8–10, 28–29, 31, and the first part of 11 are assigned. These chapters radically oppose morality, knowledge, and any political system, and nostalgically prize and idealize a tribal utopia in which human beings were free of any moral and political coercion and competition when their lives were in harmony with their inborn nature.[9] The mixture of these different interpretations in the chapters often confuses the reader and makes it impossible for one to get hold of the philosophical coherence of Zhuangzi's writings. My interpretation, supported by the authentic works of Zhuangzi as Graham and Liu have identified them, focuses on Zhuangzi's religiosity of liberation and life affirmation. That is the ultimate concern of all his philosophical undertaking, which distinguishes Zhuangzi from other thinkers of the time. This thematic approach makes the reading of the *Book of Zhuangzi* less confusing.

During the Han Dynasty (206 BCE–220 CE), Zhuangzi had little importance in the circle of Daoist study dominated by Huang-Lao texts and practices. These put emphasis on the primacy of the Dao of political rulership in association with Legalism, as well as the Dao of all kinds of popular religious practices such as divination and the cult of personal immortality or longevity. Zhuangzi's philosophy became distinctively influential and the reception of him as a leading figure of Daoism next to Laozi began in the Wei Jin Period (220–420). After He Yan (何偃, 190–249), Wang Bi (王弼, 226–249), Ruan Ji (阮籍, 210–263), Ji Kang (稽康, 224–263), and other contemporaries created a philosophical movement historically called "*Wei-Jinxuanxue*" (魏晋玄学), or "the philosophy of Wei Jin period." It centered on the cosmological origin and ontological being, which traced itself back to the philosophies of Laozi and Zhuangzi. Almost every prominent scholar of that time was fond of Zhuangzi and made commentaries on his writings. The most important works among them are the commentaries and interpretations of Xiang Xiu (227–272) and Guo Xiang (252–312). Xiang's commentary of twenty-six chapters was lost, and so Guo's commentary became the most publicly accepted version along with his edition of the *Book of Zhuangzi.* However, Xiang and Guo have been often mentioned together as the most influential school of Zhuangzi study inasmuch as they had very similar understandings of Zhuangzi, and Guo's commentary was very much inspired by and based on Xiang's interpretation.[10]

Contrary to Wang Bi's interpretation of Laozi's *wu* or nonbeing as an ontological Dao, Guo says neither *wu* nor *you* should be conceived as ontological or cosmological being, for Zhuangzi does not advocate any idea of such being. Guo proposed his interpretation of Zhuangzi based on the idea of the "self-born"or "self-creation" (*zisheng,*) and "self-transformation" (*zihua, duhua*). In chapter 2, Guo says, "non-being is nothing that cannot produce things; being [by itself] has no birth, therefore it cannot produce birth [of things]. What then is it that gives birth to things? Everything is self-born." (Guo, 1, 50). With the idea of *zisheng*, Guo revealed Zhuangzi's objection to the traditional pursuit of the cosmological origin and metaphysical Being. *Ziran* is nothing other than "self-born" and "self-transformation," which "does not have recourse to the external Dao, or rely on the internal self" (Guo, 1, 251). When one realizes this self-born and self-transforming nature of oneself, one could be free from dependence on things and go *xiaoyaoyou* around heaven, earth, and the human world. The interpretation of Xiang and Guo has also shown an effort to associate or reconcile Zhuangzi's philosophy and Confucian teaching. They believed that the Confucian teaching of morality and the Daoist doctrine of *ziran* were not different but actually the same. Morality functions in dealing with the outside world and other people, while *ziran* works in dealing with one's innate peace and self-transformation of spirit. With both, according to Xiang and Guo, one is able to reach the state of a sage who possesses "sagehood inside and kingship outside."

Xiang's and Guo's interpretations of Zhuangzi are among of the best works so far on Zhunagzi's thought. They almost recreated the historical Zhuangzi and his philosophy by which many generations of intellectuals in Chinese history were inspired and affected. However, their achievements were overshadowed by their attempt to reconcile Zhuangzi with the Confucian Dao as a sociopolitical ideal. Xiang and Guo could not perfectly understand Zhuangzi's ultimate state of spirituality or religiosity. Zhuangzi was conceived and interpreted more as an ideal or flawless sage who could do everything right rather than a free dancer who was beyond ordinary language, rational knowledge, social norms, and political parties. Without this transcending spirit of liberation, according to Zhuangzi, a complete life of *xiaoyao* would be impossible.

Xiang and Guo represented the highpoint of Zhuangzi study in ancient China. Perhaps because of the rapid assimilation and growth of Buddhism in China, *Wei-Jinxuanxue* gradually declined and disappeared in the Southern and Northern Dynasty (420–589). Since then, many individual scholars kept studying Zhuangzi and left behind numerous commentaries and exegesis, but they mostly followed Xiang's and Guo's mode of interpretation. On the other hand, with the development of religious Daoism, Zhuangzi was depicted as a Daoist deity (*shenxian*, 神仙) and "true person of southern China"(*nanhua zhenren*, 南华真人) and his book called "The Authentic Scripture of the Southern Flower" (*nanhuazhenjing*, 南华真经). At the same time, Confucianism as the state ideology and religion was strengthened and more and more privileged by the royal family, who subsequently suppressed the development of other schools of thought. From the fifth century on, the *Book of Zhuangzi* was either read as a Chinese reference to Buddhist principles or as a masterpiece of classical literature and poetry. The limitations of the development of religious Daoism and its departure from its philosophical origins could not help but distract even Daoists, and prevented them from deepening and expanding the study of Zhuangzi. Zhuangzi and his philosophy were more and more marginalized from the mainstream of social and intellectual life, and his influence became limited to artists, poets, Buddhist scholars, independent scholars, retired officials, and strange hermits. Until today, Zhuangzi's position in China's intellectual life has not changed much.

Compared to the criticism and misunderstanding that Zhuangzi has received throughout history, his philosophical and religious achievements have been little recognized. Zhuangzi has been seen as an eccentric and unconventional thinker. His indifference to political agendas and material interests, his critique of common beliefs or obsession with language, knowledge, and morality, his encouragement of living spontaneously, were judged incompatible with the mainstream tradition led by Confucius, Laozi, and others whose fundamental concerns were how to rule or govern (*zhi*) society for people's interests and thus keep the hierarchical order of the world intact. This incompatibility invoked all kinds of critique against Zhuangzi. As Wu Kuang-ming points out,

> Zhuangzi's contemporary Hui Shi declaimed that Zhuangzi's words are "big and useless" and should be discarded by everyone. Zhu Xi accused Zhuangzi of frivolous licentiousness and selfishness. Wang Yang-ming did not even bother to mention Zhuangzi by name. He merely lumped Daoism and Buddhism together as views of quietist withdrawal from the serious business of living. Modern Communist Chinese scholars variously accused Zhuangzi of pessimism, subjective idealism, crass materialism, nihilism, and so on. (*Chuang Tzu: World Philosopher at Play*, 13)

In addition, according to Wang Shu-min's *Peeping into Zhuangzi*, Zhuangzi was considered by many a successor or companion of Yangzi (扬朱, 390–319 BCE) who was thought to be the first egoist or solipsist in Chinese history. Yang Xiong (扬雄, 53 BCE–18 CE), Zhu Xi (朱熹, 1130–1200), and even the great twentieth-century historian of Chinese philosophy Fung Yu-lan all like to associate Zhuangzi and his notion of *ziran* with the Yangist soverignty of self and licentiousness of physical desire (Wang Shu-min, 10–11). Some see Zhuangzi's words as empty or useless. Wang Chong (王充, 27–97) in his *Lunheng* (论衡) criticizes the Daoist idealization of *ziran,* claiming that it cannot guide one's words and actions in accordance with concrete, tangible things, and therefore it cannot be trusted ("On Nature"). Even Guo Xiang has said that Zhuangzi's words are hard to experience or practice, despite the fact that they are perfect (Guo, 1, 3). These criticisms, based on a misreading and misunderstanding of Zhuangzi, have negatively affected the Chinese study of Zhuangzi throughout history, and have lately been inherited as prejudices misguiding modern readers of Zhuangzi, especially the revolutionaries and communists. "Escapist," "skeptic," "agnostic," "relativist," "anarchist" are often synonymous with Zhuangzi and his thought.

My study shows that all these charges and interpretations are inappropriate if we read Zhuangzi closely. First, my interpretation reveals Zhuangzi's
unique religiosity, which pursues individual transformation and self-cultivation
in order to free one within the world from all kinds of oppression caused by
our own artificial production. Dao is for Zhuangzi not an empty word, but
a higher perspective beyond the ordinary obsessions of political, economic
interest and intelligent competition. Zhuangzi never teaches us to abandon or
renounce social, political, or moral life. What he suggests is that we overcome
ourselves, that we should not be passive or subjugated slaves manipulated by
the power of authority, which is, after all, constructed by ourselves. In this
respect, I interpret Zhuangzi's philosophy as a philosophy of spiritual freedom
and liberation. Second, my project shows that Zhuangzi deconstructs the
metaphysical understanding of Dao as something determinate and absolute. In
spite of this, many Chinese commentators still read Zhuangzi as a conventional
metaphysician. My reading of Zhuangzi's affirmation of difference through
oneness challenges the traditional unitarism of China, which has been considered one of the greatest obstacles in the development of a democratic,
liberal, and pluralistic community out of its hierarchical system. Third, my
concrete analysis of Zhuangzi's critique of language, knowledge, and morality
has extracted from this ancient text some thoughts that can provide alternative
solutions to the problems and crises of humanity we are confronting today.
For example, Zhuangzi's application of "goblet words" could help us to recognize more about the nature of human language and the possible way to
expand the space and function of language in explaining something paradoxical, even divinely mysterious workings. After all, as shown in the preceding chapters, Zhuangzi is a positive and affirmative thinker who differs
fundamentally from relativism, escapism, nihilism, skepticism, and so on. What
he wanted to do was to dismantle all that is illusive, repressive, and dogmatic,
free himself from the cage constructed by human beings, and become one
with the spontaneity of the natural world of ten-thousand-things. All these
are either missing or overlooked by most of the Zhuangzi scholars throughout
Chinese history. The present interpretation will at least challenge traditional
and prevalent conceptions about Zhuangzi's philosophy.

In recent China, Nietzsche's name is not strange at all. In fact, he may
be more popular among young students than Zhuangzi or any other philosophers. As early as 1902, two years after his death, Nietzsche was introduced
to the Chinese for the first time by Liang Qi-chao (梁启超). Two years later,
Wang Guo-wei (王国维) published three articles: "Nietzsche's Notion of
Education," "A Biography of Nietzsche: the Great Reformer of German
Culture," and "The Teaching of Nietzsche," in the journal, *The World of Education* (1904), nos. 71, 76, and 78–79. Wang had studied Schopenhauer, so he
understood Nietzsche as a Schopenhauer follower, but he did appreciate
Nietzsche's rejection of metaphysics. Lu Xun (鲁迅) read Nietzsche when he
was studying in Japan in 1902. He found some of Nietzsche's ideas, such as
the *Übermensch*, genealogy, which he understood as an "evolution" theory of

morality, individualism, and extreme subjectivism, helpful in his effort to awaken Chinese self-consciousness, which was for him the most urgent task in the national liberation and social development of China.

Cheng Fang in his recent book, *Nietzsche in China* (1993), says there are three waves of the "Nietzsche cult" or "Nietzsche fever" (*Nicaire*, 尼采热) in twentieth-century China. The first phase was the period of 1915–1925, before and after the May-Fourth Movement in 1919. The representatives of this wave included Lu Xun, Chen Du-xiu, Li Shi-cen, Xie Wu-liang, Mao Dun, Fu Si-nian, Tian Han, and Cai Yuan-pei. They translated Nietzsche's works, wrote articles and books on Nietzsche, using Nietzsche's philosophy as a weapon to reevaluate and subvert the Confucian tradition as a whole. They accused Chinese culture, hitherto dominated by Confucianism, of being a culture of slavery (Chen Du-xiu). They said they needed Nietzsche's master morality and will to power to generate a Chinese Enlightenment (Xie Wu-liang, Fu Si-nian). During this period, the main motif for Chinese intellectuals was how to make the nation strong and powerful in order to prevent it from becoming a colony of the imperialist countries. Nietzsche's theory of *Übermensch*, the will to power, revaluation, master morality, and individualism was put forward as remedy and cure for the sick and weak Chinese nation.

The second wave occurred during World War II with a number of intellectuals such as Lin Yu-tang, Yu Da-fu, Liang Zong-dai, Guo Mo-ruo, Liu En-jiu, and Zhu Guang-qian. After China was occupied by Japan, fighting against the Japanese and liberating the nation was the only occupation of the Chinese people in their endeavor to regain their dignity and independence. Through Nietzsche as a mirror, some Chinese intellectuals saw the weakness and decadence of Chinese culture and Chinese people as the cause of China's fall from historical glory. In contrast to those Marxists who tried to establish a new political apparatus and distribution of means of production, Chinese Nietzscheans insisted on changing the "national disposition" or national consciousness (*guominxing*, 国民性). Li Shi-cen, in his *Outline of the Philosophy of the Übermensch*), said.

> We Chinese, due to our phlegmatic disposition, have been despised by the peoples of other countries. Lacking the outrage to advance and deficient in creativity, we are docile slaves of custom, merely out of cringing timidity. Bringing up such docile slaves is a waste of the country's money, giving birth to them is a waste of the race's energy. I suggest that we might perhaps find the salvation of these phlegmatic vassals in the thought of Nietzsche, who is so reviled, abused and refuted by our countrymen. (*Nietzsche and Asian Thought*, 156–57)

During this period, criticism of Nietzsche also started to sprout because of the relation of Nietzsche's philosophy to Hitler and Nazism. Some Marxists and nationalists claimed that the disaster of the war was the indirect outcome of Nietzsche's philosophy incorporated in the body of Nazism. They even thought that Nietzsche should show up in International Court with other Nazi war criminals (Cheng Fang, 162). Marxist thinkers who followed their Russian teachers began to criticize Nietzsche's philosophy by means of dialectical and historical materialism. Nietzsche was charged as a subjective idealist, philosopher of will or voluntarist, Nazi, racist, sexist, egoist or solipsist, nihilist, and finally a spokesman of the declining capitalism in the West. This kind of criticism later became the official and standard description of Nietzsche and his philosophy in China after 1949.

The third wave of the "Nietzsche cult" began in the late 1970s after Mao's death and the "economic reform" led by Deng Xiaoping. Awakening from a continuous nightmare of communist revolution and Cultural Revolution, the Chinese people, especially the young generation, realized that China was totally out of the international race to modernization and their lives had been little improved since the revolution. What is wrong with Chinese culture? Where is the meaning of life? Are Chinese people their own masters as the communists claimed? What is the value of the individual? Along with the older themes of national development and political and economic reform first raised by the May Fourth Movement, the call for individuality (self-value) and creativity (freedom of choice) raised the new wave of the "Nietzsche cults." In order to catch up with other nations and become a developed, strong country, it was felt that the Chinese people needed to reevaluate all values, change the collectivist tradition that had lasted more than five thousand years, and elevate individual strength and self consciousness, which are precisely the preconditions for a free, democratic, and productive society. From then on, many young intellectuals studied Nietzsche and wrote introductory books and articles that have aroused people's attention to Nietzsche's philosophy in today's China (cf. Cheng Fang, 324–56). But still, as David A. Kelley remarks, "[T]he Nietzscheanizing of the Chinese mind was, then, as much the recovery of a May Fourth beachhead as a new assimilation"(*Nietzsche and Asian Thought*, 168).

The problems I have with the various Chinese "Nietzsche Cults" are as follows. First, there was and is too much enthusiasm for the pragmatic purpose of social change for any serious attention to be paid to the need for an intensive study of Nietzsche's philosophy as a whole. Many who had read only a few passages or part of Nietzsche began making use of Nietzsche directly. Such practical mentality often distracts Chinese scholars from their scholarly work and disables them from reaching the depths of comprehension of Nietzsche's philosophy. Second, most Chinese Nietzscheans still maintain an attachment to the metaphysical tradition of philosophical reflection. What they have tried to do is to absolutize Nietzsche's *Übermensch*, the will to power (often understood as will *and* power), as the necessary result of a radical "revaluation." They customarily appeal to Nietzschean terms such as the "*Übermensch*" and "the will to power" as representations of new "transcendental values" that apparently were not so for Nietzsche himself. Third, under the influence of the official Marxist critique of Nietzsche, many have confused

Nietzsche's philosophy with different doctrines, such as evolution theory, social Darwinism, Nazism, voluntarism, cultural nihilism, and so on. By way of comment, I would like to cite David A. Kelley's observation:

> [V]ulgarization of Nietzsche is one of the conspicuous modes of his influence in China. We have seen that this takes different forms. Very common is a crude political interpretation of the will to power. Even where this error is consciously avoided, as in the case of Li Shicen, there is a disappointing blindness to Nietzsche's literary strategies and use of irony. This is true even of Lu Xun, who had by far the deepest natural affinity with the master. It is symptomatic of the post-Marxist return to the May Fourth in China that Nietzschean motifs are commonly found embedded in romantic metanarratives, as typified in Liu Xiaobo's pathos of the solitary self. One seeks in vain for careful attention to the theme of "disarticulation of the self" which marked Nietzsche's own passionate self-distancing from romanticism. (*Nietzsche and Asian Thought*, 167–68)

The interpretation of Nietzsche in this study provides a more comprehensive study than any of the work done in China. Its aim has been to understand Nietzsche within an overall picture of his philosophy and cultural context and thus to find out what he in fact achieved through his philosophizing "with a hammer." I have shown that Nietzsche's project is beyond any political intention of destruction or reconstruction of an existing system. His attempt is to deliver the human mind out of the hegemony of any ideological or metaphysical tradition, which favors "the other world" and denies our life on earth. I have intensively analyzed Nietzsche's critique of truth, language, morality as the philosophical preparation of his new values of the *Übermensch*, the will to power, eternal recurrence, and Dionysian religiosity, the ultimate freedom, and liberation as life affirmation. By providing an interpretation of Nietzsche in the context of modern and postmodern motifs, my study can help Chinese readers to familiarize themselves with how other people understand Nietzsche and to discover what might be wrong with previous readings.

Moreover, I believe that this study sheds light on the field of both Zhuangzi and Nietzsche studies in China. The Marxist method that divides philosophers in history into two opposite "armies," idealism and materialism or Platonism and Democritism, is clearly abandoned in this study. Instead, I have incorporated methods such as hermeneutics, genealogy, deconstruction, and comparison along with an interpretive perspective of religiosity.

PHILOSOPHICAL RELIGIOSITY

In this concluding section I would like to return to my introduction of the idea of religiosity. Religiosity has been the special perspective or horizon from which I have tried to interpret and compare the philosophies of Zhuangzi and Nietzsche. I have argued that Zhuangzi's and Nietzsche's philosophies bear great similarities with respect to a special religiosity, a religiosity that makes them differ from what has been held to be "religious" in both traditional philosophy and religion. My attempt is to show that this phenomenon of "religiosity" was a significant and creative part of both Zhuangzi's and Nietzsche's philosophical thinking, which has been either overlooked or underestimated by most commentators. In this section I wish to further clarify the term *religiosity* and its potential significance for the studies of philosophy and religion.

Recently, a few new books on Nietzsche have appeared showing substantial attention among English scholars to the religious aspect in Nietzsche's philosophy. These books include *Contesting Spirit: Nietzsche, Affirmation, Religion*, by Tyler T. Roberts (1998), *Nietzsche and the Gods*, edited by Weaver Santaniello (2001), and *Nietzsche, Metaphor, Religion*, by Tim Murphy (2001). Many have contributed their investigations on Nietzsche's intellectual relation to Christianity (Tyler T. Roberts, Thomas H. Brobjer, and Jerry S. Clegg), Jewish God and Judaism (Tim Murphy, Edith Wyschogrod, and Stephen L. Hood), Buddhism (Robert G. Morrison and Graham Parkes), Islam (Herry Bayman), and more importantly, of course, Greek Gods and Greek tragedy (Lawrence J. Hatab, John Sallis, and Weaver Santaniello). By "reexamination of Nietzsche's 'philosophy' of religion"(Murphy, 9) some of these scholars have confidently in their works served to "challenge impulsive claims that Nietzsche was 'atheist' or 'irreligious,' rendering such statements as needing dire qualific ation"(Santaniello, xvi). I highly appreciate their study and very much share their awareness of Nietzsche's serious thinking or religion, which is indeed a significant part of my notion of religiosity. Nevertheless, the religiosity I have discussed in this book does not parallel what they called Nietzsche's "philosophy" of religion, or "the place of religion" in his philosophy (Roberts). In what follows, therefore, I tend to make reference specifically to Tyler T. Roberts's book *Contesting Spirit: Nietzsche, Affirmation, Religion*, contrasting it to my understanding of "religiosity" or "philosophical religiosity" in both Nietzsche and Zhuangzi's philosophy.

Roberts's work mainly deals with the relationship between Nietzsche's writing and the theme of religion. Roberts's insights into these matters have been helpful in disclosing the religious elements in Nietzsche's thought. In fact, they have emphasized that apart from these elements, Nietzsche cannot be satisfactorily understood. Nonetheless, Roberts's work, as well as other works aforementioned, has not encompassed the sense of religiosity I have explored.

This book is said to be the first sustained examination in English of the place of religion in Nietzsche's writing.[11] Roberts finds in Nietzsche's writing, especially in his series of prefaces written in 1886 for new editions of his early works, "a glancing equivocation between religion and anti-religion" (4). Throughout his writings, according to Roberts, "Nietzsche led a philosophical life that resisted the religious traditions that have shaped Western civilization, only at the same time that he accomplished a transformative renewal of their discipline and passions" (ibid.). In Roberts's reading, Nietzsche went through a paradoxical *pathos* of religion and antireligion in his thinking. Most readers and commentators have only noticed the latter and failed to take into account the former. This is why Roberts calls for reexamining "the place of religion in Nietzsche's writing."

In order to do this, Roberts puts into question first the concept of "religion" and its changes of meaning in the history of Western culture. He remarks that we fail to understand Nietzsche to the extent that we do not question "the way we depend upon the construct of 'religion' in order to order and settle the world" (6). The word *religion* has a history, "in the course of which it has taken on specific meanings in specific contexts" (ibid.) For example, the Christian church came to distinguish its practices as the "true religion" in contradistinction to paganism; and in a strangely similar way philosophers and scientists in the modern era have sought to distinguish the religious from the secular through the dogmas of scientific knowledge and praxis. In contrast to the *secular*,

> *religion* as a noun rather than an adjective comes to the fore to refer to cultural complexes marked by rituals, beliefs, books, and gods. The word takes its modern meaning at the intersection of the encounter between Christianity and what we called "other religions," and between Christianity and the anti-traditional and naturalistic impulses of modernity. It is enmeshed, therefore, with issues of power, politics, and culture as it is deployed to mark these differences. *Religion* becomes a highly charged term, playing a crucial role in negotiating giant encounters and shifts of worldviews, the ramifications of which are felt in the very way we understand modernity, enlightenment, progress, pluralism and tradition. (6)

Religion, according to Roberts, is imagined and reimagined in broader senses as the cultural complexes within and around which it transforms. In other words, the meaning of religion is no longer confined to the relationship between God and human beings or specific forms of rituals and beliefs. It has come over the centuries to include art, philosophy, and cultural institutions with which a certain type of people shape their understanding of existence, life, and the world. By this exercise in what Johnathan Z. Smith has called "imagining religion," says Roberts, "by reintroducing the complex of ideas and practices that the concept *religion* allows us to deploy, and by critically interrogating this concept, one can follow the complexity of Nietzsche's vision with more precision than a simply secular reading affords" (7).

With the concept of religion thus appropriately broadened, Roberts asserts the "equivocation between religion and anti-religion" in Nietzsche's writing. He indicates that Nietzsche's antireligious critique is somehow religious, for Nietzsche's affirmation of life and "the eternal joy of becoming" is somehow ascetic, mystical, leaving his writing full of religious language. Because of Nietzsche's celebration of self-discipline and ideas concerning the spiritual transfiguration of the body, he is conceived by Roberts as "indebted, in a positive way, to Christian asceticism" (90). Because of Nietzsche's affirmation of life as joy and suffering, his longing for eternity, and his worship of creating gods, Roberts attributes to him a "mysticism" which is "about *meeting* the human and what is other than human" (127). In addition, Nietzsche's Dionysian spirit, love of antiquity, especially Greek tragedy, exaltation of the *Übermensch* and the will to power, all show his complex of religion and anti-religion. In other words, though Nietzsche rejects monotheist religions such as Christianity, he advocates polytheistic beliefs such as we find in classical Greek religion. Moreover, Roberts states, "when one says 'Yes' out of the deepest suffering and deepest joy, when one says to the 'demon' who proclaims eternal recurrence, 'You are a god,' one declares divinity. The divine reveals itself to the affirmer in the sense that to affirm is to deify" (198). Roberts has in this last point in particular a precise understanding of the place of religion in Nietzsche's writing.

Roberts's analysis of "imagining religion" in a reexamination of the relation of religion to Nietzsche's thought is very helpful. His project offers a possible way to open the borders between religion and philosophy as they have been conceived in Western thought for so long. According to Nietzsche, philosophy and religion were undifferentiated within the great art form of tragedy, which was a direct reflection of the "Dionysian spirit" of Greek life. It was Socrates and Plato who "invented" rational or logocentric philosophy and theology by denying the this-worldly experience of life. After the death of God, modern philosophy and sciences in the West "liberated" themselves from their dependence on religion and more and more treated religion as something irrational, illogical, mystical, and superstitious. In the field of mainstream philosophy and science, the religious elements of the human world were marginalized and even excluded from the practice of scientific method, and thus from the field of possible knowledge. We must not lose sight of the fact that Nietzsche's critique of modernity, which amounts to a critique of nihilism, also entails the critique of rationalist and positivist approaches to truth and reality. Throughout his writings, he disclosed the similarity between rational philosophy, positivist science, and the Christian religion, for he held them to be different systems of beliefs which in their respective manners attempted to establish one or another kind of ideal world. On the other hand, as I have said, Nietzsche made room for "religiosity" to reenter the realm of human life. For Nietzsche, such a reentry seems necessary, for the only way to undercut nihilism is by a deifying affirmation of life. Roberts is therefore correct in arguing that unless the concept of religion was questioned we would not fully understand Nietzsche.

In Chinese history, there was never any clear line between religion and philosophy. *Zongjiao* (宗教), which is actually a contemporary translation, made first by Japanese and adopted by Chinese, of the Western term *religion*, literally means the teaching (*jiao*) of truth or tradition (*zong*). For the majority of so called "Chinese religions" such as Confucianism, Daoism, and many schools of Chinese Buddhism, there is no supreme God in the other world, but spirits who live among us human beings and are examples of good and evil that we can follow in our everyday lives. The ultimate purpose of *zongjiao* is to help people to transform their state of mind to a thorough awareness of the nature of this world in order to live a life that is free from sufferings and boundaries in this world. With this respect, *zongjiao* and its aspiration for spiritual transformation, as Robert E. Allinson pointed out correctly, do not require specific religious forms or elements, for example, a supreme Being, doctrine, revealed scripture, etc., which are normally required by conventional religions in the West (Allinson, 7–9). On the other hand, a philosophical exploration of the secret of nature and the meaning of life is at the same time a religious one. In this sense, *zongjiao* or religion in Chinese tradition is philosophy (*zhexue*, 哲学, also adopted from the Japanese translation). Since philosophy is not, in Chinese tradition, the pursuit of objective knowledge but the pursuit and learning of the way (Dao) of living, it is inseparable from *zongjiao* or religion. *Zhexue* is the Chinese word used in contemporary language for philosophy, with *xue* meaning "learning" and *zhe* referring to "wisdom" or "knowledge." In antiquity, this was merely referred to as *xue*, or "learning." But alternative appellations for philosophy referred to it as the "learning" or "technique" of Dao (*daoshu*). Zhuangzi's philosophy could be called either *zongjiao* or *daoshu* in terms of its teaching of spiritual freedom and human liberation. The Chinese tradition did not develop any Aristotelian system of metaphysics and epistemology. The advantage of this kind of thinking is that in the overlapping between religion and philosophy we may find some way to overcome the limitation of rational knowledge, and, just as Zhuangzi has performed in his philosophy, seek a reintegration of religiosity into philosophical reflection in the Chinese intellectual context.

Having noted my areas of agreement with Roberts, but also with this Chinese background in mind, I must now indicate that my project and thesis differ substantially from that of Roberts with respect to religiosity. First, Roberts's use of religiosity is very much indebted to the conventional Christian concept of religion, though he attempts to bring to its aid "religion" in the modern and postmodern contexts. When he talks about "spiritual sensibility," "faith," "affirmation," and finally "asceticism" and "mysticism" in Nietzsche's thought, he clearly has in mind religion in this conventional Christian sense. The perspective of religiosity as I discussed in this study, however, has little to do with such refinements of concepts from within the conventional contexts employed by Roberts, centered as they are in a divine Other, in an institutionalized and hierarchical order, in an orthodox doctrine of principle and practice. Here religiosity is being viewed as much more anthropocentric. In this approach, an inquiry into religiosity as such is an inquiry into what prompts people to hold something as sacred as opposed to something else. In other words, religiosity in general is not the "content" of what one believes in as "religious." Rather, it is what has driven, enticed, tempted one to hold something as especially worthy of affirmation; it is like the "will to truth," a "will to hold as sacred." What is seen here as religiosity in Zhuangzi and Nietzsche is a kind of "innate passion," as Kierkegaard called it, to seek and feel something sacred or divine that they believe was hidden, distorted, or repressed in forgoing conventional religions and philosophies. The religiosity, to this extent, of Nietzsche and Zhuangzi is not a "spiritual sentiment" toward what is other than human, but is directed toward human existence and life, toward liberation and spiritual freedom as human beings living in a human, at times all-too-human world. It is this religiosity that prompts and initiates Zhuangzi and Nietzsche to examine, interpret, and evaluate the world critically and philosophically. The religiosity to be found in Zhuangzi and Nietzsche, therefore, is not what Roberts sees as the "equivocation" or "psychological balance" between religion and anti-religion. For Zhuangzi and Nietzsche, there is no ambiguity, equivocation, or ambivalence in their religiosity, their longing or aspiration for freedom and liberation, for an "improvement of mankind," as Nietzsche dubbed it (HE, 217), or for *xiaoyaoyou* in Zhuangzi's account. By getting hold of such a religiosity as a guiding thread of reading Zhuangzi and Nietzsche, we are able to understand or delve into the real depths of their philosophies.

Secondly, we must consider what is the "content" of the specific religiosity of Zhuangzi and Nietzsche. What do they hold as sacred which singles them out for a study such as this one? The religiosity that motivates Nietzsche and Zhuangzi, their "ultimate concern" or "existential character of religious experience"(Tillich, 11–12),[12] is the affirmation of this world and this life as opposed to the tendency of Christianity or Confucianism respectively to denigrate both in order to advocate a way of living that both these thinkers believed amounted to life-denial. Both Zhuangzi and Nietzsche made their philosophies unique and evocative inasmuch as their special religiosity, the religiosity that subverts what the entire tradition represented as religious, turns the religious sentiment and urge for spiritual transformation back to this world and this life. Everything, every moment in this world and this life, body, instinct, chaos, contradiction, appearance, all condemned and marginalized in the history of conventional philosophy and religion, should be affirmed and celebrated as sacred and divine. Therefore, Zhuangzi's and Nietzsche's religiosity, plainly displayed in their writings, strives to reach liberation by affirming life religiously, in the sense that this affirmation of life rests not on some logical proof or confession of faith, but an affirmation "of things seen." Without the light of such religiosity we could hardly have a good grip on the core of their philosophies. The life they resolutely affirm and say Yes to is not the "religious life" or "ascetic deal," which Roberts tries to attribute to Nietzsche's religiosity, but the life we actually enjoy and suffer everyday. It is to live resolutely and religiously in terms of believing in oneself and the flux of life into which one is born and where one's destiny lies. This is what Zhuangzi's and Nietzsche's religiosity is all about.

Third, this religiosity, which affirms life, tends toward a dissolving of the boundaries between the secular and sacred. This kind of religiosity is not about the tension between being religious and antireligious (Roberts). Rather it revolves around a tension between two different religiosities, one that bifurcates the world into the secular and sacred, and the other that unites the world into the sacred secular. So the issue for Nietzsche as well as Zhuangzi is not the dichotomy of religion and the secular; that is a dichotomy established by the rules of either/or thinking. The issue of religious versus secular should fall "under erasure." Anti-religion, if it serves any purpose for Nietzsche at all, is a kind of strategy he uses to reevaluate so-called secular life and transform it into something sacred and divine. The anti-Christ is also part of Nietzsche's religiosity which is designed to overcome or remove the artificial distinction between sacred and profane, religious and secular. Zhuangzi too tried to dissolve the separation between Dao and everyday life. It is not that there is something sacred or divine above the secular life. Rather, the secular life in which we live and die is itself sacred. It is sacred not because God created it but because we live it and affirm it religiously. After we attain the enlightenment of such an affirmation of secular life, the secular becomes religious and the religious becomes secular, or to borrow a Mahayana Buddhist expression, *samsara* becomes/is *nirvana*, and *nivarna* becomes/is *samsara*. Clearly, in this kind of religiosity, religions of another world, or an ideal world, are torn asunder, not through any crusade or persecution or colonization, which would only manifest the hatred of life these traditional religions exhibit, but through an affirmation of what these religions have least wished to affirm.

Fourth, the method of Zhuangzi's and Nietzsche's religiosity is a philosophical critique, a critique of the metaphysics, language, and values propounded by past systems they deemed life-denying. In order to reach the state of ultimate liberation of human existence, one should get rid of all the oppositional constructions concerning morality, language, metaphysics, and even religion itself that these traditions propounded. Therefore, for Zhuangzi and Nietzsche, critique as a means to access liberation has no intention to establish another Truth, Being, God, or Reality or system of metaphysics, because they are acutely aware that any such knowledge cannot represent or correspond to the "absolute." The attempt to posit one absolute over against another absolute would merely leave us entrapped in an illusory world. The state of liberation Zhuangzi and Nietzsche proposed and practiced is a state surpassing or ascending beyond conventional concepts of knowledge, language, and morality. It is not a state of certainty or clarity of knowledge but a wholehearted transformation of self into the flux of life and becoming one with the world of becoming. In contrast to traditional philosophers, Nietzsche and especially Zhuangzi do not critique one kind of tradition in favor of another but place the whole setting of human knowledge, language, and religion into question and finally transcend the very boundaries of those kinds of conflict. Critique is not the refutation of something with the establishment of a contrary truth in view, and thus, the method of this religiosity is this particular brand of critique.

On the other hand, critique is also a part of affirmation. According to Zhuangzi and Nietzsche, the world and life that we affirm are constantly moving, changing, and becoming; nothing in this world can be fixed and uniform. The state of freedom or *xiaoyaoyou* amounts to the state of mind that has no fixed dogma or uniform rule to prevent its being one with the eternal flow of becoming. Nietzsche's notion of revaluation, the will to power, and eternal return, Zhuangzi's notion of self-transformation (*zihua*) and no-self (*wuwuo*) represents a kind of critique which is a part of transformation. Critique, in terms of a constant move of overcoming all kinds of fixation, certainty, and finality, is in fact a different type of affirmation of life as becoming. As the affirmation of life as becoming, this critique confers a sacred "Yes" upon the differences and plurality of the world.

Fifth, we must envision what sort of role this philosophical religiosity can play in the current and future discipline of philosophy. For as we have seen, the philosophical religiosity of Zhuangzi and Nietzsche was not merely dedicated to the universal critique of all worldviews, but was meant to be a path (*Dao*) of liberation and an ever-creative desire for empowerment (*Wille zur Macht*). Reluctant to call philosophical religiosity itself a worldview or an ontology in its own right, especially given the fact that this study has shown that this "way of liberation" was practiced in very different historical contexts, I would prefer to say that philosophical religiosity is a method. The critical stance that it takes is a means of safeguarding the human in the midst of competing philosophical, moral, nationalistic, politico-economic, and social interests that would fix and isolate the human within their own various doctrines of truth, right, stability, progress, or hegemony. In the case of Zhuangzi, traditional Confucian, Moist, and even Daoist pictures of the natural order rendered human beings mere agents in a cosmic-moral scheme, effective only insofar as they were obedient subjects, good "sons of the son of heaven," servants of social stability through the practice of "universal love," or passive hermits wandering about nothingness. In contemporary China, the communist model of human existence as perfected through loyalty to the party mission by "serving the people, heart and soul" has been supplanted by a nihilism of consumerism. In the case of Nietzsche, traditional Christian anthropology made human beings into worshippers of the otherworldly, and in their ardor not to sin against heaven, they sinned against the earth and one another. One hundred years after Nietzsche's warnings against nihilism, the period of the "last man" would seem to be upon us, with all beliefs and desires eliminated, and the interests of a new economic colonialism uniting social sentiment under the banner of "progress," and production, a banner under which everyone, in Zarathustra's words, is to feel the same, be the same, with every dissenter going voluntarily into a madhouse. Philosophical religiosity does not safeguard the human by establishing any new doctrines of language, difference, or fundamental otherness in order to keep the intellectual endeavors of the academic establishment open, as deconstruction might. It remains reflective and critical in a philosophical spirit by not allowing any doctrine of human existence governed by metaphysical, social, and moral norms to become entrenched and "universally binding." At the same time, human life must be assessed and valued on its own fluctuating, dynamic terms. Human liberation is bound up with an axiological appreciation, indeed a reverent wonder at the seamless continuity of human existence in the ever-creative natural process. The "ultimate concern" with the value of human existence is the method-ological center of philosophical religiosity. Whether this dedication to the human itself constitutes another view can certainly be asked, just as it can be asked whether hermeneutics, for instance, is not simultaneously a view of interpretation and a method of interpreting. But philosophical religiosity never loses sight of the attempts at hegemony over the human, whether those attempts take the form of metaphysics, morality, socialization, or political coercion. Its various criticisms of these attempts at hegemony all take place for the sake of keeping watch over the genuinely human, and its potential for genuine spiritual liberation, a liberation that takes place in the world, in the very center of its own existence. In this light, life affirmation does not con-stitute a "regulative ideal" in a Kantian sense, that is, an ideal that is to be accomplished after human existence becomes "something else" at the end of some philosophical or metahistorical process. Life affirmation is not even some "other" or "transformed" state of human life, or the hypostatizing of some such transformed state as the goal of human efforts. Life affirmation is not a "philosophy of as if," but a "philosophy of as is," insofar as its whole point is the realization that human beings can either deny themselves the spiritual freedom of transformation they already possess at bottom, or they can embrace it. Life affirmation, as I have shown in my entire study, is for Zhuangzi and Nietzsche more like a "religious faith," which believes simply in life as the spontaneous flux of becoming and treats this life in this world, no matter what has happened or will happen in it, as the most divine and sacred. It is at this point of their religiosity that Zhuangzi and Nietzsche have in their philosophy overcome and transcended all the skeptical, relativist, negative, and nihilist dispositions toward and perspectives of life. A positive and affirmative view of life and the world was constructed respectively by each philosopher based on his passionate and honest faith in life.

Finally, this exploration of the thesis of religiosity, specifically the philo-sophical religiosity in Zhuangzi and Nietzsche, is an attempt to achieve a "fusion of horizons" between philosophy and religion. Although Nietzsche proclaimed the death of God, he also was the prolepsis to the "end of philosophy." On his "path of thinking," reason and knowledge finally found the limits of their own efforts to discover the "absolute truth." By shedding light on the issue of philosophical religiosity through examining the cases of Zhuangzi and Nietzsche, this study has been an attempt to look for an opportunity or possibility of a "fusion of horizons" between two intellectual and spiritual endeavors that have been separated for so long.

I found Tillich's remark in his *Systematic Theology* exceptionally inspiring when he talked about the "convergence"after he analyzed the divergence between philosophy and theology. He sees from both sides some converging trends are at work. Let's take a look from the side of philosophy:

> The philosopher, like the theologian, "exists," and he cannot jump over the concreteness of his existence and his implicit theology. He is conditioned by his psychological, sociological, and historical situation. And, like every human being, he exists in the power of an ultimate concern ... for without an ultimate concern his philosophy would be lacking in passion, seriousness, and creativity. . . . More often it is the character of the ontological principles, or a special section of a system, such as epistemology, philosophy of nature, politics and ethics, philosophy of history, etc., which is most revealing for the discovery of the ultimate concern and the hidden theology within it. Every creative philosopher is a hidden theologian (sometimes even a declared theologian). He is a theologian in the degree to which his existential situation and his ultimate concern shape his philosophical vision. . . . There is hardly a historically significant philosopher who does not show these marks of a theologian. (24–25)

Here, the "hidden theology" and "hidden theologian" within those philosophies Tillich mentioned in terms of their ultimate concerns would be considerably analogous to what I meant by "religiosity," of course, if we remove his Christian fundamentals out of the words. It is true that creative philosophers such as Zhuangzi and Nietzsche do have ultimate concerns behind their philosophical writings. It is also true, after we have investigated both philosophers under the guidance of their religiosity, that Zhuangzi and Nietzsche are "hidden theologians" in the degree to which their existential situation and their ultimate concerns "shape" their "philosophical visions" (ibid.) We cannot understand and interpret the philosophies completely without finding out their specific "hidden theology." The "hidden theology" or religiosity in Nietzsche and Zhuangzi challenge both conventional philosophy and religion, and do make their converging trend "at work."

Religiosity thereby transgresses the territory of philosophy and transforms it from a purely speculative or reflective wonder to an open, free, affirmative wisdom of life. On the other hand, the religiosity Zhuangzi and Nietzsche experimented with is specifically philosophical, inasmuch as they brought traditional religion back to the earth and elevated life as it is to the sacred through the ardent labor of critique. As Nietzsche has expressed explicitly in his *Gay Science,*

We *are* something different from scholars, although it is unavoidable for us to be also, among other things, scholarly. We have different needs, grow differently, and also have a different digestion: we need more, we also need less. How much a spirit needs for its nourishment, for there is no formula; but if its taste is for independence, for adventures for which only the swiftest are a match, it is better for such a spirit to live in freedom with little to eat than unfree and stuffed. It is not fat but the greatest possible suppleness and strength that a good dancer desires from his nourishment—and I would know what the spirit of a philosopher might wish more to be than a good dancer. For the dance is his ideal, also his art, and finally also his only piety, his "service of God." (*GS*, 381)

In Zhuangzi and Nietzsche, the "good dancers" of free spirit, philosophy and religion, converge, and in this "fusion of horizons" the very understanding of both philosophy and religion can be rethought, reevaluated, and transformed.

NOTES

CHAPTER 1. INTRODUCTION

1. Nietzsche's name was known in China as early as the beginning of the twentieth century, introduced first by Lian Qi-chao (1902), then by Wang Guo-wei in association with his favorite philosopher Schopenhauer (1904). During and after the May Fourth Movement in 1919, many great Chinese thinkers of the time were influenced by Nietzsche's philosophy, such as Chen Du-xiu, Li Da-zhao, and especially Lu Xun, who was even described as the "Nietzsche of China." But Chinese interpretations of Nietzsche concentrated mainly on Nietzsche's radical critique and extremist language, especially phrases such as "God is dead," "revaluation of all values," "will to power," and "slave morality," all of which very much echoed the Chinese desire for strength after China had been defeated by the West in one campaign after another since the Opium War in the 1840s. During the 1980s, the same themes, issues, and problems were recreated after the failure of Mao's experiment with communism. Nietzsche once again captured the consciousness of Chinese intellectuals who could not endure the humiliation of being a weak and undeveloped nation. See also chapter 5.

2. In China, people are less likely to be confused with religion (*zongjiao*, 宗教) and religiosity (*zongjiaoxing*, 宗教性, or *zongjiaogan*, 宗教感) because most indigenous Chinese religions, such as Confucianism and Daoism, do not have a definite concept of God but rather of the sacredness of this life and this world. This cultural background suggests why I prefer the word *religiosity* to characterize the spirit of these two philosophers. There will be a further discussion of the term in chapter 5.

3. In Fall 1984, a series of lectures was held by the Beijing Seminary of Culture, established in the same year. I was invited as a representative on behalf of The Center of East-West Comparative Cultures (Shanghai) to celebrate the opening of the seminary. Chen Guying's lecture was one of the first series. His lecture later was published as a part of his book *Nietzsche—a Tragic Philosopher*, and translated by James Sellman and published as "Zhuangzi and Nietzsche: Plays of Perspectives," in Parks, ed., *Nietzsche and Asian Thought*, 115–29.

4. It is difficult to give a general account of these perspectives because each of them is different. I would like to borrow Peter R. Sedgwick's division of the "traditions" of Nietzsche interpretation: (1) *"The 'German tradition'*: readings which tend to

situate Nietzsche within the context of issues in modern philosophy, aesthetics and social theory as delineated by the writings of Kant, Goethe and Marx respectively." These include Heidegger, Gadamer, Jaspers, and some work of Marxists such as Lukacs and the Frankfurt School. (2) *The 'French tradition'*: this includes the readings of Bataille, the existentialists, and the postmodern, poststructuralist, and deconstructive approaches. "Here questions of language, style, rhetoric, and force are often highlighted in relation to Nietzsche's texts, as well as the constitution of human subjectivity in the context of psychoanalysis or social relations of power." (3) *"The 'Anglo-American tradition'*: epitomized by Arthur Danto, Walter Kaufmann, and R. J. Collingdale, which tends to relate Nietzsche's work more to classically determined conceptions of truth, politics and subjectivity as they have been addressed within the domain of Anglo-American analytic philosophy. A more recent variant on this model can be found in Richard Rorty's view of Nietzsche as a Jamesean pragmatist and iconoclastic 'strong texualist,' whose thought can be opposed to the practice of analytic philosophy" (Sedgwick, ed., *Nietzsche: A Critical Reader*, 2).

5. Some did suspect Nietzsche's message of "God is dead" was in a way "search for God." Heidegger once suggested that Nietzsche was "the last German philosopher who was passionately in search of God." The problem seems clear to me that they try to use the traditional and Christian concept of God to explore Nietzsche's antireligious and anti-Christian religiosity. See also Michel Haar, *Nietzsche and Metaphysics*, chapter 7, "Metamorphosis of the Divine." He seemingly noticed Nietzsche's religiosity and its influence in Nietzsche's thinking, but he still confused such religiosity with a mood for "metaphysical consolation" or a search for "the God of metaphysics" (133). A few books published in English recently began to discuss Nietzsche's philosophy in relation to religion; I will comment on these works in chapter 5.

6. See Kuang-ming Wu, *Chuang Tzu: World Philosopher at Play*, "Prelude" (1–25). Wu has listed nine misunderstandings of Zhuangzi in Chinese history, from ancient times until today. I think most of his critique is quite right and I myself found those same problems in my research.

7. These accusations can be easily found in any textbook published in China between the 1950s and 1980s. It has been changed recently, as more and more scholars began to unleash themselves from the fetter of official dogmatism and reinterpret Zhuangzi and other Chinese philosophers in a more scholarly fashion.

8. Whether Zhuangzi was the author of the book and which chapters were exactly his writing are still unsolved riddles. In the case of Nietzsche, the body of his writings, those published by himself and the posthumous notes (*Nachlass*), presents more authentically his thought. Since the authors are dead, perhaps no satisfactory answer is possible.

9. The translations of Zhuangzi I consult are major sources for English readers: James Legge, Burton Watson, Victor H. Mair, A. C. Graham (Inner Chapters), Fung Yulan (Inner Chapters with Guo Xiang's commentary), and some of Kuang-ming Wu's.

10. Many commentators may have noticed some religious elements in both Zhuangzi and Nietzsche's writings. However, they did not see as I do a special religiosity as a basic sentiment that indeed flows as "blood" in the corpuses of their writings. I will go back to this in chapter 5.

CHAPTER 2. ZHUANGZI'S DAO

1. There were two "Meng Cheng" (蒙城) or town of Meng in early China, one was in Song State (now Henan Province) and another in Chu State (now Anhui Province). I chose the conjecture that Zhuangzi was from Chu State with the group of scholars such as Ji Kang (稽康), Su Shi (苏轼), and Zhu Xi (朱熹). See also Sun Yi-kai, 76–82. Another reason given to argue that Zhuangzi was from Chu is that Zhuangzi's overall style of writing seems to be more coincide with the Chu culture than Song culture; the latter emphasizes ritual and mores whereas the former likes poetry, music, and myth. See also Lang Qing-xiao, 2–3, for opposing remarks.

2. This version was edited and exegeted by Guo Xiang. Before Guo Xiang (郭象, 252–312) there were other versions such as Sima Biao (司马彪, ?–306) with fifty-eight chapters and Xiang Xiu's (向秀, 227–272) with twenty-eight chapters, but we cannot find those versions anymore because they were lost. I follow the consensus in general that the inner chapters need to be treated differently from the rest of the chapters. Nonetheless, we should remember the fact that it was not Zhuangzi himself who edited the Book of Zhuangzi. There is no definite evidence to say exclusively that the inner chapters as they are in Guo Xiang's edition are all written by Zhuangzi, or that nothing in the other chapters comes from his teaching directly. Nor could we prove there is no possibility at all that a number of the bamboo slips were misplaced here and there in the past. Though I used outer and miscellaneous chapters as supplementary sources in most cases, I did sometimes quote passages from these chapters, as pieces of the evidence of the inner chapters with qualifications.

3. Chapters 27 and 33 were often said to be the introduction chapters to Zhuangzi's teaching, as Wuang Fu-zhi had point out. Most scholars agree that both chapters are perhaps the best explanation of Zhuangzi's thought among other chapters from *Outer* and *Miscellaneous Chapters*.

4. See Liu Xiao-gan, *Classifying the Zhuangzi Chapters*. viii–xix, 83–99, and Lang Qing-xiao, 18–33. See also my chapter 5 section 2. The passages I cited other than *Inner Chapters* are the part that basically explains and develops thought from the *Inner Chapters* and does "not raise important points of their own or points clearly different from those of the *Inner Chapters*" (Liu, 87).

5. The sense "to guide" is found earliest in a bronze text (*Yuding*, 禹鼎) at the turn of the first millennium BCE. Later a hand element, *cun* (寸), was added for this usage as 导. See Eno, "Cook Ding's Dao and the Limits of Philosophy," in Kjellberg and Ivanhoe, eds., *Essays on Skepticism, Relativism, and Ethics in the Zhuangzi*, 145.

6. Evidently, during the mid and late Zhou Dynasty these connotations of the term *Dao* had been commonly understood and used in various contexts. It is very easy to become confused if one does not read the word *Dao* carefully within the right context of the text. Therefore, the above clarification of the term *Dao* will help us to sort out the proper meaning of Dao in Chinese classics, especially in the *Book of Zhuangzi*.

7. Fu said that his analysis of the concept of Dao was inspired by Tang Jun-yi (唐君毅). Tang extracted six meanings of the concept of Dao in Laozi's philosophy: (1) Dao as universal principle; (2) Dao as metaphysical reality or being; (3) Dao as manifestation of Dao; (4) Dao as virtue; (5) Dao as the way of cultivating virtue and other aspects of life; (6) Dao as the state of things and the stature of heart/mind and personality. Tang's emphasis is more on moral or personal cultivation and transformation

in comparison with Fu. See Charles Fu, "Laozi, Zhuangzi, and Chan Buddhism—A Hermeneutic Experiment on the Philosophical Coherence from Dao to Chan, *From Western Philosophy to Chan Buddhism*, 403–408.

8. "Metaphysics" here is not exactly the same term that Aristotle and Greek philosophers used to apply to a systematic explanation of the principle or reality behind the phenomenal world. But evidently enough, there were similar kinds of thinking during the pre-Qing period that were to articulate and meditate the original reality or universal principle, normally called Dao, that was believed to be the ultimate being or truth of all natural and social phenomena. This kind of thinking was called "*xing-er-shang-xue*" (形而上学), meaning the learning of something that is beyond forms. Lately, the Western term *metaphysics* has been translated into Chinese by this. It has already said in the *Book of Change* that "that which is beyond forms is named Dao, and that which are under forms are named things" (*Yizhuan*, 易传, *Xici*, 系辞). In this respect, we should admit there were at least, if not systematic metaphysics and ontology, some kind of metaphysical and ontological thinking developed as early as the mid Zhou period. However, we should not confuse these early Chinese thoughts with Aristotle's idea of metaphysics. And I will apply the terms such as "metaphysics" and "ontology" in a very strict Chinese sense of "*xing-er-shang-xue*" and "*bengtilun*" (本体论).

9. *Guanzi* (管子) was written by the first Chinese academy called the Jixia (稷下) Academy at Qi State during the Warrior State period (357–301 BCE). This book collected various thoughts from different schools and historical thinkers, especially that of Guanzi. Guanzi was a famous and gifted minister of Qi State in the seventh century BCE and one of the earliest philosophers in Chinese history. His theory of the universe and the early utterance of *tiandao* were seen as very close to the Daoist philosophy.

10. The textual evidence is plentiful to show the importance of the term *Dao*, which appears more than one hundred times in *Zuo Zuan*, (左传) or *Narratives of Zuo*, approximately one hundred times in *Analects*, more than 160 times in *Mo Jing* (墨经), seventy times in *Dao De Jing*, and about 150 times in *Mencius*. See also Liu Xiao-gan, 9–10.

11. *Daoshu* (道术), the art of Dao, cannot really carry the exact meaning of the word. *Shu* can be understood as art, technique, strategy, tactic, and so on, but in *Zhuangzi*, especially in the chapter 33, *Tianxia*, *daoshu* connotes the meaning of learning, understanding, and perspective as well. So here I think *daoshu* refers to "the perspectives of Dao" rather than art or technique of Dao. And in this particular sentence, the author used another word "*fangshu*, 方术" meaning the art of magic to mock those who thought they possessed the true Dao.

12. Many who failed to see Zhuangzi's uniqueness from Laozi were perhaps influenced by Sima Qian's remark that "the essence of Zhuangzi's teaching is affiliated to the words of Laozi" (*Shi Ji, the Biography of Lao, Zhuang, Shen, Han*, 老庄申韩列传) Even Charles Fu has said that the entire philosophy of Zhuangzi could be considered a great philosophical footnote to Laozi's Dao. But in his various papers on Laozi and Zhuangzi, he admits that differences between Laozi and Zhuangzi were distinctive, and Zhuangzi developed Laozi's philosophy "creatively." See his "Taoist Metaphysics and Heidegger," *Journal of Chinese Philosophy* 3 (1976).

13. Charles W. Fu, "Laozi, Zhuangzi, Guo Xiang, and Zen—A Hermeneutic Exploration on the Philosophical Consistency from Daoism to Zen Buddhism," *From Western Philosophy to Zen Buddhism* (Dongda Press, 1986), 408–15.

14. *Ziran*, unlike the English word *nature*, which could stand for "essence" or "reality," refers to the natural or spontaneous happening and becoming of the world. It literally means "self/*zi*–so/*ran*" or [something] "done or be (*ran*) by itself (*zi*)." In Laozi and Zhuangzi this self-so-ness or suchness precisely refers to the world of "*nature*" and "spontaneity," or "auto/*zi*-matic/*ran*," but never "the *nature* of the world." Since this is one of the key concepts in Zhuangzi's philosophy, I will elaborate further on it later in this chapter.

15. Wing-Tsit Chan's translation: "Man models himself after earth, earth models itself after Heaven, Heaven models itself after Tao, Tao models itself after Nature." The key word is *fa* (法) or law.

16. See Charles Wei-Hsun Fu, "Creative Hermeneutics: Taoist Metaphysics and Heidegger."

17. The term *ziran* appeared two times in the Inner Chapters (5 and 6). Some would say that the concept of ziran was not yet developed there. But if we read the Inner Chapters carefully enough in combination with other terms such as *ziji* (自己, stop by itself), *zisheng* (自生, self producing or becoming), *zishi* (自适, self adjusting), *zihua* (自化, self-transformation), etc., the very concept of ziran as such is quite complete.

18. Though not in the exact words as "flow of life" or "universal flux," the idea of an ever-changing, ever-transforming world is stated explicitly and implicitly throughout the Inner Chapters. The images of water (rivers and lakes), air (*qi*), wind (the music of heaven), are often appeared to depict the ever-changing flux. The words he used to designate such flowing nature are *hua* (化, change, transformation), *bian* (辨/变, change), *wuchang* (无常, impermanence), *sheng* (生, birth, becoming), *wucheng* (无成, no-completion), *wuhui* (无毁, no-destruction), *wuqiong* (无穷, infinite, endless), etc. The word *you* or wandering, *cheng* (乘, ride), *shi* (适, adapt), *yin* (因, in accord with), *sui* (随, follow), etc., on the other hand, are used frequently in the Book of Zhuangzi to describe the state of mind that is one with the flow of life or the flux of nature.

19. *Tong*, literally through or throughness has multiple meanings in Chinese such as to walk (*xing*, 行), to reach (*da*, 达), to open (*kaitong*, 开通), to permeate (*rongtong*, 融通), thorough (*zhoubian*, 周遍), common (*gongtong*, 共通), clearing or enlightenment (*ming*, 明), and many more. I prefer a literal translation here to other contextual renderings simply because in Zhuangzi *tong* serves as one of the ultimate philosophical concepts that encompasses all the possible meanings listed above.

20. Guo Xiang is perhaps the first one to envision Zhuangzi's notion of one differently from Laozi's. This is why I said that my interpretation is partly indebted to him. Yet I do not agree with his interpretation in many places. For example, Guo emphasizes the sameness (One) behind the differences while I see at the same time Zhuangzi's one as togetherness or unity of differences. Guo's one identifies rights and wrongs by identifying their common nature (xing, 性) of argumentation while mine goes beyond self and others by way of throughness. Guo cannot eventually escape metaphysical trap while Zhuangzi attains the state of *xiaoyaoyou*.

21. Many would argue that Zhuangzi has never made clear whether the metaphysical Dao exists. In fact many Chinese commentators would like to argue that Zhuangzi has his own metaphysical Dao in mind, based on some textual evidences in the Book of Zhuangzi (5/3; 11/3 [*zhidao zhi jin yao yao ming ming*, 至道之精窈窈冥冥]; 11/5 [*wu er bu wu*, 物而不物, *duyou*, 独有]; 12/1 [*dao jian yü tian*, 道兼于天];

12/8; 13/1 [*tian dao*, 天道]; 13/6; 22/5; 22/6; 22/8; 23/6; 24/15). But if one has a close look at those writings one notices that they all sound like Laozi. Some of them are simply citations from *DaoDeJing*. A more obvious fact is that there is only one paragraph found in the entire *Inner Chapters*, and this paragraph does not seem coherent with the context and sounds odd in chapter 5. According to the whole text, especially the *Inner Chapters*, I think the "antimetaphysical" intention of Zhuangzi is explicit, though he did not answer the question whether such a Dao exists.

On the other hand, many scholars (interestingly enough most of them are from the West) assign Zhuangzi to the category of Skeptic and Relativist, and certainly Antimetaphysician (Hansen, Ivanhoe, etc.; see *Essays on Skepticism, Relativism, and Ethics in the Zhuangzi*, ed. Paul Kjellberg and Philip J. Ivanhoe. And *Experimental Essays on Chuang-tzu*, ed. Victor H. Mair).

Zhuangzi might have been aware that any definite assertion about metaphysics could itself be metaphysical. If one says that the metaphysical Dao does not exist, one needs to go through an entire logical or nonlogical process to prove it. When one says that everything is relative, one needs to prove the relativity is relative as well, and after this is done, relativity finally becomes universality and absolute. This may be the tragic nature of metaphysics and human knowledge. Zhuangzi has no intention at all to make any metaphysical or antimetaphysical assertion of the world, he just deconstructs all those metaphysical notions and returns to nature itself by his means of *wuwu*, which leads to a higher understanding of the nature and ourselves with no more discussion of metaphysics. So here Dao as *wuwu* or *wuwu* as Dao means also the ultimate state of a liberated human mind which accords perfectly with nature. We cannot get out of such dilemmas within the structure of common knowledge, Zhuangzi says. The only dao that can help is to realize the nature of knowledge and the limit or boundary of knowing (like a Kantian critique), by means of which we may be able to reach the stage of liberation.

22. These are three small nations. According to Ling Xi-yi, there is no evidence about them in the classical scriptures; their stories are merely allegories (Chen Gu-ying, 79).

23. Chad Hansen, "A Tao of Tao in Chuang-Tzu," in *Experimental Essays on Chuang-tzu*, 30–31.

24. As a matter of fact, according to chapter 33, "Tian Xia," the idea of "equalizing all things" came from another school of Daoism lead by Peng Meng (彭蒙) and Shen Dao (慎到). Both of them were prestigious scholars and Daoist thinkers at the Jixia Academy of the Qi State (357–301 BCE).

25. Zhuangzi's critique of knowledge is closely related his critique of language. I will investigate his notion of language in detail in the next section.

26. *Jingjie* is the word I would like to use as my Chinese translation of "perspective" specifically in Zhuangzi and Nietzsche's notions of perspective and perspectivism. Perspective in Zhuangzi and Nietzsche means a special or different level of worldview or understanding of things and the world. Different from relativists, both Zhuangzi and Nietzsche maintain that perspectives and interpretations have different levels and quality that will determine one's stage of enlightenment (Zhuangzi) or quantum of will to power (Nietzsche).

27. Heaven, earth, and the four directions together called *Liuhe* (六合), which stands for the universe.

28. Many are puzzled by this word, interpreting it reluctantly as "virtue." But according to the context, the word *de* is best understood in its original meaning as "gain." So I translated *de* in this particular circumstance as "consequence" which means something gained from the linguistic distinctions of things. See also Chen, 78, where he interpreted it as "*biaoxian* (表现)," or phenomena.

29. Maybe this was the way that the ministers and the officials had to follow in talking to the emperor, because the emperor was not supposed to be wrong or take advice from others.

30. Cui Yi-ming, in his *Existence and Wisdom—A Modern Interpretation of Zhuangzi's Philosophy*, points out that the sentence "*shiweiqiai* (是为耆艾)" should be read as "take the word 'elder' as an example." I think his reading is closer to what Zhuangzi intended to say and makes more sense of the whole paragraph.

31. Wang Fu-zhi says, "*yuyan, chongyan* and others are same, they are all *zhiyan . . .*" (Wang, 248). Before Wang, *zhiyan* was understood as the third type of words in addition to the other two. I think Wang is right, *zhiyan* is not merely a type of words, such as Sima Biao suggested as "broken" or "dismembered" words, but is rather Zhuangzi's new discourse for his own philosophy.

32. Ref. Wang Bi's commentary, Watson's translation, Guo Qing-fan, Fung You-lan, 63. This paragraph also parallels the paragraph in *Qi Wu-lun* 2/6, 2/4: *dao xin zhi er chen* (道行之而成)*; yan fei chui* (言非吹), etc.

33. It may be interesting to compare Zhuangzi to Derrida a little bit here: Derrida tries to legitimize the oppressed *other* to speak or interpret the text on its own as equally and freely as the privileged *self* used to do. Zhuangzi tries to help people go beyond the differences of language and reach the unity and equality of the differences (*tianjun*, 天钧 and *tianni*, 天倪, natural equality and diversity). Derrida stays in the language to enhance relativism and pluralism, Zhuangzi tends to overcome relativism by forgetting language.

34. Watson calls it "the injury of the Way," which is inappropriate, because here the sentence means "do less for Dao" (*weiDao*, 为道); *Sun* (损) here means to lessen the subjective effort to reveal or realize Dao, but not to "injure" Dao itself, because Dao does nothing but self-so (*wuwei*).

35. The authors of the *Outer* and *Miscellaneous Chapters* of the *Zhuangzi* have condemned morality, both Confucian and Moist, overwhelmingly, by developing and even exaggerating both Laozi's and Zhuangzi's ideas. See chapter 8; 10; 11; 13; 14. Actually, in the *Inner Chapters*, Zhuangzi hardly used any radical or extremist words to attack or renounce the idea of morality. What he tries to point out is that moral goodness is not the nature of our life; therefore, we should transcend it in order to free ourselves from any kind of bondage.

Here the problem of Laozi and Zhuangzi is the same—on the one hand they claimed that the creation of ideas and norms confused human mind and society; on the other hand, they admitted that the creation of morality was due to the degeneration of human beings. What does this mean? What is the causal relationship between morality and degeneration? Laozi said, morality is established when Dao perishes, great fallacy comes when wisdom is created (ch. 18). Perhaps what they tried to say was that the creation of morality was a *sign* of degeneration, like Nietzsche.

36. Here I follow the common rendering of *de* as "virtue" in the original sense of "virtuality." Since in modern English virtuality is often associate with the meaning of

"virtual reality," I do not use it to replace "virtual." But it is worth noting that *de* or virtue here in Zhuangzi, just as " virtuality" in its original sense, refers to essence or effect of existence (from middle English *virtuall*). From its Latin root (*virtus*), the word also contains the meaning of "excellence" or "excellent function," as Plato and Aristotle denoted in their virtue ethics. Both meanings are suitable to Zhuangzi's use of "*de*" as the actual manifestation of Dao. Unlike Confucius and other Chinese thinkers, Zhuangzi did not use "*de*" as virtue in terms of conventional morality but simply the genuine, effective, and excellent existence of being.

37. Most translations of this chapter title are inappropriate. They mistakenly interpreted *Fu* as "sign" (Watson), "seal" (Legge), "evidence" (Fung). Here *Fu* actually means conformity, harmony, or uniformity. From Guoxian down to Wang Fuzhi and Guo Qingfan, they all interpreted *chong fu* as two dimensions of *de*: abundant inside (a person) and conformable with the outside world.

38. In the same chapter, Zhuangzi used another word to describe *De Chong Fu*, called *Caiquan* (才全), or "talent and quality completed", and *debuxing* (德不形), or "virtue without forms" or "virtue never shows off".

39. *Ming* (冥), usually explained as sea (*ming*) in this passage (see Chen, 1, note 1). But *ming* literally stands for "darkness," "obscurity," "mysterious places," "nether world," and so on. Watson translates it as "darkness," which seems inappropriate because a place we do not know is not necessarily dark. I like Ji Kang's interpretation: "*mingmowuya*" (溟漠无涯) or "boundless, mysterious place." This is closer to Zhuangzi's characteristic and metaphorical use of words. The word *sea* cannot connote the more profound meaning of *ming* here; it is a metaphorical or symbolical place rather than an exact "sea."

40. Fang Yi-zhi said that "*Kun* (鲲) is small fish, Zhuangzi used it as the name of big fish" (Wang Fu-zhi, 1). Watson is right in his note: "*Kun* means fish roe. So Zhuangzi begins with a paradox—the tiniest fish imaginable is also the largest fish imaginable" (30).

41. Many translated *Xiao Yao You* "carefree wandering." Though not wrong, the translation misses some of the richness of the expression. First, "carefree" only caught the word *xiao*, without the meaning of "distance" or *yao*. *Yao* is indispensable in this phrase, because it suggests a meaning that "*xiao*" cannot cover. So when we use the word carefree, it must include *yao*—distance or openness. *You* is also more than just wandering. In classic Chinese, *you* often relates to the work of art and game playing. Confucius's "*youyuyi*" (游于艺) or "play in the arts" (*Analects*, 7/6) is a good example.

42. *Shenren* (神人) refers to a spiritual and mythical person which later was used frequently by religious Daoism. In Zhuangzi *shenren* is no more than an enlightened Daoist sage though sometimes described metaphorically. It says, "There is a Holy Man living on faraway Kushe mountain, with skin like ice or snow, and gentle and shy like a virgin. He does not eat the five grains, but sucks the wind, drinks the dew, climbs up on the clouds and mist, rides a flying dragon, and wanders beyond the four seas. By concentrating his spirit, he can protect creatures from sickness and plague and make the harvest plentiful." (Watson, 33). I would rather interpret this kind of mythic fiction symbolically and metaphorically.

43. I will elaborate more on Zhuangzi's practical aspect in chapter 4.

44. *Liuqi* (六气), literally "six breathes (energies)": *Yin*, *Yang*, wind, rain, cloud, and sunlight (Sima Biao).

45. *Weng* (闻, hear or heard) was also a special word for the student of Dao in ancient China. It refers not to the physical or sensual reflection but an internal enlightenment of the truth of Dao. So "hearing" Dao is a common use of a metaphor, indicating learning, understanding, and attaining Dao, as Confucius meant when he said: "Hear the Dao in the morning, I can die [without regret] in the evening" (*Analects*, 4/5).

CHAPTER 3. NIETZSCHE'S PHILOSOPHY OF LIFE AFFIRMATION

1. Jacques Derrida, "Interpreting Signatures (Nietzsche/Heidegger)," in Sedgwick, ed., *Nietzsche: A Critical Reader*, 63.

2. Ibid.

3. Gilles Deleuze, *Nietzsche and Philosophy*, 1. Deleuze sees Nietzsche's main project as to introduce the concepts of sense and value into philosophy, and thus to "pose the problem of critique in terms of values." Deleuze's definition of evaluation is worth mentioning here: "Evaluation is defined as the differential element of corresponding values, an element which is both critical and creative. Evaluations, in essence, are not values but ways of being, modes of existence of those who judge and evaluate, serving as principles for the values on the basis of which they judge. This is why we always have the beliefs, feelings and thoughts that we deserve given our way of being or our style of life." Also see Nietzsche's *GM* (III, 11), where he used the term *mode of existence* to explain the meaning of *valuation*.

4. We cannot take Nietzsche's words *all values* literally as every value (i.e., money, wine, etc.) in our life. What Nietzsche criticizes and revalues are those prevailing, predominating, and highest values of a particular society, such as metaphysics, truth, morality, beauty, human nature, virtue, freedom, and so on. They are the values in a society that tend to lead to cultural ideologies; they determine for what purposes life is lived in a particular culture.

5. Arthur Danto, in his *Nietzsche as Philosopher*, claims that since Nietzsche rejected truth as absolute reality and objectively valid value he is a nihilist. Nishitani too thinks that Nietzsche tried to overcome nihilism by living through nihilism (*The Self-Overcoming of Nihilism*). I think we cannot perceive Nietzsche as a nihilist—first, his mission of revaluation is to overcome nihilism; second, the problem of nihilism is the denial of life as it is, which is directly against his Yes-saying type of affirmation; third, we cannot say one is a nihilist because his goal is to overcome nihilism, just as we cannot say that Marx is a capitalist.

6. Robert John Ackermann points out correctly: "We have two Nietzsches to deal with—first is attacking the prevailing value tables, and the other is trying to produce progressive new value tables.... Many of the alleged contradictions in Nietzsche can be traced to this device of the double concept, and problems in interpretation can often be traced to failure to notice Nietzsche's double concepts." *Nietzsche—a Frenzied Look*, 5; 9. I think this is an accurate way to look at Nietzsche's contradictory characters.

7. Walter Kaufmann in his *Nietzsche* answered, "No." He was wrong because (1) he misunderstood Nietzsche's concept of value as mere virtue, so that he could not think of any new virtue that was created by Nietzsche (110). He forgot that Nietzsche was not a moral teacher but an immoralist. Are not the traits he posited in Zarathustra, the *Übermensch*, the dancer, and laughter "new values"? Even in terms of virtues? (2) He did not see a "reverse" as a kind of creating new value (111). On my understanding, to reverse the prevalent valuations is itself creation. Are not Yes saying, life affirmation, and "the meaning of the earth" new values? (3) He did not realize that revaluation is itself a new value, a new perspective that has produced Nietzsche's new philosophy. Can we still say that Nietzsche did not offer any new value?

8. Nietzsche said: "In fact, the problem of the origin of evil pursued me even as a boy of thirteen: at an age in which you have 'half childish trifles, half God in your heart,' I devoted to it my first childish literary trifle, my first philosophical effort—and as for the 'solution' of the problem I posed at that time, well, I gave the honor to God, as was only fair, and made him the *father* of evil" (*GM*, 17).

9. See David C. Hoy: "Nietzsche, Hume, and the Genealogical Method," in Yovel, ed., *Nietzsche as Affirmative Thinker*, 20–38. David C. Hoy may be right in saying, "that hitting on this method allowed him to bring together in a coherent framework points that were scattered in previous works" (21). But it is not right to say "his own adaptation of the method of genealogy was motivated by his reaction to Paul Rée's *Origin of the Moral Sensations*" (20). The method that later he called genealogy was applied long before the *GM* was published. In *GM*, Nietzsche for the first time named his unique method "genealogy."

10. These essays include "The Philosopher: Reflections on the Struggle between Art and Knowledge," "On the Pathos of Truth," "The Philosopher as Cultural Physician," "On the Truth and Lies in a Nonmoral Sense," "Philosophy in Hard Times," "The Struggle between Science and Wisdom" (they are compiled now under the title of *Philosophy and Truth*, ed. and trans Daniel Breazeale), and *Philosophy in the Tragic Age of the Greeks*.

11. See Eric Blondel, *Nietzsche: the Body and Culture—Philosophy as a Philological Genealogy*, 16–17: "Nietzsche borrows the term from Greek antiquity, and evokes especially Hesiod's genealogy in the *Theogony* . . ."

12. In his *Nietzsche, Genealogy, History*, Michel Foucault distinguishes two words, *Ursprung* and *Herkunft*. The former refers more to the origin in which resides the ultimate nature or thing-in-itself and from which everything has generated as it is. This is often the origin that philosophical historians and metaphysicians tend to construct and recuperate. Nietzsche's genealogy, on the contrary, likes to trace origins as *Herkunft*, which refers to *descent*, "the ancient affiliation to a group, sustained by the bonds of blood, tradition, or social class." "Genealogy does not resemble the evolution of a species and does not map the destiny of a people. On the contrary, to follow the complex course of descent is to maintain passing events in their proper dispersion; it is to identify the accidents, the minute deviations—or conversely, the complete reversals—the errors, the false appraisals, and the faulty calculations that give birth to those things that continue to exist and have value for us; it is to discover that truth or being does not lie at the root of what we know and what we are, but the exteriority of accidents." (*Foucault Reader*, ed. Paul Rabinow, 81). I agree with Foucault that *Herkunft*

and *Entstehung* (another word for "origin") are more exact than *Ursprung* in recording the true object of genealogy for Nietzsche.

13. Ibid., 76.

14. Deleuze, *Nietzsche and Philosophy*, 2.

15. Heidegger tells us: "Nietzsche once says, in a brief observation found among the early sketches (1870–71) for his first treatise, 'My philosophy an *inverted Platonism*: the farther removed from true being, the purer, the finer, the better it is . . .' (IX, 190). That is an astonishing preview in the thinker of his entire later philosophical position. For during the last years of his creative life he labors at nothing else than the over-turning of Platonism" (*Nietzsche*, I, 153–54). John Sallis argues that Heidegger mis-treated the writings of young Nietzsche as *only* a preview, for the attempt at inverting Platonism in *BT* is at the same time twisting free from it. (See John Sallis, *Crossing: Nietzsche and the Space of Tragedy*, 3–5).

16. In his "self-criticism," Nietzsche says: "It is clear what task I first dare to touch with this book. How I regret now that in those days I still lacked the courage (or immodesty?) to permit myself in every way an individual language of my own for such individual views and hazards—and that instead I tried laboriously to express by means of Schopenhauerian and Kantian formulas strange and new valuations which were basically at odds with Kant's and Schopenhauer's spirit and taste!" (6). We should read his words carefully, because they sometime sound too metaphysical or smell somehow "offensively Hegelian" (see also *EH*). However, the immaturity of *BT* can never eclipse its significance in Nietzsche's whole creative life as an original philosopher.

17. See Maudemarie Clark, *Nietzsche on Truth and Philosophy*. She takes this as a serious issue in Nietzsche study and argues with other commentators to maintain that Nietzsche does not renounce the existence of truth all together.

18. Traditional philosophers, up to and even including Heidegger, ask what Being is in fact, because they have no doubt that Being exists in opposition to the world of appearances. Nietzsche, on the contrary, does not believe in the existence of Being as such. Being is only an empty human concept or lie which was first motivated by the tendency to deny life and this world. This is why Nietzsche was interested in question-ing the concept of Being, its origin and the detrimental uses to which it has been put by human beings.

19. Some would say Nietzsche used the term *intelligible character* here ironically. For he had criticized the idea found in Kant and taken over by Schopenhauer, which played on the Platonic notion of the "intelligible realm" as one of the central problems of metaphysics. But here, I think Nietzsche used the term differently in reference to "the intelligible character" of the world, the part of the world that humans live and interpret. In this respect, will to power is not seen as universal or cosmological essence of the world at large, but the nature of the world only when it was viewed according to its "intelligible character."

20. Cf. Maudemarie Clark, *Nietzsche on Truth and Philosophy*, ch.7, "Will to Power." She says the passage cited "presents a detailed argument for the cosmological doctrine of will to power, and is the only passage in all of Nietzsche's published writings to do so. I argue, however, that if we look at the argument carefully, we find overwhelming reasons to deny that Nietzsche accepts it" (212–13).

21. See Walter Kaufmann, *Nietzsche: Philosopher, Psychologist, Antichrist*, 308. He also recommends later that: Klages, in his chapter on the *Überwindungsmotiv*, makes a point worth quoting in this connection: "Altogether, *Zarathustra* is an enraptured and uncanny exegesis of the proposition '*über*'. Over-fullness, over-goodness, over-time, over-kind, over-wealth, over-hero, to over-drink—those are a few out of the great number of over-words, some of which are newly coined and some of which are used over again—and they are just as many variations of the one exclusively meant: overcoming" (309).

22. Heidegger is right in saying: "Who is Nietzsche's Zarathustra? He is the advocate of the Dionysian. That is to say: Zarathustra is the teacher who teaches the Eternal Recurrence of the Same in, and for the sake of, his doctrine of the Superman" ("Who is Nietzsche's Zarathustra" in *The New Nietzsche*, ed. David B. Allison, 77). But I cannot accept Heidegger's interpretation that Nietzsche's eternal recurrence "thinks the permanentizing of what becomes," and since what becomes becomes the same itself (identity) or being, the doctrine of eternal recurrence is a part of Nietzsche's system of metaphysics (see also *Nietzsche*, Volume III, Part II). For Nietzsche, what eternally recurs is not identity or Being but life itself as becoming—what has happened will happen again; and what the doctrine of eternal recurrence is up to is not the proof of Being but the affirmation of life as it is (it was, it has been, it will be).

23. Athur C. Danto analyzed in depth the cosmological arguments from the Nachlass (204–209). Kaufmann took seriously Nietzsche's statement that eternal return is the "most scientific of all possible hypotheses" (*WP*, 55; cf. Kaufmann, 326). According to Ivan Soll, Nietzsche's concern is only the psychological acceptance of the doctrine of eternal recurrence as a test in affirming life, not a cosmological acceptance of it (322–33). Bernard Magnus perceived the idea a "myth" or "counter-myth" to the Platonic myth of another world (154), and Alexander Nehamas said that it is "not a theory but a view of the self" (chapter 5), where by "theory" Nehamas means a "cosmological theory." Milan Kundera writes, in the world of eternal return the weight of unbearable responsibility lies heavy on every move we make (*Lightness*, 3–5). For the discussion of this issue see also Maudemarie Clarke, 246–54, and Robert Jhon Ackermann, 155–63).

24. For example, Alen White (64–71), Michel Haar (21), Gilles Deleuze (27–29), Laurence Lampert (165–69), Robert John Ackermann (164–67), etc. Michel Haar even said that Nietzsche's Eternal Recurrence is the "the future religion" for the strong (11). This is very close to my interpretation of the idea of Eternal Recurrence. But I would not call it "religion" because Nietzsche never intended to establish a new religion, in addition to his Dionysian spirit (religiosity) of ultimate affirmation.

25. Lawrence J. Hatab has keenly pointed out, "Nietzsche's thought, of course, is not overly religious in any customary way, and yet his early interest in Apollo and Dionysus and his continued reference to Dionysus in later texts show at least that a 'deity,' in the sense of an extrahuman site of meaning and significance, would not be anathema to his purposes. This is especially true if we notice the connection between early Greek religion and a Nietzschean affirmation of finite life conditions—which becomes fully dramatized in the 'narrative' of eternal recurrence" (Santaniello, 53).

CHAPTER 4. AN INTERPLAY BETWEEN
ZHUANGZI AND NIETZSCHE

1. Nietzsche's acquaintance with Hinduism and Buddhism perhaps came from his study of Schopenhauer and from his longtime friend Paul Deussen who became the leading authority on Upanishadic philosophy in Germany. See Carl Pletsch, *Young Nietzsche* (79–93) and Freny Mistry, *Nietzsche and Buddhism* (12–18), and especially Mervyn Sprung, "Nietzsche's Trans-European Eye," in *Nietzsche and Asian Thought*, 76–90.

2. See Sarah Kofman, *Nietzsche and Metaphor*, 17–18.

3. *Tianlai* (天籟) is blowing itself while "*renlai* (人籟) is flute and *dilai* (地籟) holes." Blowing itself does not have any position and particular sound as a pure blowing, so that it can make all different sounds come into play. Likewise, real language (*tianlai*) does not have a particular meaning, signified or presence to "obey"; it just speaks, signifies, and presents. This is the nature of the language of "the language without words" in Zhuangzi. Unfortunately, this aspect has not been fully exposed so far in many commentaries.

4. Some commentators, such as Cheng Gu-ying and Shi Deqing, misunderstand the first sentence of this passage. They mistake "*dazhi*" (大知) for "great knowledge" which Zhuangzi would advocate, so they easily interpret "*xianxian*" (閑閑) as profound and comprehensive. Graham follows: "Great knowledge, is free and easy," which has misled some students to think that "Zhuangzi writes as a seeker of great knowledge" (Kjellberg and Ivanhoe, 30). Watson does the same with some hesitation: "Great understanding is broad and unhurried." My reading is different, closer to Wang Fu-zhi. *Dazhi* and *xiaozhi* (小知) are not opposite knowledge that we should prefer but different forms of knowledge that we should get beyond. And it is also evident in the context of the following sentences that he uses the same style of contrasting big and small, such as "big and small words," "big and small fears," to show the same problem.

5. Zhuangzi and Nietzsche have been made controversial in this for a long time. See preceding chapters.

6. Some Western scholars mistakenly projected onto Zhuangzi an idea of "skillfulness" to rescue him from the charge of relativism or skepticism. Lee H. Yearley even asserts: "Skillful activity, then, clearly points to the highest spiritual state" (Essays on Skepticism, Relativism, and Ethics in the Zhuangzi, 164). Just the opposite, Zhuangzi and Daoism object to skillfulness because it would generate "fixed mind" and "cunning heart," which could only harm our health and nature. At the outset of the cook Ding story, which is those scholars' basic textual evidence, Ding said clearly: "What I care for is Dao which goes beyond skill."

7. Some conceived Zhuangzi as a kind of escapist and ascetic (see Chen Guying, "Zhuangzi and Nietzsche"). In my opinion, Zhuangzi has an antigovernment and antisocial attitude but he never, at least in his *Inner Chapters*, suggests we should withdraw from social life. Different from ascetics or escapists, he emphasizes spiritual cultivation and liberation of individuals. Once you are liberated you can live anywhere you wish and be anything you want to be. There is no need to escape life, as some religions advocate. Zhuangzi may be disengaged from political positions, but he never renounces life within the world.

8. The translation "superman" and the exaggerations of it depicted in literature and movies are responsible for the misconceptions about Nietzsche's idea of *Übermensch*, who in fact has nothing to do with this sort of "superman."

CHAPTER 5. CONVERGING NEW WORLDS

1. Jacques Derrida, "Qual Quelle," in *Margins of Philosophy*, 305.

2. Michel Foucault asserts that it was "Nietzsche the philologist" who first connected "the philosophical task with a radical reflection upon language." See *The Order of Things*, 305, and "Nietzsche, Freud, Marx," in *Transforming the Hermeneutic Context: From Nietzsche to Nancy*, 59–67.

3. Michel Foucault, "Nietzsche, Freud, Marx," 66.

4. Jacques Derrida, "Differance," 11, in *Margins of Philosophy*.

5. Michel Foucault, "Nietzsche, Freud, Marx," 66.

6. For example, see Chen Chung-ying, "A Taoist Interpretation of 'Differance' in Derrida"; Chien Chi-hui, " 'Theft's Way': A Comparative Study of Chuang-tzu's Tao and Derridean 'Trace,' " *Journal of Chinese Philosophy* 17, no. 1 (1990):31–49; Mark Berkson, "Language: the Guest of Reality—Zhuangzi and Derrida on Language, Reality, and Skillfulness," in *Essays on Skepticism, Relativism, and Ethics in the Zhuangzi*; Xie S. B. and Chen J. M., "Derrida, Jacque and Chuang-tzu, Some Analogies in Their Deconstructionist Discourse on Language and Truth," *Canadian Review of Comparative Literature—Revue Canadienne de Litterature Comparee* 19, no. 3 (1992):363–76; Michelle Yeh, "The Deconstructive Way: A Comparative Study of Derrida and Chuang-tzu," *Journal of Chinese Philosophy* 10, no. 2:95–126, 1989; and also Zhang Long-xi, *The Dao and the Logos*.

7. Shrift, *Nietzsche and the Question of Interpretation*, 79; Foucault, *The Order of hings*, 305.

8. Derrida, *Margins of Philosophy*, "Differance," 17.

9. Liu Xiao-gan, *Classifying the Zhuangzi Chapters*, chapter 3, 83–156, also the "Foreword" by Donald J. Munro. Munro has compared Liu's analysis with Graham's and found the two are close: Graham calls the first the "school of Zhuangzi," the second "Syncretist," and divides the third into two, "Primitivist" and "Yangist" schools. I have problems with his use of the term *primitivist*. For Zhuangzi and his followers, old times were better not because they were "primitive" but because the people of that time knew Dao and lived with and as Dao manifested spontaneously. I also feel hesitant to relate Zhuangzi to Yangism. First, I doubt that there has ever been a Yangism in history, and second, there is too little evidence to actually decide what Yangzi's theory is except for some fragments scattered about referring to him as an irresponsible "egoist." See also Zhang Cheng-qiu's *Investigating the Chapters of the Book of Zhuangzi*.

10. There was a rumor that Guo's commentary was a copy of Xiang's (Liu Yi-qing, *Shi Shuo Xin Yü*), but not much evidence could prove such a charge. About the relationship between the two and their commentaries, see Lang Qing-xiao, *Zhuangzi Xue An*, 326–29; Tang Yong-tong, *Wei Jin Xuan Xue Lun Gao*, 103.

11. As Roberts has observed, "[T]his is not to say that commentators never remark on a certain spiritual, prophetic, or even religious pathos in Nietzsche's thought. But

even among those who do, very few studies have treated this aspect of Nietzsche's thought in any real depth, and most seem satisfied that this sensibility has little impact on the overall anti-religious nature of his ideas. Exceptions are Jaspers 1961 and, more recently, Valadier 1975 and Figl 1984. There remains no sustained examination of the issue in English. Stambaugh 1994 examines some of the mystical tendencies of Nietzsche's writing and Makarushka 1994 offers an analysis of religious language in some of Nietzsche's texts. Neither study, however, undertakes a detailed and comprehensive exploration of the problem of religion in Nietzsche. There are a number of theological thinkers who find Nietzsche a valuable resource for postmodern religious thought, though they also have not supplied any detailed studies of Nietzsche's thought. See especially Altizer and Hamilton 1966, Taylor 1984, Winquist 1995, and Raschke 1996" (5, note 5). I would add Michel Haar, though while his interpretation has closely examined Nietzsche's religiosity, he finally included religiosity within the old term *metaphysics*. I would also add Hans Küng's *Does God Exist*, which explored religious and antireligious elements in Nietzsche's philosophy from a theologian's perspective in particular.

12. What I meant by "ultimate concern" is quite the same as Paul Tillich's definition. He said, "The religious concern is ultimate; it excludes all other concerns from ultimate significance; it makes them preliminary. The ultimate concern is unconditional, independent of any conditions of character, desire, or circumstance"(Tillich, 11–12).

SELECTED REFERENCES

Ackermann, Robert John. *Nietzsche: A Frenzied Look*. Amherst: The University of Massachusetts Press, 1990.

Allinson, Robert E. *Chuang-tzu for Spiritual Transformation*. Albany: State University of New York Press, 1989.

———, ed. *Understanding the Chinese Mind*. New York: Oxford University Press, 1989.

Allison, David B., ed. *The New Nietzsche: Contemporary Styles of Interpretation*. Cambridge: MIT Press, 1985.

Alt, Wayne E. "Logic and Language in the Chuang-tzu." *Asian Philosophy* 1, no. 1 (1991): 13–16.

Ashcroft, B., G. Griffiths, and H. Tiffin, eds. *The Post-Colonial Studies Reader*. London and New York: Routledge, 1995.

Bataille, Georges. *On Nietzsche*. Translated by Bruce Boone. New York: Paragon House, 1992.

Behle, Ernst. *Confrontations: Derrida/Heidegger/Nietzsche*. Translated by Steven Taubeneck, Stanford: Stanford University Press, 1991.

Blondel, Eric. *Nietzsche: The Body and Culture, Philosophy as a Philological Genealogy*. Translated by Sean Hand, Stanford: Stanford University Press, 1991.

Caputo, John D. *Radical Hermeneutics: Repetition, Deconstruction, and the Hermeneutic Project*. Bloomington and Indianapolis: Indiana University Press, 1987.

Chan, Wing-Tsit. *A Source Book in Chinese Philosophy*, Princeton: Princeton University Press, 1963.

Chang Chung-yuan. "The Philosophy of Taoism According to Chuang-tzu." *Philosophy East & West* 27, no. 4 (1977): 409–22.

Chen Chung-ying. "A Taoist Interpretation of 'Difference' in Derrida." *Journal of Chinese Philosophy* 17, no. 1 (1990): 19–30.

Chen Gu-ying. *Nietzsche: A Tragic Philosopher*. Beijing: San Lian Shu Dian Press, 1987.

———. *A Recent Annotation and Interpretation of Zhuangzi (Zhuangzi Jin Zhu JinYi*, 庄子今注今译). Beijing: Zhong Hua Shu Ju Press, 1983.

Cheng Fang. *Nietzsche in China*. Nanjing: Nanjing Press, 1993.

Cheng Xuan-ying. *Nan Hua Zhen Jing Shu (The Book of Zhuangzi)—An Explanation* 南华真经疏 *with Guo Xiang's Annotation*. Shanghai: Shanghai Classics Press, 1993.

Chien Chi-hui, " 'Theft's Way': A Comparative Study of Chuang-tzu's Tao and Derridean 'Trace'," Journal of Chinese Philosophy, 17, 1, 1990.

Clark, Maudemarie. *Nietzsche on Truth and Philosophy*. Cambridge: Cambridge University Press, 1990.

Creel, Herrlee G. *Confucius and the Chinese Way*. New York: Harper Torchbooks, 1960.

Cui Yi-ming. *Existence and Wisdom—A Modern Interpretation of Zhuangzi's Philosophy (Shengcun Yü Zhi Hui—Zhuangzi De Xian Dai Chan Shi* 生存与智慧—庄子的现代阐释*)*. Shanghai: Shanghai People's Press, 1996.

Dai, Zhen. *Verifying and Interpreting the Words in Mentius (Mengzi Zi Yi Shu Zheng,* 孟子字义疏证*)*. Beijing: Zhonghua shu Jü, 1978.

Danto, Arthur C. *Nietzsche as Philosopher*. New York: Columbia University Press, 1965.

Dean, Thomas, ed. *Religious Pluralism and Truth: Essays on Cross-cultural Philosophy of Religion*. Albany: State University of New York Press, 1995.

Deleuze, Gilles. *Nietzsche and Philosophy*. Translated by Hough Tomlinson. New York: Columbia University Press, 1983.

De Man, Paul. *Allegories of Reading: Figural Language in Rousseau, Nietzsche, Rilke, and Proust*. New Haven: Yale University Press, 1979.

Derrida, Jacques. "Interpreting Signatures (Nietzsche/Heidegger)." Translated by Diane Michelfelder and Richard E. Palmer. In *Nietzsche: A Critical Reader*, ed. Peter R. Sedgwick. Cambridge: Blackwell, 1995.

———. *Margins of Philosophy*. Translated by A. Bass. Chicago: University of Chicago Press, 1982.

———. *Of Grammatology*. Translated by G. Spivak. Baltimore: Johns Hopkins University Press, 1976.

———. *Spurs: Nietzsche's Style*. Translated by B. Harlow. Chicago: University of Chicago Press, 1979.

Deutsch, Eliot, ed. *Culture and Modernity: East-West Philosophic Perspectives*. Honolulu: University of Hawaii Press, 1991.

Ferry, Luc, and Alain Renaut, eds. *Why We Are not Nietzschean*. Translated by Robert de Loaiza. Chicago and London: The Chicago University Press, 1997.

Fingarette, Herbert. *Confucius: The Secular as Sacred*. New York: Harper Torchbooks, 1972.

Foucault, Michel. "Nietzsche, Freud, Marx." Translated by Allan D. Schrift. In *Transforming the Hermeneutic Context*, ed. Gayle L. Ormiston and Alan D. Schrift. Albany: State University of New York Press, 1990.

———. "Nietzsche, Genealogy, History." Translated by Donald F. Bouchard and Sherry Simon. In *Foucault Reader*, ed. Paul Rabinow. New York: Pantheon Books, 1984.

———. *The Order of Things: An Archaeology of the Human Sciences.* Translated by Alan Sheridan-Smith. New York: Random House, 1970.

Frey-Rohn, Liliane. *Fredrich Nietzsche: A Psychological Approach to His Life and Work.* Translated by Gary Massey. Zürich: Paimon Verlag, 1988.

Fu, Charles Wei-hsun. "Creative Hermeneutics: Taoist Metaphysics and Heidegger." *Journal of Chinese Philosophy* 3 (1976): 115–43.

———. "The Trans-onto-theological Foundations of Language in Heidegger and Taoism." *Journal of Chinese Philosophy* 5 (1978): 301–33.

———. From Western Philosophy to Chan Buddhism, Sanming Press, Taiwan, 1987.

Fung Yu-Lan. *Chuang-Tzu—A New Selected Translation with an Exposition of the Philosophy of Kuo Hsiang.* New York: Paragon Book Reprint Corp., 1964.

———. *Sansongtangquanji,* 三松堂全集, Volume I. Henan, Henan People's Press, 1985.

Gillespie, M. A., and T. B. Strong, eds. *Nietzsche's New Seas: Explorations in Philosophy, Aesthetics, and Politics.* Chicago and London: Chicago University Press, 1988.

Goodman, Russel B. "Skepticism and Relativism in the Chuang-tzu." *Philosophy East & West* 5, no. 1 (1985): 21–69.

Graham, A. C. *Chuang-tzu: The Inner Chapters.* London and Boston: Unwin Paper Backs, 1981.

———. *Disputers of the Dao: Philosophical Argument in Ancient China.* Chicago and La Salle, IL: Open Court, 1989.

Guan Feng. *The Interpretation and Critique of the Inner Chapters in the Book of Zhuangzi (Zhuangzi Nei Pian Yi Jie He Pi Pan,* 庄子内篇义解和批判*).* Beijing: Zhonghua Shu Jü, 1961.

Guo Qing-fan. *A Collective Commentary of Zhuangzi (Zhuangzi Ji Jie,* 庄子集解*).* Beijing: Zhong Hua Shu Jü, 1988.

Guo Xiang. *An Annotation on Zhuangzi (Zhuangzi Zhu,* 庄子注*).* In *Nan Hua Zhen Jing* with Chen Xuan-ying's explanation. Shanghai: Shanghai Classics Press, 1993.

Gutmann, A., ed. *Multiculturalism: Examining the Politics of Recognition, essays by Chales Taylor, Anthony Appiah, Jürgen Habermas, Steven C. Rockfeller, Michael Walzer, and Susan Wolf.* Princeton: Princeton University Press, 1994.

Haar, Michel. *Nietzsche and Metaphysics.* Translated by Michael Gendre. Albany: State University of New York Press, 1996.

Habermas, Jürgen. *The Philosophical Discourse of Modernity.* Translated by Frederick Lawrence. Cambridge: MIT Press, 1971.

Hansen, Chad. *A Daoist Theory of Chinese Thought.* New York: Oxford University Press, 1992.

Havas, Randall. *Nietzsche's Genealogy: Nihilism and the Will to Knowledge.* Ithaca and London: Cornell University Press, 1995.

Heidegger, Martin. *Nietzsche.* Translated by David Farrall Krell, San Francisco: Harper and Row, 1976–1987.

Ivanhoe, Philip J. "Skepticism, Skill, and the Ineffable Tao." *Journal of the American Academy of Religion* 61, no. 4 (1993): 639–54.

———, ed. *Chinese Language, Thought, and Culture: Nivison and His Critics*. Chicago and La Salle, IL: Open Court, 1996.

Jaspers, Karl. *Nietzsche: An Introduction to the Understanding of His Philosophical Activity*. Translated by Charles F. Wallraff and Frederick J. Schmitz. Tucson: University of Arizona Press, 1965.

Kamuf, Peggy, ed. *A Derrida Reader: Between the Blinds*. New York: Columbia University Press, 1997.

Kaufmann, Walter. *Nietzsche: Philosopher, Psychologist, Antichrist*. Princeton: Princeton University Press, 1974.

Kjellberg, Paul, and Philip J. Ivanhoe, eds. *Essays on Skepticism, Relativism, and Ethics in the Zhuangzi*. Albany: State University of New York Press, 1996.

Koelb, Clayton, ed. *Nietzsche as Postmodernist: Essays Pro and Contra*. Albany: State University of New York Press, 1990.

Kofman, Sarah. *Nietzsche and Metaphor*. Translated by Duncan Large. Stanford: Stanford University Press, 1993.

Küng, Hans. *Does God Exist: An Answer for Today*. Translated by Edward Quinn, Garden City: Doubleday, 1980.

Lampert, Laurence. *Nietzsche's Teaching: An Interpretation of "Thus Spoke Zarathustra."* New Haven: Yale University Press, 1986.

Lang Qing-xiao. *A Case Study of Zhuangzi (Zhuangzi Xue An, 庄子学案)*. Tianjin: Tianjin Classics Press, 1990.

Legge, James. *The Writings of Kwang-Tze*. In *The Sacred Books of the East*: vol. XXXIX, *The Texts of Taoism*. London: Oxford University Press, 1891.

Legge, Russel D. "Chuang-tzu and the Free Man." *Philosophy East & West* 29, no. 1 (1979): 11–20.

Levine, Peter. *Nietzsche and the Modern Crisis of the Humanities*. Albany: State University of New York Press, 1995.

Lin His-I. *The Meaning of Zhuangzi (Zhuangzi Kou Yi, 庄子括义)*. Taiwan, Hung Tao Cultural Enterprise Company Limited, 1971.

Liu Da-jie. *On Wei Jin Thoughts (Wei Jin Si Xiang Lun, 魏晋四贤论)*. Shanghai: Zhonghua Shu Jü, 1939.

Liu Xiao-gan. *Classifying the Zhuangzi Chapter*. Translated by Willian E. Savage, Ann Arbor: The University of Michigan Press, 1994.

———. *Zhuangzi's Philosophy and its Evolution (Zhuangzi Zhe Xue Ji Qi Yan Bian)*. Beijing: Chinese Academy of Social Sciences Press, 1987.

Lyotard, Jean-Francois. *The Postmodern Condition: A Report on Knowledge*. Translated by Geoff Bennington and Brian Massumi. Minneapolis: University of Minnesota Press, 1984.

Magnus, Bernd. *Nietzsche's Existential Imperative*, Bloomington: Indiana University Press, 1978.

Magnus, B., J. Mileur, and S. Stewart. *Nietzsche's Case: Philosophy as/and Literature*. New York and London: Routledge, 1993.

Mair, Victor H., ed. *Experimental Essays on Chuang-tzu*. Honolulu: University of Hawaii Press, 1983.

——, trans. *Wandering on the Way: Early Taoist Tales and Parables of Chuang Tzu*. New York: Bantam Books, 1994.

Major, John S. "The Efficacy of Uselessness: A Chuang Tzu Motif." *Philosophy East & West* 25, no. 3 (1975): 265–80.

Ma Xü-lun. *Making Sense of Zhuangzi (Zhuangzi Yi Zheng)*. Taipei: Hun Tao Cultural Enterprise Company Limited, 1970.

MacIntyre, Alasdair. *After Virtue*. Notre Dame: University of Notre Dame Press, 1981.

Merton, Thomas. *The Way of Chuang-tzu*. New York: New Directions, 1965.

Mistry, Freny. *Nietzsche and Buddhism: Prolagomenon to a Comparative Study*. Berlin/New York: Walter de Gruyter, 1981.

Munro, Donald. *The Concept of Man in Early China*. Stanford: Stanford University Press, 1969.

Murphy, Tim. *Nietzsche, Metaphor, Religion*. Albany: State University of New York Press, 2001.

Nehamas, Alexander. *Nietzsche: Life as Literature*. Cambridge: Harvard University Press, 1985.

Nietzsche, Friedrich. *The Antichrist*. Translated by Walter Kaufmann in *The Portable Nietzsche*, ed. Walter Kaufmann. New York: Viking, 1968. Abbreviated *A*.

——. *Beyond Good and Evil*. Translated by Walter Kaufmann. New York: Random House, 1966. Abbreviated *BGE*.

——. *The Birth of Tragedy*. Translated by Walter Kaufmann. New York: Random House, 1967. Abbreviated *BT*.

——. *Ecce Homo*. Translated by Walter Kaufmann. New York: Random House, 1967. Abbreviated *EH*.

——. *The Gay Science*. Translated by Walter Kaufmann. New York: Random House, 1974. Abbreviated *GS*.

——. *Human, All Too Human*. Translated by R. J. Hollingdale. Cambridge: Cambridge University Press, 1986. Abbreviated *HAH*.

——. *On the Genealogy of Morals*. Translated by Walter Kaufmann and R. J. Hollingdale. New York: Random House, 1969. Abbreviated *GM*.

——. *On Truth and Lies in a Nonmoral Sense*. In *Philosophy and Truth: Selections from Nietzsche's Notebooks of the 1870s*, ed. and trans. Daniel Breazeal. New Jersey: Humanities Press, 1979. Abbreviated *TL* and *PT*, respectively.

——. *The Philosopher: Reflections on the Struggle between Art and Knowledge*. In *Philosophy and Truth: Selections from Nietzsche's Notebooks of the 1870s*, Ed. and trans. Daniel Breazeal. New Jersey: Humanities Press, 1979. Abbreviated *P* and *PT*, respectively.

——. *Philosophy in the Tragic Age of the Greeks*. Translated by Marianne Cowan. Washington, DC: Regnery Gateway, 1962.

——. *A Self-Portrait from His Letters*. Edited and translated by Peter Fuss and Henry Shapiro. Cambridge: Harvard University Press, 1971.

——. *Thus Spoke Zarathustra*. Translated by Walter Kaufmann, in *The Portable Nietzsche*, ed. Walter Kaufmann. New York: Viking, 1968. Abbreviated *Z*.

——. *Twilight of the Idols*. Translated by Walter Kaufmann in *The Portable Nietzsche*, ed. Walter Kaufmann. New York: Viking, 1968. Abbreviated *TI*.

——. *Untimely Meditations*. Translated by R. J. Hollingdale. Cambridge: Cambridge University Press, 1983. Abbreviated *UM*.

——. *The Will to Power*. Translated by Walter Kaufmann and R. J. Hollingdale. New York: Random House, 1967. Abbreviated *WP*.

Nishitani Keiji. *The Self-Overcoming of Nihilism*. Translated Graham Parkes. Albany: State University of New York Press, 1990.

Nivison, David S. *The Way of Confucianism*. Edited by W. Van Norden. Chicago and La Salle, IL: Open Court, 1996.

Ormiston, C. L., and A. D. Schrift, eds. *Transforming the Hermeneutic Context: From Nietzsche to Nancy*. Albany: State University of New York Press, 1990.

Parks, Graham, ed. *Nietzsche and Asian Thought*. Chicago: University of Chicago Press, 1991.

——. "The Wandering Dance: Chuang-tzu and Zarathustra," *Philosophy East & West* 33, no. 3 (1983): 235–50.

Pletsch, Car. *Young Nietzsche: Becoming a Genius*. New York: The Free Press, 1991.

Qian Mu. *Chuang-tzu Ts'uan Chien*. Hong Kong: Tung Nan Ying Wu Press, 1951.

——. *A General Argument on Laozi and Zhuangzi (Zhuang Lao Tong Bian)*. Jiulong: The Institute of New Asia, 1947.

Richardson, John. *Nietzsche's System*. New York and Oxford: Oxford University Press, 1996.

Roberts, Tyler T. *Confronting Spirit: Nietzsche, Affirmation, Religion*. Princeton: Princeton University Press, 1998.

Rosemont, Henry, ed. *Chinese Texts and Philosophical Contexts*. La Salle, IL: Open Court, 1991.

Rorty, Richard. *Philosophy and the Mirror of Nature*. Princeton: Princeton University Press, 1979.

——. *Philosophy Papers*, 2 vols. New York: Cambridge University Press, 1991.

Said, Edward W. *Orientalism*. New York: Vintage Books, 1979.

Sallis, John. *Crossings: Nietzsche and the Space of Tragedy*. Chicago: University of Chicago Press, 1991.

——, ed. *Deconstruction and Philosophy: The Text of Derrida*. Chicago and London: Chicago University Press, 1987.

Santaniello, Weaver, ed. *Nietzsche and the Gods*. Albany: State University of New York Press, 2001.

Sarup, Madan. *An Introductory Guide to Post-structuralism and Postmodernism*. Athens: University of Georgia Press, 1993.

Schacht, Richard. *Nietzsche*. Boston: Routledge and Kegan Paul, 1983.

Schutte, Ofelia. *Beyond Nihilism: Nietzsche without Masks*. Chicago and London: University of Chicago Press, 1984.

Schwartz, Benjamin. *The World of Thought in Ancient China*. Cambridge: Belknap Press, 1985.

Sedgwick, Peter R., ed. *Nietzsche: A Critical Reader*. Oxford and Cambridge, MAA: Blackwell, 1995.

Shrift, Allan D. *Nietzsche and the Question of Interpretation*. New York: Routledge, 1990.

——. *Nietzsche's French Legacy: A Genealogy of Poststructuralism*. New York and London: Routledge, 1995.

Sleinis, E. E. *Nietzsche's Revaluation of Values: a Study in Strategies*. Urbana: University of Illinois Press, 1994.

Soll, Ivan. "Reflections on Recurrence: A Re-examination of Nietzsche's Doctrine, *die ewige Wiederkehr des Gleichen*." In *Nietzsche: A Collection of Critical Essays*, ed. Robert Solomon, 322–42. Garden City: Doubleday, 1973.

Solomon, Robert, ed. *Nietzsche: A Collection of Critical Essays*, Garden City: Doubleday, 1973.

Stambaugh, Joan. *Nietzsche's Thought of Eternal Return*. Baltimore: The Johns Hopkins University Press, 1972.

Sun Yi-kai and Chang-song Zhen. *An Overview on Zhuangzi (Zhuangzi Tong Lun* 庄子通论*)*. Beijing: Eastern Press, 1995.

Tang Yong-tong. *On Wei-Jin Philosophy (Wei Jin Xuanxue Lungoa,* 魏晋玄学论稿*)*. Beijing, People's Press, 1957.

Thele, L. Paul. *Friedrich Nietzsche and the Politics of the Soul: A Study of Heroic Individualism*. Princeton: Princeton University Press, 1990.

Tillich, Paul. *Systematic Theology*. Three volumes in one. New York and Evanston: University of Chicago Press and Harper and Row, Publishers, 1967.

Waite, Geoff. *Nietzsche's Corps/e: Aesthetics, Politics, or, the Spectacular Technoculture of Everyday Life*. Durham and London: Duke University Press, 1996.

Waley Arthur. *Three Ways of Thought in Ancient China*. Stanford: Stanford University Press, 1982.

Wang Fu-zhi. *Interpreting Zhuangzi (Zhuangzi Jie* 庄子解*)*. Beijing: Zhong Hua Shu Jü, 1961.

Wang Shu-min. *Peeping into Zhuangzi (Zhuangzi Guan Kui* 庄子管窥*)*. Taipei: Yi Wen Press, 1978.

Wang Xian-qian. *A Collection of Interpretations of Zhuangzi (Zhuangzi Ji Jie* 庄子集解*)*. Beijing: Zhonghua Shu Jü, 1987.

Watson, Burton. *The Complete Works of Chuang Tzu*. New York: Columbia University Press, 1968.

White, Alan. *Within Nietzsche's Labyrinth*. New York: Routledge, 1990.

White, Richard J. *Nietzsche and the Problem of Sovereignty*. Urbana and Chicago: University of Illinois Press, 1997.

Wu Kuang-ming. *The Butterfly as Companion*. Albany: State University of New York Press, 1990.

——. *Chuang Tzu: World Philosopher at Play*. New York: The Crossroad Publishing Company and Scholars Press, 1982.

——. "Dream in Nietzsche and Chuang-tzu." *Journal of Chinese Philosophy* 13, no. 4 (1986): 371–78.

Xie S. B and Chen J. M, "Derrida, Jacque and Chuang-tzu, some Analogies on Language and Truth," Canadian Review of Comparative Lifesature, 19, 3, 1992.

Xu, Shen, 许慎. *Explanation of Words and Elucidation of Characters (Shuo Wen Jie Zi*, 说文解字). Beijing: Zhong Hua Shu Ju, 1963.

Yeh, Michelle, "The Deconstructive Way: A Comparative Study of Derrida and Chuang Tzu," Journal of Chinese Philosophy 10, 2, 1989.

Yovel, Y., ed. *Nietzsche as Affirmative Thinker*. Dordrecht/Boston/Lancaster: Martinus Nijhoff Publishers, 1986.

Yü Ying-shih. *History and Theory (Li-shi yu Si-xiang*, 历史与思想). Taipei: Lian-jing Publish Company, 1976.

Zhang Cheng-qiu. *Investigating the Chapters in the Book of Zhuangzi (Zhuangzi Pian Mu Kao* 庄子篇目考). Taipei: Taiwan Zhonghua Shu Jü, 1961.

Zhang Long-xi. *The Tao and the Logos: Literary Hermeneutics, East and West*. Durham: Duke University Press, 1992.

Zhang Shi. *Zhuangzi and Modernism (Zhuangzi yu Xiandaizhuyi* 庄子与现代主义). Shijiazhuang: Hebei People's Press, 1989.

Zhou, Q. "A Survey of Recent Studies on the Thought of Laozi and Zhuangzi." *Chinese Studies in Philosophy* 20, no. 3 (1989): 71–90.

Zhu, Xi. *A Collective Notes on Four Classics (Si Shu Ji Zhu*, 四书集注). Changsha: Yue Lu Shu She, 1985.

INDEX